For M.
    —J.L.

For the man I love.
    —L.T.

From Pure Joy springs all creation.
By Joy it is sustained, toward Joy it
proceeds and to Joy it returns.
                    from the Sanskrit

From a Translation of the
Septuagint, Book of Proverbs

For at the gates of the Mighty, She hath taken a seat,
and at the entrance thereof chanteth Her song:

"In the beginning, before the Lord made the Earth
When He furnished the Heavens, I was with Him;
and when He set apart His throne on the winds.
When He set to the sea its bound,
and the waters passed not the word of His mouth
I was harmonizing with Him. I was the one in whom
He delighted, and I was daily gladdened by His
presence on all occasions."

White Samvara
A Tanka
Anonymous
Nineteenth Century

DESIGNED BY JOHN LYNCH

LOVE

A CELEBRATION IN ART AND LITERATURE

EDITED BY JANE LAHR AND LENA TABORI

STEWART, TABORI & CHANG, PUBLISHERS, NEW YORK

Consulting Editor: MARYA DALRYMPLE
Photo Research: NATALIE GOLDSTEIN

We would like to thank the following friends for their help and suggestions in creating this book: Viveca Lindfors, Sheldon and Margie Harnick, John Lahr, Natalie Goldstein, Chuck Boyce, Palmer Hasty, Anne Knauth, John Lynch, Tom Wilson, Richard Williams, and Michael Liebert.

Page 1, Hoysaleswara Temple Sculpture

Page 4–5, Detail from *Equestrian* by Marc Chagall

Page 7, Detail from *Self-Portrait with Isabella Brandt in the Honeysuckle Bower* by Peter Paul Rubens

Page 8, Detail from *Scene at Houghton Farm* by Winslow Homer

Page 12, Detail from *Spring in Central Park* by William Zorach

Page 15, Detail from *King Mycerinus and Queen Kha Merer Nebty II*

Hardcover edition published in 1982 and paperback edition published in 1995 by Stewart, Tabori & Chang, a division of U.S. Media Holdings, Inc. 575 Broadway, New York, NY 10012

Library of Congress Cataloging in Publication Data

Love, a celebration in art and literature.

Includes index.
1. Love in art.   2. Love—Literary collections.
I. Lahr, Jane.   II. Tabori, Lena.
NX650.L68L6   700 82-5680
ISBN 0-941434-20-6 (Hardcover)
ISBN 1-55670-446-1 (Paperback)

Distributed in the U.S. by Stewart, Tabori & Chang, 575 Broadway, New York, N.Y. 10012. Distributed in Canada by General Publishing Company Limited, 30 Lesmill Road, Don Mills, Ontario, Canada M3B 2T6. Distributed in the U.K. by Hi Marketing, 38 Carver Road, London SE24 9LT, England. Distributed in Europe by Onslow Books Limited, Tyler's Court, 111A Wardour Street, London W1V 3TD, England. Distributed in Australia and New Zealand by Peribo Pty Limited, 58 Beaumont Road, Mount Kuring-gai, NSW 2080, Australia.

Printed in Japan

15 14 13 12 11 10 9 8 7 6 5 4 3 2 1

With special gratitude to Marya Dalrymple who provided the editorial nourishment and paid us the ultimate compliment of falling in love.

♥ ♥ ♥

CONTENTS

FOREWORD

Lena and I chose to confront the awesome theme of love after the failure of each of our marriages. In fact, so few of our friends' marriages had resulted in a deepening emotional commitment that divorce began to seem like a cultural cliché. Still, we simply could not accept Gloria Steinem's dictum that a woman without a man is like a fish without a bicycle. We both believe and delight in the concept of heterosexual love and want it to be part of our lives.

We decided to compile a book that distilled the theme of love—a book that would put people immediately in touch with their capacity to love. We looked at hundreds of works of art and literature and finally addressed Shakespeare, Colette, Millay, Vonnegut, Whitman, Brancusi, Rembrandt, Chagall, and so many others. What is love? Show us. Tell us. Teach us.

I have come to feel, after more than a year of working on this book, that true love—which is unique in that it is reciprocal—is not difficult to describe, nor is it a complex, mysterious emotion. Rather, it is exquisite, simple, and definable. Love is the act of extending oneself to nurture another. One can learn the art of loving well, as a craftsman learns a craft. But it takes a conscious act of will to learn to love. Love is a discipline.

As you read this book, you will not see examples of jealousy, inconstant love, or unrequited love. In my view, these are not true love, but distortions of love—aberrations that have long been confused with love. Forget what the songs tell you.

What you will find in this volume are the processes that are at the very heart of love—honoring, nurturing, hallowing, and affirming. Even in the form of physical expression, love can be a transcendent metaphor for creation if the hallowing of another is present. D.H. Lawrence demonstrates this perfectly in *Lady Chatterley's Lover*.

This anthology makes one assertion: Love is possible. The Koren cartoon that asks, "William, do you have the courage to love?" says it all. Love is for the stickers and the fighters, not the escape artists. Take the heroine in Neil Simon's play *Chapter Two*, who has the guts to confront her beloved but risks his abandonment. She does it and their love deepens because of her courage.

We have framed such key moments in love's evolution with visual essays. In the essay on young love, we see the emotions of two Dutch lovers sharing a glass of lemonade and experience a romantic moment between a newly wed Renaissance couple. In a rather frivolous essay on the kiss, we celebrate this physical token of love through the ages. But perhaps the most touching expressions of love can be found in the art of ancient cultures—Egyptian, Etruscan, Hindu, and Tibetan. In the visual essay that ends the book, we present some of the most outstanding examples of this art. Man and woman come together, as partners, consorts, and companions, befriending, holding, and, above all, honoring one another. Indeed, as the essay reminds us, "We two form a multitude."

—Jane Lahr

♥ ♥ ♥

Love. Jane says it's a discipline, something to be learned. An art. I thought, for a very long time, it was about kissing.

I remember when I was twelve and I caught my mother and father kissing in the kitchen. I was intensely proud. I didn't have any friends who who could say that about their parents.

And then I got kissed. For the first time. I was thirteen and at camp in Montana. That summer was filled with music, mainly Hank Snow and Hank Williams. The songs were all love songs. They told stories of heartbreak and divorce and betrayal. I listened gravely and watched curiously when one of the young wranglers took a liking to my bunkmate. Then came the night I met the head wrangler (the one who played the guitar and sang) on the way to my cabin. It was, of course, the perfect setting. The moon was high, the sky was clear, and he explained that he wanted to do something he had never done before and that I mustn't tell anyone. It was a secret. I was chosen. He kissed me. And I guarded that moment in my memory for a long time.

Years later, when I was sixteen, I fell properly in love. It was desperate, urgent, and obsessive. He wrote me poems and extraordinary, beautiful letters. I read everything I could find to try to gain an understanding of what I was feeling. *Lady Chatterley's Lover* struck home. I was clearly in over my head. But we were trying. We talked late into the night about our parents and their mistakes, and read Shelley, Byron, and Edna St. Vincent Millay. We went to the movies... *Jules and Jim, A Man and A Woman*. But we were too young. We couldn't assimilate the experience fast enough. Still, it was the first time and there was nothing frivolous about it.

Part of the problem was, and continued to be, that my only understanding of what a love relationship could be was based on what I had seen and read. That's the curious thing about love. You can only do it by doing it. And you can only learn about it by watching and seeing how it works. Although I found my mother and father kissing in the kitchen, they would be divorced by the time I was twenty-five. So I was coming to realize that kissing wasn't a guarantee. I think growing into a loving person is a little like becoming an artist. You start with yourself, then you learn by imitating the "masters"—parents, writers, filmmakers—and finally, with everyone else's experiences rattling around in your head, you begin to absorb it all and find your own form.

By the time I was twenty-three I was pretty lost. Riding off into the sunset on a white horse was obviously not the answer. And I had never achieved Lawrence's passion. So I tried marriage. I knew what it required—cooking, entertaining, sitting for hours at my husband's rehearsals. I worked, to be sure, but I worked harder at being the perfect wife; and for several years, if I found time for a five-minute bath with the door closed, I was enormously grateful. Later, a wonderful psychoanalyst would say that I had simply put a plug in the tub. I must say that, with the exception of my magical children, maybe the best way of describing that time was that I was just passing through.

My marriage came to an abrupt end the night I met the man with whom I have been deeply in love since I was thirty-one. I was unprepared despite my incubation and I fell hard. It was corny, really. But love at first sight is certainly what I succumbed to. And succumbed is the wrong word. I *knew*, like I had never known before, that this was my man, that I had been born for him. I told my husband immediately and spent the next year in turmoil. I knew only two things. I was completely out of control. And I was in perfect control for the first time in my life.

That knowledge was simple. The getting from there to here has been slow, complex, and very profound. In the space of the past several years, I have lived Anne Frank's first kiss and James Joyce's "Yes." I have learned a great lesson from Giraudoux's *Apollo of Bellac* and have been reaffirmed by Rilke's beautiful understanding of love's evolution. The poet Madgett offered the perfect word of caution and Mark Twain's *Adam and Eve* put things in context. Today I hear them all clearly as I never heard them before. They helped as we two loved each other, constantly protecting what we both knew was the most important thing to have happened to us. He met my children. And they came to love him. We began to work together. And bought a house together. And formed a business together. But it was the hanging in, the deep mutual admiration, the talking, the warmness at night, the pulling our lives together that made the inevitable inevitable. We knew that the more we invested, the more we had. And when the going got rough, Jane would give me Frieda and D.H.'s letters to read, or an e.e. cummings poem, and by giggle or by thought things would be put in perspective.

Therein lies the reason for this book. It is filled with works by artists and writers who have taught and sustained me, whose experiences have enriched my own and whose insights have made mine more profound.

I hope they may do the same for you.

—Lena Tabori

INTRODUCTION

The Diary of Adam and Eve
by Mark Twain

PART I—Extracts from Adam's Diary

Monday This new creature with the long hair is a good deal in the way. It is always hanging around and following me about. I don't like this; I am not used to company. I wish it would stay with the other animals. ... Cloudy today, wind in the east; think we shall have rain ... *We?* Where did I get that word?—I remember now—the new creature uses it.

Tuesday Been examining the great waterfall. It is the finest thing on the estate, I think. The new creature calls it Niagara Falls—why, I am sure I do not know. Says it *looks* like Niagara Falls. That is not a reason, it is mere waywardness and imbecility. I get no chance to name anything myself. The new creature names everything that comes along, before I can get in a protest. And always the same pretext is offered—it *looks* like the thing. There is the dodo, for instance. Says the moment one looks at it one sees at a glance that it "looks like a dodo." It will have to keep that name, no doubt. It wearies me to fret about it, and it does no good, anyway. Dodo! It looks no more like a dodo than I do.

Wednesday Built me a shelter against the rain, but could not have it to myself in peace. The new creature intruded. When I tried to put it out it shed water out of the holes it looks with, and wiped it away with the back of its paws, and made a noise such as some of the other animals make when they are in distress. I wish it would not talk; it is always talking. That sounds like a cheap fling at the poor creature, a slur; but I do not mean it so. I have never heard the human voice before, and any new and strange sound intruding itself here upon the solemn hush of these dreaming solitudes offends my ear and seems a false note. And this new sound is so close to me; it is right at my shoulder, right at my ear, first on one side and then on the other, and I am used only to sounds that are more or less distant from me.

Friday The naming goes recklessly on, in spite of anything I can do. I had a very good name for the estate, and it was musical and pretty—GARDEN OF EDEN. Privately, I continue to call it that, but not any longer publicly. The new creature says it is all woods and rocks and scenery, and therefore has no resemblance to a garden. Says it *looks* like a park, and does not look like anything *but* a park. Consequently, without consulting me, it has been new-named—NIAGARA FALLS PARK. This is sufficiently high-handed, it seems to me. And already there is a sign up:

> KEEP OFF
> THE GRASS

My life is not as happy as it was.

Saturday The new creature eats too much fruit. We are going to run short, most likely. "We" again—that is *its* word; mine, too, now, from hearing it so much. Good deal of fog this morning. I do not go out in the fog myself. The new creature does. It goes out in all weathers, and stumps right in with its muddy feet. And talks. It used to be so pleasant and quiet here.

Sunday Pulled through. This day is getting to be more and more trying. It was selected and set apart last November as a day of rest. I had already six of them

Adam and Eve
Anonymous American artist
Circa 1830

per week before. This morning found the new creature trying to clod apples out of that forbidden tree.

Monday   The new creature says its name is Eve. That is all right, I have no objections. Says it is to call it by, when I want it to come. I said it was superfluous, then. The word evidently raised me in its respect; and indeed it is a large, good word and will bear repetition. It says it is not an It, it is a She. This is probably doubtful; yet it is all one to me; what she is were nothing to me if she would but go by herself and not talk.

Tuesday   She has littered the whole estate with execrable names and offensive signs:

THIS WAY TO THE WHIRLPOOL
THIS WAY TO GOAT ISLAND
CAVE OF THE WINDS THIS WAY

She says this park would make a tidy summer resort if there was any custom for it. Summer resort—another invention of hers—just words, without any meaning. What is a summer resort? But it is best not to ask her, she has such a rage for explaining.

Friday   She has taken to beseeching me to stop going over the Falls. What harm does it do? Says it makes her shudder. I wonder why; I have always done it —always liked the plunge, and coolness. I supposed it was what the Falls were for. They have no other use that I can see, and they must have been made for something. She says they were only made for scenery —like the rhinoceros and the mastodon.

I went over the Falls in a barrel—not satisfactory to her. Went over in a tub—still not satisfactory. Swam the Whirlpool and the Rapids in a fig-leaf suit. It got much damaged. Hence, tedious complaints about my extravagance. I am too much hampered here. What I need is change of scene.

Saturday   I escaped last Tuesday night, and traveled two days, and built me another shelter in a secluded place, and obliterated my tracks as well as I could, but she hunted me out by means of a beast which she has tamed and calls a wolf, and came making that pitiful noise again, and shedding that water out of the places she looks with. I was obliged to return with her, but will presently emigrate again when occasion offers. She engages herself in many foolish things; among others, to study out why the animals called lions and tigers live on grass and flowers, when, as she says, the sort of teeth they wear would indicate that they were intended to eat each other. This is foolish, because to do that would be to kill each other, and that would introduce what, as I understand it, is called "death"; and death, as I have been told, has not yet entered the Park. Which is a pity, on some accounts.

Sunday   Pulled through.

Monday   I believe I see what the week is for: it is to give time to rest up from the weariness of Sunday. It seems a good idea... She has been climbing that tree again. Clodded her out of it. She said nobody was looking. Seems to consider that a sufficient justification

for chancing any dangerous thing. Told her that. The word justification moved her admiration—and envy, too, I thought. It is a good word.

Tuesday   She told me she was made out of a rib taken from my body. This is at least doubtful, if not more than that. I have not missed any rib... She is in much trouble about the buzzard; says grass does not agree with it; is afraid she can't raise it; thinks it was intended to live on decayed flesh. The buzzard must get along the best it can with what it is provided. We cannot overturn the whole scheme to accommodate the buzzard.

Saturday   She fell in the pond yesterday when she was looking at herself in it, which she is always doing. She nearly strangled, and said it was most uncomfortable. This made her sorry for the creatures which live in there, which she calls fish, for she continues to fasten names on to things that don't need them and don't come when they are called by them, which is a matter of no consequence to her, she is such a numskull, anyway; so she got a lot of them out and brought them in last night and put them in my bed to keep warm, but I have noticed them now and then all day and I don't see that they are any happier there than they were before, only quieter. When night comes I shall throw them outdoors. I will not sleep with them again, for I find them clammy and unpleasant to lie among when a person hasn't anything on.

Sunday   Pulled through

Tuesday   She has taken up with a snake now. The other animals are glad, for she was always experimenting with them and bothering them; and I am glad because the snake talks, and this enables me to get a rest.

Friday   She says the snake advises her to try the fruit of that tree, and says the result will be a great and fine and noble education. I told her there would be another result, too—it would introduce death into the world. That was a mistake—it had been better to keep the remark to myself; it only gave her an idea—she could save the sick buzzard, and furnish fresh meat to the despondent lions and tigers. I advised her to keep away from the tree. She said she wouldn't. I foresee trouble. Will emigrate.

Wednesday   I have had a variegated time. I escaped last night, and rode a horse all night as fast as he could go, hoping to get clear out of the Park and hide in some other country before the trouble should begin; but it was not to be. About an hour after sun-up, as I was riding through a flowery plain where thousands of animals were grazing, slumbering, or playing with each other, according to their wont, all of a sudden they broke into a tempest of frightful noises, and in one moment the plain was a frantic commotion and every beast was destroying its neighbor. I knew what it meant—Eve had eaten that fruit, and death was come into the world... The tigers ate my horse, paying no attention when I ordered them to desist, and they would have eaten me if I had stayed—which I didn't, but went away in much haste...I found this place, outside the Park, and was fairly comfortable for a few days, but she has found me out. Found me out, and has named the place Tonawanda—says it *looks* like that. In fact I was sorry she came, for there are but meager pickings here, and she brought some of those apples. I was obliged to eat them, I was so hungry. It was against my principles, but I find that principles have no real force except when one is well fed...She came curtained in boughs and bunches of leaves, and when I asked her what she meant by such nonsense, and snatched them away and threw them down, she tittered and blushed. I had never seen a person titter and blush before, and to me it seemed unbecoming and idiotic. She said I would soon know how it was myself. This was correct. Hungry as I was, I laid down the apple half-eaten—certainly the best one I ever saw, considering the lateness of the season—and arrayed myself in the discarded boughs and branches, and then spoke to her with some severity and ordered her to go and get some more and not make such a spectacle of herself. She did it, and after this we crept down to where the wild-beast battle had been, and collected some skins, and I made her patch together a couple of suits proper for public occasions. They are uncomfortable, it is true, but stylish, and that is the main point about clothes...I find she is a good deal of a companion. I see I should be lonesome and depressed without her, now that I have lost my property. Another thing, she says it is ordered that we work for our living hereafter. She will be useful. I will superintend.

Ten Days Later   She accuses *me* of being the cause of our disaster! She says, with apparent sincerity and truth, that the Serpent assured her that the forbidden fruit was not apples, it was chestnuts. I said I was innocent, then, for I had not eaten any chestnuts. She said the Serpent informed her that "chestnut" was a figurative term meaning an aged and moldy joke. I turned pale at that, for I have made many jokes to pass the weary time, and some of them could have been of that sort, though I had honestly supposed that they were new when I made them. She asked me if I had made one just at the time of the catastrophe. I was obliged to admit that I had made one to myself, though not aloud. It was this. I was thinking about the Falls, and I said to myself, "How wonderful it is to see that vast body of water tumble down there!" Then in an instant a bright thought flashed into my head, and I let it fly, saying, "It would be a deal more wonderful to see it tumble *up* there!"—and I was just about to kill myself with laughing at it when all nature broke loose in war and death and I had to flee for my life. "There," she said, with triumph, "that is just it; the Serpent mentioned that very jest, and called it the First Chestnut, and said it was coeval with the creation." Alas, I am indeed to blame. Would that I were not witty; oh, that I had never had that radiant thought!

Next Year   We have named it Cain. She caught it while I was up country trapping on the North Shore of the Erie; caught it in the timber a couple of miles from our dug-out—or it might have been four, she isn't cer-

tain which. It resembles us in some ways, and may be a relation. That is what she thinks, but this is an error, in my judgment. The difference in size warrants the conclusion that it is a different and new kind of animal—a fish, perhaps, though when I put it in the water to see, it sank, and she plunged in and snatched it out before there was opportunity for the experiment to determine the matter. I still think it is a fish, but she is indifferent about what it is, and will not let me have it to try. I do not understand this. The coming of the creature seems to have changed her whole nature and made her unreasonable about experiments. She thinks more of it than she does of any of the other animals, but is not able to explain why. Her mind is disordered—everything shows it. Sometimes she carries the fish in her arms half the night when it complains and wants to get to the water. At such times the water comes out of the places in her face that she looks out of, and she pats the fish on the back and makes soft sounds with her mouth to soothe it, and betrays sorrow and solicitude in a hundred ways. I have never seen her do like this with any other fish, and it troubles me greatly. She used to carry the young tigers around so, and play with them, before we lost our property, but it was only play; she never took on about them like this when their dinner disagreed with them.

Sunday   She doesn't work, Sundays, but lies around all tired out, and likes to have the fish wallow over her; and she makes fool noises to amuse it, and pretends to chew its paws, and that makes it laugh. I have not seen a fish before that could laugh. This makes me doubt...I have come to like Sunday myself. Superintending all the week tires a body so. There ought to be more Sundays. In the old days they were tough, but now they come handy.

Wednesday   It isn't a fish. I cannot quite make out what it is. It makes curious devilish noises when not satisfied, and says "goo-goo" when it is. It is not one of us, for it doesn't walk; it is not a bird, for it doesn't fly; it is not a frog, for it doesn't hop; it is not a snake, for it doesn't crawl, I feel sure it is not a fish, though I cannot get a chance to find out whether it can swim or not. It merely lies around, and mostly on its back, with its feet up. I have not seen any other animal do that before. I said I believed it was an enigma; but she only admired the word without understanding it. In my judgment it is either an enigma or some kind of a bug. If it dies, I will take it apart and see what its arrangements are. I never had a thing perplex me so.

Three Months Later   The perplexity augments instead of diminishing. I sleep but little. It has ceased from lying around, and goes about on its four legs now. Yet if differs from the other four-legged animals, in that its front legs are unusually short, consequently this causes the main part of its person to stick up uncomfortably high in the air, and this is not attractive. It is built much as we are, but its method of traveling shows that it is not of our breed. The short front legs and long hind ones indicate that it is of the kangaroo family, but it is a marked variation of the species, since the true kangaroo hops, whereas this one never does. Still it is a

curious and interesting variety, and has not been catalogued before. As I discovered it, I have felt justified in securing the credit of the discovery by attaching my name to it, and hence have called it *Kangaroorum Adamiensis*.... It must have been a young one when it came, for it has grown exceedingly since. It must be five times as big, now, as it was then, and when discontented it is able to make from twenty-two to thirty-eight times the noise it made at first. Coercion does not modify this, but has the contrary effect. For this reason I discontinued the system. She reconciles it by persuasion, and by giving it things which she had previously told me she wouldn't give it. As already observed, I was not at home when it first came, and she told me she found it in the woods. It seems odd that it should be the only one, yet it must be so, for I have worn myself out these many weeks trying to find another one to add to my collection, and for this one to play with; for surely then it would be quieter and we could tame it more easily. But I find none, nor any vestige of any; and strangest of all, no tracks. It has to live on the ground, it cannot help itself; therefore, how does it get about without leaving a track? I have set a dozen traps, but they do no good. I catch all small animals except that one; animals that merely go into the trap out of curiosity, I think, to see what the milk is there for. They never drink it.

Three Months Later   The Kangaroo still continues to grow, which is very strange and perplexing. I never knew one to be so long getting its growth. It has fur on its head now; not like kangaroo fur, but exactly like our hair except that it is much finer and softer, and instead of being black is red. I am like to lose my mind over the capricious and harassing developments of this unclassifiable zoological freak. If I could catch another one—but that is hopeless; it is a new variety, and the only sample; this is plain. But I caught a true kangaroo and brought it in, thinking that this one, being lonesome, would rather have that for company than have no kin at all, or any animal it could feel a nearness to or get sympathy from in its forlorn condition here among strangers who do not know its ways or habits, or what to do to make it feel that it is among friends; but it was a mistake—it went into such fits at the sight of the kangaroo that I was convinced it had never seen one before. I pity the poor noisy little animal, but there is nothing I can do to make it happy. If I could tame it—but that is out of the question; the more I try the worse I seem to make it. It grieves me to the heart to see it in its little storms of sorrow and passion. I wanted to let it go, but she wouldn't hear of it. That seemed cruel and not like her; and yet she may be right. It might be lonelier than ever; for since I cannot find another one, how could *it?*

Five Months Later   It is not a kangaroo. No, for it supports itself by holding to her finger, and thus goes a few steps on its hind legs, and then falls down. It is probably some kind of a bear; and yet it has no tail—as yet—and no fur, except on its head. It still keeps on growing—that is a curious circumstance, for bears get their growth earlier than this. Bears are dangerous—since our catastrophe—and I shall not be

detail from
Peaceable Kingdom
of the Branch
by Edward Hicks
1830–1840

satisfied to have this one prowling about the place much longer without a muzzle on. I have offered to get her a kangaroo if she would let this one go, but it did no good—she is determined to run us into all sorts of foolish risks, I think. She was not like this before she lost her mind.

A Fortnight Later   I examined its mouth. There is no danger yet: it has only one tooth. It has no tail yet. It makes more noise now than it ever did before—and mainly at night. I have moved out. But I shall go over, mornings, to breakfast, and see if it has more teeth. If it gets a mouthful of teeth it will be time for it to go, tail or no tail, for a bear does not need a tail in order to be dangerous.

Four Months Later   I have been off hunting and fishing a month, up in the region that she calls Buffalo; I don't know why, unless it is because there are not any buffaloes there. Meantime the bear has learned to paddle around all by itself on its hind legs, and says "poppa" and "momma." It is certainly a new species. This resemblance to words may be purely accidental, of course, and may have no purpose or meaning; but even in that case it is still extraordinary, and is a thing which no other bear can do. This imitation of speech, taken together with general absence of fur and entire absence of tail, sufficiently indicates that this is a new kind of bear. The further study of it will be exceedingly interesting. Meantime I will go off on a far expedition among the forests of the north and make an exhaustive search. There must certainly be another one somewhere, and this one will be less dangerous when it has company of its own species. I will go straightway; but I will muzzle this one first.

Three Months Later   It has been a weary, weary hunt, yet I have had no success. In the mean time, without stirring from the home estate, she has caught another one! I never saw such luck. I might have hunted these woods a hundred years, I never would have run across that thing.

Next Day   I have been comparing the new one with the old one, and it is perfectly plain that they are the same breed. I was going to stuff one of them for my collection, but she is prejudiced against it for some reason or other; so I have relinquished the idea, though I think it is a mistake. It would be an irreparable loss to science if they should get away. The old one is tamer than it was and can laugh and talk like the parrot, having learned this, no doubt, from being with the parrot so much, and having the imitative faculty in a highly developed degree. I shall be astonished if it turns out to be a new kind of parrot; and yet I ought not to be astonished, for it has already been everything else it could think of since those first days when it was a fish. The new one is as ugly now as the old one was at first; has the same sulphur-and-raw-meat complexion and the same singular head without any fur on it. She calls it Abel.

Ten Years Later   They are *boys*; we found it out long ago. It was their coming in that small, immature shape that puzzled us; we were not used to it. There are some girls now. Abel is a good boy, but if Cain had stayed a bear it would have improved him. After all these years, I see that I was mistaken about Eve in the beginning; it is better to live outside the Garden with her than inside it without her. At first I thought she talked too much; but now I should be sorry to have that voice fall silent and pass out of my life. Blessed be the chestnut that brought us near together and taught me to know the goodness of her heart and the sweetness of her spirit!

PART II—Eve's Diary

(*Translated from the original*)

Saturday   I am almost a whole day old, now. I arrived yesterday. That is as it seems to me. And it must be so, for if there was a day-before-yesterday I was not there when it happened, or I should remember it. It could be, of course, that it did happen, and that I was not noticing. Very well; I will be very watchful now, and if any day-before-yesterdays happen I will make a note of it. It will be best to start right and not let the record get confused, for some instinct tells me that these details are going to be important to the historian some day. For I feel like an experiment, I feel exactly like an experiment; it would be impossible for a person to feel more like an experiment than I do, and so I am coming to feel convinced that that is what I *am*—an experiment; just an experiment, and nothing more.

Then if I am an experiment, am I the whole of it? No, I think not; I think the rest of it is part of it. I am the main part of it, but I think the rest of it has its share in the matter. Is my position assured, or do I have to watch it and take care of it? The latter, perhaps. Some instinct tells me that eternal vigilance is the price of supremacy. [That is a good phrase, I think, for one so young.]

Everything looks better to-day than it did yesterday. In the rush of finishing up yesterday, the mountains were left in a ragged condition, and some of the plains were so cluttered with rubbish and remnants that the aspects were quite distressing. Noble and beautiful works of art should not be subjected to haste; and this majestic new world is indeed a most noble and beautiful work. And certainly marvelously near to being perfect, notwithstanding the shortness of the time. There are too many stars in some places and not enough in others, but that can be remedied presently, no doubt. The moon got loose last night, and slid down and fell out of the scheme—a very great loss; it breaks my heart to think of it. There isn't another thing among the ornaments and decorations that is comparable to it for beauty and finish. It should have been fastened better. If we can only get it back again—

But of course there is no telling where it went to. And besides, whoever gets it will hide it; I know it because I would do it myself. I believe I can be honest in all other matters, but I already begin to realize that the core and center of my nature is love of the beautiful, a passion for the beautiful, and that it would not be safe to trust me with a moon that belonged to another person and that person didn't know I had it. I could give up a moon that I found in the daytime, because I should be afraid some one was looking; but if I found it in the dark, I am sure I should find some kind of an excuse for not saying anything about it. For I do love moons, they are so pretty and so romantic. I wish we had five or six; I would never go to bed; I should never get tired lying on the moss-bank and looking up at them.

Stars are good, too. I wish I could get some to put in my hair. But I suppose I never can. You would be surprised to find how far off they are, for they do not look it. When they first showed, last night, I tried to knock some down with a pole, but it didn't reach, which astonished me; then I tried clods till I was all tired out, but I never got one. It was because I am left-handed and cannot throw good. Even when I aimed at the one I wasn't after I couldn't hit the other one, though I did make some close shots, for I saw the black blot of the clod sail right into the midst of the golden clusters forty or fifty times, just barely missing them, and if I could have held out a little longer maybe I could have got one.

So I cried a little, which was natural, I suppose, for one of my age, and after I was rested I got a basket and started for a place on the extreme rim of the circle, where the stars were close to the ground and I could get them with my hands, which would be better, anyway, because I could gather them tenderly then, and not break them. But it was farther than I thought, and at last I had to give it up; I was so tired I couldn't drag my feet another stop; and besides, they were sore and hurt me very much.

I couldn't get back home; it was too far and turning cold; but I found some tigers and nestled in among them and was most adorably comfortable, and their breath was sweet and pleasant, because they live on strawberries. I had never seen a tiger before, but I knew them in a minute by the stripes. If I could have one of those skins, it would make a lovely gown.

To-day I am getting better ideas about distances. I was so eager to get hold of every pretty thing that I giddily grabbed for it, sometimes when it was too far off, and sometimes when it was but six inches away but seemed a foot—alas, with thorns between! I learned a lesson; also I made an axiom, all out of my own head—my very first one: *The scratched Experiment shuns the thorn*. I think it is a very good one for one so young.

I followed the other Experiment around, yesterday afternoon, at a distance, to see what it might be for, if I could. But I was not able to make out. I think it is a man. I had never seen a man, but it looked like one, and I feel sure that that is what it is. I realize that I feel more curiosity about it than about any of the other reptiles. If it is a reptile, and I suppose it is; for it has frowsy hair and blue eyes, and looks like a reptile. It has no hips; it tapers like a carrot; when it stands, it spreads itself apart like a derrick; so I think it is a reptile, thought it may be architecture.

I was afraid of it at first, and started to run every time it turned around, for I thought it was going to chase me; but by and by I found it was only trying to get away, so after that I was not timid any more, but tracked it along, several hours, about twenty yards

behind, which made it nervous and unhappy. At last it was a good deal worried, and climbed a tree. I waited a good while, then gave it up and went home.

To-day the same thing over. I've got it up the tree again.

Sunday It is up there yet. Resting, apparently. But that is a subterfuge: Sunday isn't the day of rest; Saturday is appointed for that. It looks to me like a creature that is more interested in resting than in anything else. It would tire me to rest so much. It tires me just to sit around and watch the tree. I do wonder what it is for; I never see it do anything.

They returned the moon last night, and I was *so* happy! I think it is very honest of them. It slid down and fell off again, but I was not distressed; there is no need to worry when one has that kind of neighbors; they will fetch it back. I wish I could do something to show my appreciation. I would like to send them some stars, for we have more than we can use. I mean I, not we, for I can see that the reptile cares nothing for such things.

It has low tastes, and is not kind. When I went there yesterday evening in the gloaming it had crept down and was trying to catch the little speckled fishes that play in the pool, and I had to clod it to make it go up the tree again and let them alone. I wonder if *that* is what it is for? Hasn't it any heart? Hasn't it any compassion for those little creatures? Can it be that it was designed and manufactured for such ungentle work? It has the look of it. One of the clods took it back of the ear, and it used language. It gave me a thrill, for it was the first time I had ever heard speech, except my own. I did not understand the words, but they seemed expressive.

When I found it could talk I felt a new interest in it, for I love to talk; I talk, all day, and in my sleep, too, and I am very interesting, but if I had another to talk to I could be twice as interesting, and would never stop, if desired.

If this reptile is a man, it isn't an *it*, is it? That wouldn't be grammatical, would it? I think it would be *he*. I think so. In that case one would parse it thus: nominative, *he*; dative, *him*; possessive, *his'n*. Well, I will consider it a man and call it he until it turns out to be something else. This will be handier than having so many uncertainties.

Next week Sunday All the week I tagged around after him and tried to get acquainted. I had to do the talking, because he was shy, but I didn't mind it. He seemed pleased to have me around, and I used the sociable "we" a good deal, because it seemed to flatter him to be included.

Wednesday We are getting along very well indeed, now, and getting better and better acquainted. He does not try to avoid me any more, which is a good sign, and shows that he likes to have me with him. That pleases me, and I study to be useful to him in every way I can, so as to increase his regard. During the last day or two I have taken all the work of naming things off his hands, and this has been a great relief to him, for he has not gift in that line, and is evidently very grateful. He can't think of a rational name to save him, but I do not let him see that I am aware of his defect. Whenever a new creature comes along I name it before he has time to expose himself by an awkward silence. In this way I have saved him many embarrassments. I have no defect like his. The minute I set eyes on an animal I know what it is. I don't have to reflect a moment; the right name comes out instantly, just as if it were an inspiration, as no doubt it is, for I am sure it wasn't in me half a minute before. I seem to know just by the shape of the creature and the way it acts what animal it is.

When the dodo came along he thought it was a wildcat—I saw it in his eye. But I saved him. And I was careful not to do it in a way that could hurt his pride. I just spoke up in a quite natural way of pleased surprise, and not as if I was dreaming of conveying information, and said, "Well, I do declare, if there isn't the dodo!" I explained—without seeming to be explaining—how I knew it for a dodo, and although I thought maybe he was a little piqued that I knew the creature when he didn't, it was quite evident that he admired me. That was very agreeable, and I thought of it more than once with gratification before I slept. How little a thing can make us happy when we feel we have earned it!

Thursday My first sorrow. Yesterday he avoided me and seemed to wish I would not talk to him. I could not believe it, and thought there was some mistake, for I loved to be with him, and loved to hear him talk, and so how could it be that he could feel unkind toward me when I had not done anything? But at last it seemed true, so I went away and sat lonely in the place where I first saw him the morning that we were made and I did not know what he was and was indifferent about him; but now it was a mournful place, and every little thing spoke of him, and my heart was very sore. I did not know why very clearly, for it was a new feeling; I had not experienced it before, and it was all a mystery, and I could not make it out.

But when night came I could not bear the lonesomeness, and went to the new shelter which he has built, to ask him what I had done that was wrong and how I could mend it and get back his kindness again; but he put me out in the rain, and it was my first sorrow.

Sunday It is pleasant again, now, and I am happy; but those were heavy days; I do not think of them when I can help it.

I tried to get him some of those apples, but I cannot learn to throw straight. I failed, but I think the good intention pleased him. They are forbidden, and he says I shall come to harm; but so I come to harm through pleasing him, why shall I care for that harm?

Monday This morning I told him my name, hoping it would interest him. But he did not care for it. It is strange. If he should tell me his name, I would care. I think it would be pleasanter in my ears than any other sound.

He talks very little. Perhaps it is because he is not bright, and is sensitive about it and wishes to conceal it. It is such a pity that he should feel so, for brightness is nothing; it is in the heart that the values lie. I wish I could make him understand that a loving good heart is riches, and riches enough, and that without it intellect is poverty.

Although he talks so little, he has quite a considerable vocabulary. This morning he used a surprisingly good word. He evidently recognized, himself, that it was a good one, for he worked it in twice afterward, casually. It was not good casual art, still it showed that he possesses a certain quality of perception. Without a doubt that seed can be made to grow, if cultivated.

Where did he get that word? I do not think I have ever used it.

No, he took no interest in my name. I tried to hide my disappointment, but I suppose I did not succeed. I went away and sat on the moss-bank with my feet in the water. It is where I go when I hunger for companionship, some one to look at, some one to talk to. It is not enough—that lovely white body painted there in the pool—but it is something, and something is better than utter loneliness. It talks when I talk; it is sad when I am sad; it comforts me with its sympathy; it says, "Do not be downhearted, you poor friendless girl; I will be your friend." It *is* a good friend to me, and my only one; it is my sister.

That first time that she forsook me! ah, I shall never forget that—never, never. My heart was lead in my body! I said, "She was all I had, and now she is gone!" In my despair I said, "Break, my heart; I cannot bear my life any more!" and hid my face in my hands, and there was no solace for me. And when I took them away, after a little, there she was again, white and shining and beautiful, and I sprang into her arms!

That was perfect happiness; I had known happiness before, but it was not like this, which was ecstasy. I never doubted her afterward. Sometimes she stayed away—maybe an hour, maybe almost the whole day, but I waited and did not doubt; I said, "She is busy, or she is gone a journey, but she will come." And it was so: she always did. At night she would not come if it was dark, for she was a timid little thing; but if there was a moon she would come. I am not afraid of the dark, but she is younger than I am; she was born after I was. Many and many are the visits I have paid her; she is my comfort and my refuge when my life is hard—and it is mainly that.

Tuesday All the morning I was at work improving the estate; and I purposely kept away from him in the hope that he would get lonely and come. But he did not.

At noon I stopped for the day and took my recreation by flitting all about with the bees and the butterflies and reveling in the flowers, those beautiful creatures that catch the smile of God out of the sky and preserve it! I gathered them, and made them into wreaths and garlands and clothed myself in them while I ate my luncheon—apples, of course; then I sat in the shade and wished and waited. But he did not come.

But no matter. Nothing would have come of it, for he does not care for flowers. He calls them rubbish, and cannot tell one from another, and thinks it is superior to feel like that. He does not care for me, he does not care for flowers, he does not care for the painted sky at eventide—is there anything he does care for, except building shacks to coop himself up in from the good clean rain, and thumping the melons, and sampling the grapes, and fingering the fruit on the trees, to see how those properties are coming along?

I laid a dry stick on the ground and tried to bore a hole in it with another one, in order to carry out a scheme that I had, and soon I got an awful fright. A thin, transparent bluish film rose out of the hole, and I dropped everything and ran! I thought it was a spirit, and I *was* so frightened! But I looked back, and it was not coming; so I leaned against a rock and rested and panted, and let my limbs go on trembling until they got steady again; then I crept warily back, alert, watching, and ready to fly if there was occasion; and when I was come near, I parted the branches of a rose-bush and peeped through—wishing the man was about, I was looking so cunning and pretty—but the sprite was gone. I went there, and there was a pinch of delicate pink dust in the hole. I put my finger in, to feel it, and said *ouch!* and took it out again. It was a cruel pain. I put my finger in my mouth; and by standing first on one foot and then the other, and grunting, I presently eased my misery; then I was full of interest, and began to examine.

I was curious to know what the pink dust was. Suddenly the name of it occurred to me, though I had never heard of it before. It was *fire!* I was as certain of it as a person could be of anything in the world. So without hesitation I named it that—fire.

I had created something that didn't exist before; I had added a new thing to the world's uncountable properties; I realized this, and was proud of my achievement, and was going to run and find him and tell him about it, thinking to raise myself in his esteem—but I reflected, and did not do it. No—he would not care for it. He would ask what it was good for, and what could I answer? For if it was not *good* for something, but only beautiful, merely beautiful—

So I sighed, and did not go. For it wasn't good for anything; it could not build a shack, it could not improve melons, it could not hurry a fruit crop; it was useless, it was a foolishness and a vanity; he would despise it and say cutting words. But to me it was not despicable; I said, "Oh, you fire, I love you, you dainty pink creature, for you are *beautiful*—and that is enough!" and was going to gather it to my breast. But refrained. Then I made another maxim out of my own head, though it was so nearly like the first one that I was afraid it was only a plagiarism: *"The burnt Experiment shuns the fire."*

I wrought again; and when I had made a good deal of fire-dust I emptied it into a handful of dry brown grass, intending to carry it home and keep it always and play with it; but the wind struck it and it sprayed up and spat out at me fiercely, and I dropped it and ran. When I looked back the blue spirit was towering up and stretching and rolling away like a cloud, and instantly I thought of the name of it—*smoke!*—though, upon my word, I had never heard of smoke before.

Soon, brilliant yellow and red flares shot up through the smoke, and I named them in an instant—*flames*— and I was right, too, though these were the very first flames that had ever been in the world. They climbed the trees, they flashed splendidly in and out of the vast and increasing volume of tumbling smoke, and I had to clap my hands and laugh and dance in my rapture, it was so new and strange and so wonderful and so beautiful!

He came running, and stopped and gazed, and said not a word for many minutes. Then he asked what it was. Ah, it was too bad that he should ask such a direct question. I had to answer it, of course, and I did. I said it was fire. If it annoyed him that I should know and he must ask, that was not my fault; I had no desire to annoy him. After a pause he asked:

"How did it come?"

Another direct question, and it also had to have a direct answer.

"I made it."

The fire was traveling farther and farther off. He went to the edge of the burned place and stood looking down, and said:

"What are these?"

"Fire-coals."

He picked up one to examine it, but changed his mind and put it down again. Then he went away. *Nothing* interests him.

But I was interested. There were ashes, gray and soft and delicate and pretty—I knew what they were at once. And the embers; I knew the embers, too. I found my apples, and raked them out, and was glad; for I am very young and my appetite is active. But I was disappointed; they were all burst open and spoiled. Spoiled apparently; but it was not so; they were better than raw ones. Fire is beautiful; some day it will be useful, I think.

Friday   I saw him again, for a moment, last Monday at nightfall, but only for a moment. I was hoping he would praise me for trying to improve the estate, for I had meant well and had worked hard. But he was not pleased, and turned away and left me. He was also displeased on another account: I tried once more to persuade him to stop going over the Falls. That was because the fire had revealed to me a new passion —quite new, and distinctly different from love, grief, and those others which I had already discovered—*fear*. And it is horrible!—I wish I had never discovered it; it gives me dark moments, it spoils my happiness, it makes me shiver and tremble and shudder. But I could not persuade him, for he has not discovered fear yet, and so he could not understand me.

Extract from Adam's Diary

Perhaps I ought to remember that she is very young, a mere girl, and make allowances. She is all interest, eagerness, vivacity, the world is to her a charm, a wonder, a mystery, a joy; she can't speak for delight when she finds a new flower, she must pet it and caress it and smell it and talk to it, and pour out endearing names upon it. And she is colormad: brown rocks, yellow sand, gray moss, green foliage, blue sky; the pearl of the dawn, the purple shadows on the mountains, the golden islands floating in crimson seas at sunset, the pallid moon sailing through the shredded cloud-rack, the star-jewels glittering in the wastes of space—none of them is of any practical value, so far as I can see, but because they have color and majesty, that is enough for her, and she loses her mind over them. If she could quiet down and keep still a couple of minutes at a time, it would be a reposeful spectacle. In that case I think I could enjoy looking at her; indeed I am sure I could, for I am coming to realize that she is a quite remarkably comely creature—lithe, slender, trim, rounded, shapely, nimble, graceful; and once when she was standing marble-white and sun-drenched on a boulder, with her young head tilted back and her hand shading her eyes, watching the flight of a bird in the sky, I recognized that she was beautiful.

Monday noon   If there is anything on the planet that she is not interested in it is not in my list. There are animals that I am indifferent to, but it is not so with her. She has no discrimination, she takes to all of them, she thinks they are all treasures, every new one is welcome.

When the mighty brontosaurus came striding into camp, she regarded it as an acquisition, I considered it a calamity; that is a good example of the lack of harmony that prevails in our views of things. She wanted to domesticate it, I wanted to make it a present of the homestead and move out. She believed it could be tamed by kind treatment and would be a good pet; I said a pet twenty-one feet high and eighty-four feet long would be no proper thing to have about the place, because, even with the best intentions and without meaning any harm, it could sit down on the house and mash it, for any one could see by the look of its eye that it was absent-minded.

Still, her heart was set upon having that monster, and she couldn't give it up. She thought we could start a dairy with it, and wanted me to help her milk it; but I wouldn't; it was too risky. The sex wasn't right, and we hadn't any ladder anyway. Then she wanted to ride it, and look at the scenery. Thirty or forty feet of its tail was lying on the ground, like a fallen tree, and she thought she could climb it, but she was mistaken; when she got to the steep place it was too slick and down she came, and would have hurt herself but for me.

Was she satisfied now? No. Nothing ever satisfies her but demonstration; untested theories are not in her line, and she won't have them. It is the right spirit, I concede it; it attracts me; I feel the influence of it; if I were with her more I think I should take it up myself. Well, she had one theory remaining about this colossus: she thought that if we could tame him and make him friendly we could stand him in the river and use him for a bridge. It turned out that he was already plenty tame enough—at least as far as she was concerned—so she tried her theory, but it failed: every time she got him properly placed in the river and went ashore to cross over on him, he came out and followed her around like a pet mountain. Like the other animals. They all do that.

Friday   Tuesday—Wednesday—Thursday—and to-day: all without seeing him. It is a long time to be alone; still, it is better to be alone than unwelcome.

I *had* to have company—I was made for it, I think —so I made friends with the animals. They are just charming, and they have the kindest disposition and the politest ways; they never look sour, they never let you feel that you are intruding, they smile at you and wag their tail, if they've got one, and they are always ready for a romp or an excursion or anything you want to propose. I think they are perfect gentlemen. All these days we have had such good times, and it hasn't been lonesome for me, ever. Lonesome! No, I should say not. Why, there's always a swarm of them around—sometimes as much as four or five acres—you can't count them; and when you stand on a rock in the midst and look over the furry expanse it is so mottled and splashed and gay with color and frisking sheen and sun-flash, and so rippled with stripes, that you might think it was a lake, only you know it isn't; and there's storms of sociable birds, and hurricanes of whirring wings; and when the sun strikes all that feathery commotion, you have a blazing up of all the colors you can think of, enough to put your eyes out.

We have made long excursions, and I have seen a great deal of the world; almost all of it, I think; and so I am the first traveler, and the only one. When we are on the march, it is an imposing sight—there's nothing like it anywhere. For comfort I ride a tiger or a leopard, because it is soft and has a round back that fits me, and because they are such pretty animals; but for long distance or for scenery I ride the elephant. He hoists me up with his trunk, but I can get off myself; when we are ready to camp, he sits and I slide down the back way.

The birds and animals are all friendly to each other, and there are no disputes about anything. They all talk, and they all talk to me, but it must be a foreign language, for I cannot make out a word they say; yet they often understand me when I talk back, particularly the dog and the elephant. It makes me ashamed. It shows that they are brighter than I am, and are therefore my superiors. It annoys me, for I want to be the principal Experiment myself—and I intend to be, too.

I have learned a number of things, and am educated, now, but I wasn't at first. I was ignorant at first. At first it used to vex me because, with all my watching, I was never smart enough to be around when the water was running uphill; but now I do not mind it. I have experimented and experimented until now I know it never does run uphill, except in the dark. I know it does in the dark, because the pool never goes dry, which it would, of course, if the water didn't come back in the night. It is best to prove things by actual experiment; then you *know*; whereas if you depend on guessing and supposing and conjecturing, you will never get educated.

Some things you *can't* find out; but you will never know you can't by guessing and supposing: no, you have to be patient and go on experimenting until you find out that you can't find out. And it is delightful to have it that way, it makes the world so interesting. If there wasn't anything to find out, it would be dull. Even trying to find out and not finding out is just as interesting as trying to find out and finding out, and I don't know but more so. The secret of the water was a treasure until I *got* it; then the excitement all went away, and I recognized a sense of loss.

By experiment I know that wood swims, and dry leaves, and feathers, and plenty of other things; therefore by all that cumulative evidence you know that a rock will swim; but you have to put up with simply knowing it, for there isn't any way to prove it—up to now. But I shall find a way—then *that* excitement will go. Such things make me sad; because by and by when I have found out everything there won't be any more excitements, and I do love excitements so! The other night I couldn't sleep for thinking about it.

At first I couldn't make out what I was made for, but now I think it was to search out the secrets of this wonderful world and be happy and thank the Giver of it all for devising it. I think there are many things to learn yet—I hope so; and by economizing and not hurrying too fast I think they will last weeks and weeks. I hope so. When you cast up a feather it sails away on the air and goes out of sight; then you throw up a clod and it doesn't. It comes down, every time. I have tried it and tried it, and it is always so. I wonder why it is? Of course it *doesn't* come down, but why should it *seem* to? I suppose it is an optical illusion. I mean, one of them is. I don't know which one. It may be the feather, it may be the clod; I can't prove which it is, I can only demonstrate that one or the other is a fake, and let a person take his choice.

By watching, I know that the stars are not going to last. I have seen some of the best ones melt and run down the sky. Since one can melt, they can all melt; since they can all melt, they can all melt the same night. That sorrow will come—I know it. I mean to sit up every night and look at them as long as I can keep awake; and I will impress those sparkling fields on my memory, so that by and by when they are taken away I can by my fancy restore those lovely myriads to the black sky and make them sparkle again, and double them by the blur of my tears.

AFTER THE FALL

When I look back, the Garden is a dream to me. It was beautiful, surpassingly beautiful, enchantingly beautiful; and now it is lost, and I shall not see it any more.

The Garden is lost, but I have found *him*, and am content. He loves me as well as he can; I love him with all the strength of my passionate nature, and this, I think, is proper to my youth and sex. If I ask myself why I love him, I find I do not know, and do not really much care to know; so I suppose that this kind of love is not a product of reasoning and statistics, like one's love for other reptiles and animals. I think that this must be so. I love certain birds because of their song; but I do not love Adam on account of his singing—no, it is not that; the more he sings the more I do not get reconciled to it. Yet I ask him to sing, because I wish to learn to like everything he is interested in. I am sure I can learn, because at first I could not stand it, but now I can. It sours the milk, but it doesn't matter; I can get used to that kind of milk.

It is not on account of his brightness that I love him—no, it is not that. He is not to blame for his brightness, such as it is, for he did not make it himself; he is as God made him, and that is sufficient. There was a wise purpose in it, *that* I know. In time it will develop, though I think it will not be sudden; and besides, there is no hurry; he is well enough just as he is.

It is not on account of his gracious and considerate ways and his delicacy that I love him. No, he has lacks in these regards, but he is well enough just so, and is improving.

It is not on account of his industry that I love him—no, it is not that. I think he has it in him, and I do not know why he conceals it from me. It is my only pain. Otherwise he is frank and open with me, now. I am sure he keeps nothing from me but this. It grieves me that he should have a secret from me, and sometimes it spoils my sleep, thinking about it, but I will put it out of my mind; it shall not trouble my happiness, which is otherwise full to overflowing.

It is not on account of his education that I love him—no, it is not that. He is self-educated, and does really know a multitude of things, but they are not so.

It is not on account of his chivalry that I love him—no, it is not that. He told on me, but I do not blame him; it is a peculiarity of sex, I think, and he did not make his sex. Of course I would not have told on him, I would have perished first; but that is a peculiarity of sex, too, and I do not take credit for it, for I did not make my sex.

Then why is it that I love him? *Merely because he is masculine*, I think.

At bottom he is good, and I love him for that, but I could love him without it. If he should beat me and abuse me, I should go on loving him. I know it. It is a matter of sex, I think.

He is strong and handsome, and I love him for that, and I admire him and am proud of him, but I could love him without those qualities. If he were plain, I should love him; if he were a wreck, I should love him; and I would work for him, and slave over him, and pray for him, and watch by his bedside until I died.

Yes, I think I love him merely because he is *mine* and is *masculine*. There is no other reason, I suppose. And so I think it is as I first said; that this kind of love is not a product of reasonings and statistics. It just *comes*—none knows whence—and cannot explain itself. And doesn't need to.

It is what I think. But I am only a girl, and the first that has examined this matter, and it may turn out that in my ignorance and inexperience, I have not got it right.

FORTY YEARS LATER

It is my prayer, it is my longing, that we may pass from this life together—a longing which shall never perish from the earth, but shall have place in the heart of every wife that loves, until the end of time; and it shall be called by my name.

But if one of us must go first, it is my prayer that it shall be I; for he is strong, I am weak, I am not so necessary to him as he is to me—life without him would not be life; how could I endure it? This prayer is also immortal, and will not cease from being offered up while my race continues. I am the first wife; and in the last wife I shall be repeated.

AT EVE'S GRAVE

ADAM: Wheresoever she was, *there* was Eden.

YOUNG LOVE

Paolo and Francesca
by William Dyce
1837

"This bud of love, by summer's ripening breath,
May prove a beauteous flower when next we meet."

William Shakespeare

above

Persian Fresco at Isfahan
Safavid Period
Sixteenth Century

opposite

A Bridal Pair
Anonymous German artist
Circa 1470

Hindu Temple Sculpture
Khajurāho, India
Tenth to Eleventh Century

opposite, detail
Jealousy and Flirtation
by Haynes King
1874

The Glass of Lemonade
by Gerard Terborch
1663–1664

Speak Memory
by Vladimir Nabokov

On the browner and wetter part of the *plage*, that part which at low tide yielded the best mud for castles, I found myself digging, one day, side by side with a little French girl called Colette.

She would be ten in November, I had been ten in April. Attention was drawn to a jagged bit of violet mussel shell upon which she had stepped with the bare sole of her narrow long-toed foot. No, I was not English. Her greenish eyes seemed flecked with the overflow of the freckles that covered her sharp-featured face. She wore what might now be termed a playsuit, consisting of a blue jersey with rolled-up sleeves and blue knitted shorts. I had taken her at first for a boy and then had been puzzled by the bracelet on her thin wrist and the corkscrew brown curls dangling from under her sailor cap.

She spoke in birdlike bursts of rapid twitter, mixing governess English and Parisian French. Two years before, on the same *plage*, I had been much attached to Zina, the lovely, sun-tanned, bad-tempered little daughter of a Serbian naturopath—she had, I remember (absurdly, for she and I were only eight at the time), a *grain de beauté* on her apricot skin just below the heart, and there was a horrible collection of chamber pots, full and half-full, and one with surface bubbles, on the floor of the hall in her family's boardinghouse lodgings which I visited early one morning to be given by her as she was being dressed, a dead hummingbird moth found by the cat. But when I met Colette, I knew at once that this was the real thing. Colette seemed to me so much stranger than all my other chance playmates at Biarritz! I somehow acquired the feeling that she was less happy than I, less loved. A bruise on her delicate, downy forearm gave rise to awful conjectures. "He pinches as bad as my mummy," she said, speaking of a crab. I evolved various schemes to save her from her parents, who were *"des bourgeois de Paris"* as I heard somebody tell my mother with a slight shrug. I interpreted the disdain in my own fashion, as I knew that those people had come all the way from Paris in their blue-and-yellow limousine (a fashionable adventure in those days) but had drably sent Colette with her dog and governess by an ordinary coachtrain. The dog was a female fox terrier with bells on her collar and a most waggly behind. From sheer exuberance, she would lap up salt water out of Colette's toy pail. I remember the sail, the sunset and the lighthouse pictured on that pail, but I cannot recall the dog's name, and this bothers me.

During the two months of our stay at Biarritz, my passion for Colette all but surpassed my passion for Cleopatra. Since my parents were not keen to meet hers, I saw her only on the beach; but I thought of her constantly. If I noticed she had been crying, I felt a surge of helpless anguish that brought tears to my own eyes. I could not destroy the mosquitoes that had left their bites on her frail neck, but I could, and did, have a successful fistfight with a red-haired boy who had been rude to her. She used to give me warm handfuls of hard candy. One day, as we were bending together over a starfish, and Colette's ringlets were tickling my ear, she suddenly turned toward me and kissed me on the cheek. So great was my emotion that all I could think of saying was, "You little monkey."

I had a gold coin that I assumed would pay for our elopement. Where did I want to take her? Spain? America? The mountains above Pau? *"Là-bas, là-bas, dans la montagne,"* as I had heard Carmen sing at the opera. One strange night, I lay awake, listening to the recurrent thud of the ocean and planning our flight. The ocean seemed to rise and grope in the darkness and then heavily fall on its face.

Of our actual getaway, I have little to report. My memory retains a glimpse of her obediently putting on rope-soled canvas shoes, on the lee side of a flapping tent, while I stuffed a folding butterfly net into a brown-paper bag. The next glimpse is of our evading pursuit by entering a pitch-dark *cinéma* near the Casino (which, of course, was absolutely out of bounds). There we sat, holding hands across the dog, which now and then gently jingled in Colette's lap, and were shown a jerky, drizzly, but highly exciting bullfight at San Sebastián. My final glimpse is of myself being led along the promenade by Linderovski. His long legs move with a kind of ominous briskness and I can see the muscles of his grimly set jaw working under the tight skin. My bespectacled brother, aged nine, whom he happens to hold with his other hand, keeps trotting out forward to peer at me with awed curiosity, like a little owl.

Among the trivial souvenirs acquired at Biarritz before leaving, my favorite was not the small bull of black stone and not the sonorous seashell but something which now seems almost symbolic—a meerschaum penholder with a tiny peephole of crystal in its ornamental part. One held it quite close to one's eye, screwing up the other, and when one had got rid of the shimmer of one's own lashes, a miraculous photographic view of the bay and of the line of cliffs ending in a lighthouse could be seen inside.

And now a delightful thing happens. The process of recreating that penholder and the microcosm in its eyelet stimulates my memory to a last effort. I try again to recall the name of Colette's dog—and, triumphantly, along those remote beaches, over the glossy evening sands of the past, where each footprint slowly fills up with sunset water, here it comes, here it comes, echoing and vibrating: Floss, Floss, Floss!

Colette was back in Paris by the time we stopped there for a day before continuing our homeward journey; and there, in a fawn park under a cold blue sky, I saw her (by arrangement between our mentors, I believe) for the last time. She carried a hoop and a short stick to drive it with, and everything about her was extremely proper and stylish in an autumnal, Parisian, *tenue-de-ville-pour-fillettes* way. She took from her governess and slipped into my brother's hand a farewell present, a box of sugar-coated almonds, meant, I knew, solely for me; and instantly she was off, tap-tapping her glinting hoop through light and shade, around and around a fountain choked with dead leaves, near which I stood. The leaves mingle in my memory with the leather of her shoes and gloves, and there was, I remember, some detail in her attire (perhaps a ribbon on her Scottish cap, or the pattern of her stockings) that reminded me then of the rainbow spiral in a glass marble. I still seem to be holding that wisp of iridescence, not knowing exactly where to fit it, while she runs with her hoop ever faster around me and finally dissolves among the slender shadows cast on the graveled path by the interlaced arches of its low looped fence.

Scene at Houghton Farm
by Winslow Homer
Circa 1878

She Loves Me
Lyrics by Sheldon Harnick

Well, well, well, . . .
Will wonders never cease?

She loves me.
And to my amazement
I love it,
knowing that she loves me.
She loves me.
True, she doesn't show it.
How could she,
when she doesn't know it?

Yesterday she loathed me—Bah!
Now today she likes me—Hah!
And tomorrow, tomorrow—Ah. . . .

My teeth ache
from the urge to touch her.
I'm speechless,
for I mustn't tell her.
It's wrong now,
but it won't be long now
before my love discovers
that she and I are lovers.
I imagine how surprised she's bound to be.
She loves me.
She loves me.

I love her.
Isn't that a wonder?
I wonder
why I didn't want her.
I want her,
that's the thing that matters.
And matters
are improving daily.

Yesterday I loathed her—Bah!
Now today I love her—Hah!
And tomorrow, tomorrow—Ah. . . .

I'm tingling
such delicious tingles.
I'm trembling,
what the heck does that mean?
I'm freezing,
that's because it's cold out,
but still I'm incandescent
and like some adolescent,
I'd like to scrawl on every wall I see.
She loves me.
She loves me.

Anne Frank: The Diary of a Young Girl
by Anne Frank

Darlingest Kitty, remember yesterday's date for it is a very important day in my life. Surely it is an important day for any girl when she receives her first kiss. Then it is just as important for me too. How did I suddenly come by this kiss? Well, I will tell you. Yesterday evening at eight o'clock I was sitting with Peter on his divan. It wasn't long before his arms went around me. "Let's move up a bit," I said. "Then I don't bump my head against the cupboard." He moved up, almost into the corner. I laid my arm under his and across his back, and he just about buried me, because his arm was hanging on my shoulder. Now we've sat like this on other occasions, but never so close as yesterday. He held me firmly against him, my left shoulder was against his chest, and already my heart began to beat faster, but we had not finished yet. He didn't rest until my head was on his shoulder and his against it. When I sat upright again, after about five minutes, he took my head in his hands and laid it against him once more. Oh, it was so lovely. I couldn't talk much the joy was too great. He stroked my cheek and arm a bit awkwardly, played with my curls, and our heads lay touching most of the time. I can't describe the feeling that ran through me all the while. I was too happy for words and I believe he was as well. We got up about half-past eight. Peter took off his gym shoes, so that he wouldn't make noise when he went through the house and I stood beside him. How it came about so suddenly, I don't know, but before we went downstairs, he kissed me. Through my hair, half on my left cheek, half on my ear. I tore downstairs without looking around, and am simply longing for tonight.

Yours, Anne Frank

Daphnis and Chloé
by Pierre Bonnard
1902

Gigi
by Colette

"Don't forget you are going to Aunt Alicia's. Do you hear me, Gilberte? Come here and let me do your curls. Gilberte, do you hear me?"

"Couldn't I go there without having my hair curled, Grandmama?"

"I should think not," said Madame Alvarez quietly. She took an old pair of curling irons, with prongs ending in little round metal knobs, and put them to heat over the blue flame of a spirit lamp while she prepared the tissue papers.

"Grandmama, couldn't you do my hair in waves down the side of my head for a change?"

"Out of the question. Ringlets at the very ends—that's as far as a girl of your age can possibly go. Now sit down on the footstool."

To do so, Gilberte folded up under her the heronlike legs of a girl of fifteen. Below her tartan skirt, she revealed ribbed cotton stockings to just above the knees, unconscious of the perfect oval shape of her kneecaps. Slender calf and high arched instep—Madame Alvarez never let her eyes run over these fine points without regretting that her granddaughter had not studied dancing professionally. At the moment, she was thinking only of the girl's hair. She had corkscrewed the ends and fixed them in tissue paper, and was now compressing the ash-blond ringlets between the heated knobs. With patient, soft-fingered skill she gathered up the full magnificent weight of finely kept hair into sleek ripples that fell to just below Gilberte's shoulders. The girl sat quite still. The smell of the heated tongs and the whiff of vanilla in the curling papers made her feel drowsy. Besides, Gilberte knew that resistance would be useless. She hardly ever tried to elude the restraints exercised by her family.

"Is Mama singing Frasquita today?"

"Yes. And this evening in *Si j'étais Roi*. I have told you before, when you're sitting on a low seat you must keep your knees close to each other and lean both of them together, either to the right or to the left, for the sake of decorum."

"But, Grandmama, I've got on my drawers and my petticoat."

"Drawers are one thing, decorum is another," said Madame Alvarez. "Everything depends on the attitude."

"Yes, I know. Aunt Alicia has told me often enough," Gilberte murmured from under her tent of hair.

"I do not require the help of my sister," said Madame Alvarez testily, "to instruct you in the elements of propriety. On that subject, thank goodness, I know rather more than she does."

"Supposing you let me stay here with you today, Grandmama, couldn't I go see Aunt Alicia next Sunday?"

"What next!" said Madame Alvarez haughtily. "Have you any other *purposal* to make to me?"

"Yes, I have," said Gilberte. "Have my skirts made a little longer, so I don't have to fold myself up in a Z every time I sit down. You see, Grandmama, with my skirts too short, I have to keep thinking of my you-know-what."

"Silence! Aren't you ashamed to call it your you-know-what?"

"I don't mind calling it by any other name, only—"

Madame Alvarez blew out the spirit lamp, looked at the reflection of her heavy Spanish face in the looking glass above the mantelpiece, and then laid down the law: "There is no other name."

A skeptical look passed across the girl's eyes. Beneath the cockleshells of fair hair they showed a lovely dark blue, the color of glistening slate. Gilberte unfolded with a bound.

"But, Grandmama, all the same, look! If only my skirts were just that much longer! Or if a small frill could be added!"

"That *would* be nice for your mother, to be seen with a great mare who looks at least eighteen! In her profession! Where are your brains!"

"In my head," said Gilberte. "Since I hardly ever go out with Mama, what would it matter?"

She pulled down her skirt, which had climbed up toward her slim waist, and asked, "Can I go in my everyday coat? It's good enough."

"That wouldn't show that it's Sunday! Put on your serge coat and blue sailor hat. When will you learn what's what?"

On her feet, Gilberte was as tall as her grandmother.

Reclining Girl
by Richard Williams
1964

Madame Alvarez had taken the name of a Spanish lover now dead and, accordingly, had acquired a creamy complexion, an ample bust, and hair lustrous with brilliantine. She used too white a powder, and her heavy cheeks had begun to draw down her lower eyelids a little, so that eventually she took to calling herself Inez. Her family pursued their fixed orbit around her. Her unmarried daughter Andrée, forsaken by Gilberte's father, now preferred the sober life of a second-lead singer in a state-controlled theater to the fitful opulence of a life of gallantry. Aunt Alicia—none of her admirers, it seemed, had ever mentioned marriage—lived alone, on an income she pretended was modest. The family had a high opinion of Alicia's judgment and of her jewels.

Madame Alvarez looked her granddaughter up and down, from the felt sailor hat trimmed with a quill to the ready-made cavalier shoes.

"Can't you ever manage to keep your legs together? When you stand like that, the Seine could flow between them. You haven't the shadow of a stomach, and yet you somehow contrive to stick it out. And don't forget your gloves, I beg of you."

Gilberte's every posture was still governed by the unconcern of childish innocence. At times she looked like Robin Hood, at others like a stone angel, or again like a boy in skirts; but she seldom resembled a nearly grown-up girl. "How can you expect to be put into long skirts when you haven't the sense of a child of eight?" Madame Alvarez would ask. And Andrée would sigh, "I find Gilberte so discouraging." To which Gilberte would answer quietly, "If you didn't find *me* discouraging, then you'd find something else." For she was sweet and gentle, resigned to a stay-at-home life and to seeing few people outside the family. As for her features, no one could yet predict their final mold. A large mouth, which showed beautiful strong white teeth when she laughed, no chin to speak of, and, between high cheekbones, a nose—"Heavens, where did she get that button?" whispered her mother under her breath. "If you can't answer that question, my girl, who can?" retorted Madame Alvarez. Whereupon Andrée, who had become prudish too late in life and disgruntled too soon, relapsed into silence, automatically stroking her sensitive larynx. "Gigi is just a bundle of raw material," Aunt Alicia affirmed. "It may turn out very well—and, just as easily, all wrong."

"Grandmama, there's the bell! I'll open the door on my way out. Grandmama," Gigi shouted from the passage, "it's Uncle Gaston!"

She came back into the room with a tall, youngish-looking man, her arm linked through his, chattering to him with the childish pomposity of a schoolgirl out of class.

"What a pity it is, Tonton, that I've got to desert you so soon! Grandmama wishes me to pay a call on Aunt Alicia. Which motorcar are you using today? Did you come in the new four-seater-de-Dion-Boutan-with-the-collapsible-hood? I hear it can be driven simply with one hand! Goodness, Tonton, those are smart gloves, and no mistake! So you've had a fight with Liane, Tonton?"

"Gilberte," scolded Madame Alvarez, "what business of yours can that be?"

"But Grandmama, everybody knows about it. The whole story was in the *Gil Blas*. It began: 'A secret bitterness is seeping into the sweetened product of the sugarbeet....' At school all the girls were asking me about it, for of course they know I know you. And I can tell you, Tonton, there's not a soul at school who takes Liane's side! They all agree that she's behaved disgracefully!"

"Gilberte," repeated Madame Alvarez, "say good-bye to Monsieur Lachaille and run along!"

"Leave her alone, poor child," Gaston Lachaille sighed. "She, at any rate, intends no harm. And it's perfectly true that all's over between Liane and me. You're off to Aunt Alicia's, Gigi? Take my motorcar and send it back for me."

Gilberte gave a little cry, a jump of joy, and hugged Lachaille.

"Thank you, Tonton! Just think of Aunt Alicia's face! The concierge's eyes will be popping from her head!"

Off she went, with the clatter of a young filly not yet shod.

"You spoil her, Gaston," said Madame Alvarez.

But in this she was not altogether speaking the truth. Gaston Lachaille did not know how to "spoil" anyone—even himself. His luxuries were cut and dried: motorcars, a dreary mansion on the Parc Monceau, Liane's monthly "allowance" and birthday jewels, champagne and baccarat at Deauville in the summer, at Monte Carlo in the winter. From time to time he would drop a fat check into some charity fund, or finance a new daily paper, or buy a yacht only to resell it almost at once to some Central European monarch—yet from none of this did he get any fun. He would say as he looked at himself in the glass, "That's the face of a man who's been rooked." Because of his rather long nose and large dark eyes, he was regarded on all sides as easy game. His commercial instinct and rich man's caution stood him in good stead, however; no one had succeeded in robbing him of his pearl studs, of his massive gold or silver cigarette cases encrusted with precious stones, of his dark sable-lined greatcoat.

From the window he watched his motorcar start up. That year fashionable automobiles were being built with a slightly higher body and a rather wider top to accommodate the exaggerated hats affected by Caroline Otero, Liane de Pougy, and other conspicuous figures of 1899—and in consequence they would sway gently at every turn of the wheel.

"Mamita," said Gaston Lachaille, "you wouldn't make me a cup of camomile?"

"Two rather than one," answered Madame Alvarez. "Sit down, my poor Gaston."

From the depths of a dilapidated armchair she removed some crumpled illustrated papers, a stocking waiting to be darned, and a box of licorice candies known as *agents de change*. The jilted man settled down into the chair luxuriously while his hostess put out the tray and two cups.

"Why does the camomile they brew at home always smell of faded chrysanthemums?" sighed Gaston.

"It's simply a matter of taking pains. You may not believe it, Gaston, but I often pick my best camomile flowers in Paris, growing on waste ground, insignificant little flowers you would hardly notice. But they have a taste that is *esquisite*. My goodness, what beautiful cloth your suit is made of! That deep-woven stripe is as smart as can be. Just the sort of material your poor father liked! But, I must confess, he would never have carried it so elegantly."

Never more than once during the course of a conversation did Madame Alvarez evoke the memory of an elder Lachaille, whom she claimed to have known intimately. From her former relationship, real or invented, she drew no advantage other than the close relationship of Gaston Lachaille and the pleasure to be derived from watching a rich man enjoying the comforts of the poor when he made himself at home in her old armchair. Under their gas-blackened ceiling, these three feminine creatures never asked him for pearls, chinchillas, or solitaire diamonds, and they knew how to converse with tact and due solemnity on scandalous topics traditional and recondite. From the age of twelve, Gigi had known that Madame Otero's string of large black pearls were "dipped," that is to say, artificially tinted, whereas the three strings of her matchlessly graded pearl necklace were worth "a king's ransom"; that Madame de Pougy's seven rows lacked "life"; that Eugénie Fougère's famous diamond bolero was quite worthless; and that no self-respecting woman gadded about, like Madame Antokolski, in a coupé upholstered in mauve satin. She had obediently broken her friendship with a school friend, Lydia Poret, after the girl had shown her a solitaire, set as a ring, presented by the Baron Ephraim.

"A solitaire!" Madame Alvarez had exclaimed. "For a girl of fifteen! Her mother must be mad!"

"But, Grandmama," pleaded Gigi, "it's not Lydia's fault if the Baron gave it to her!"

"Silence! I'm not blaming the Baron. The Baron knows what is expected of him. But plain common sense should have told the mother to put the ring in a safe at the bank, while waiting."

"While waiting for what, Grandmama?"

"To see how things turn out."

"Why not in her jewel box?"

"Because one never knows. Especially since the Baron is the sort of man who might change his mind. If on the other hand he had declared himself openly, Madame Poret has only to withdraw her daughter from her studies. Until the matter has been properly cleared up, you will oblige me by not walking home with that little Poret. Who ever heard of such a thing!"

"But supposing she marries, Grandmama?"

"Marries? Marries whom, pray?"

"Why, the Baron!"

Madame Alvarez and her daughter exchanged glances of stupefaction. "I find the child so discouraging," Andrée had murmured. "She comes from another planet."

"My poor Gaston," said Madame Alvarez, "is it really true, then, that you have broken with her? In some ways, it may be the best thing for you; but in others, I'm sure you must find it most upsetting. Whom can one trust, I ask you!"

Poor Gaston listened while he drank the scalding camomile. The taste of it gave him as much comfort as the sight of the plaster rose on the ceiling, still black from the hanging lamp now "converted to electricity,"

still faithfully retaining its shader—vast frilly bell of palest green. Half the contents of a workbasket lay strewn over the dining-room table, from which Gilberte had forgotten to remove her notebook. Above the upright piano hung an enlarged photograph of Gilberte at eight months, as a pendant to a portrait in oil of Andrée, dressed for her part in *Si j'étais Roi*. The completely inoffensive untidiness, the ray of spring sunshine coming through the lace curtains, the warmth given out by a little stove kept at a low heat—all these homely things were like so many soothing potions to the nerves of a jilted and lonely millionaire.

"Are you positively in torment, my poor Gaston?"

"To be exact, I'm not in torment. I'm just very upset, as you say,"

"I have no wish to appear inquisitive," said Madame Alvarez, "but how did it all happen? I've read the papers, of course; but can one believe what they say?"

Lachaille tugged at his small, waxed mustache and ran his fingers over his thick, cropped hair.

"Oh, much the same as on previous occasions. She waited for the birthday present, then off she trotted. And, into the bargain, she had to go bury herself in such a wretched little hole in Normandy—so stupid of her! Any fool could have discovered that there were only two rooms at the inn, one occupied by Liane, the other by Sandomir, a skating instructor from the *Palais de Glace*."

"He's Polaire's teatime waltzing partner, isn't he? Oh, women don't know where to draw the line nowadays! And just after her birthday, too! Oh, it's so tactless! What could be more unladylike!"

Madame Alvarez stirred the teaspoon around and around in her cup, her little finger in the air. When she lowered her gaze, her lids did not quite cover her protuberant eyeballs, and her resemblance to George Sand became marked.

"I'd given her a 'rope,'" said Gaston Lachaille. "What you might call a rope—thirty-seven pearls. The middle one as big as the ball of my thumb."

He held out his white, beautifully manicured thumb, to which Madame Alvarez accorded the admiration due to a middle pearl.

"You certainly know how to do things in stlye," she said. "You came out of it extremely well, Gaston."

"I came out of it with a pair of horns, certainly."

Madame Alvarez did not seem to have heard him.

"If I were you, Gaston, I would try to get even with her. I would take up with some society lady."

"That's a nice pill to offer me," said Lachaille, who was absentmindedly helping himself to the *agents de change*.

"Yes, indeed, I might even say that sometimes the cure may prove worse than the disease," Madame Alvarez continued, tactfully agreeing with him. "Out of the frying pan into the fire." After which she respected Gaston Lachaille's silence.

The muffled sounds of a piano penetrated through the ceiling. Without a word, the visitor held out his empty cup, and Madame Alvarez refilled it.

"Is the family all right? What's new with Aunt Alicia?"

"Oh, my sister, you know, is always the same. She's smart enough to keep herself to herself. She says she would rather live in a splendid past than in an ugly present. Her King of Spain, her Milan of Serbia, her Khedive, her rajahs by the half dozen—or so she would have you believe! She is very considerate to Gigi. She finds her a trifle backward for her age, as indeed she is, and puts her through her paces. Last week, for instance, she taught her how to eat *homard a l'américaine* in faultless style."

"Whatever for?"

"Alicia says it will be extremely useful. The three great stumbling blocks in a girl's education, she maintains, are *homard a l'américaine*, a boiled egg, and asparagus. Bad table manners, she says, have broken up many a happy home."

"That can happen," said Lachaille dreamily.

"Oh, Alicia is no fool! And it's just what Gigi requires—she is so greedy! If only her brain worked as well as her jaws! But she might well be a child of ten! And what breathtaking scheme have you got for the Battle of Flowers? Are you going to dazzle us again this year?"

"Oh Lord no!" groaned Gaston. "I shall take advantage of my misfortune and save on the red roses."

Madame Alvarez clasped her hands.

"Oh, Gaston, you mustn't do that! If you're not there, the procession will look like a funeral!"

"I don't care what it looks like," said Gaston gloomily.

"You're never going to leave the prize banner to people like Valérie Cheniaguine? Oh, Gaston, we can't allow that!"

"You will have to. Valérie can very well afford it."

"Especially since she does it so cheaply! Gaston, do you know where she went for the ten thousand bunches thrown last year? She had three women tying them up for two days and two nights, and the flowers were bought in the flower market! In the market! Only the four wheels, and the coachman's whip, and the harness trappings bore the label of Lachaume."

"That's a trick worth remembering!" said Lachaille, cheering up. "Good Lord! I've finished the licorice!"

The tap-tap of Gilberte's marching footsteps could be heard crossing the outer room.

"Back already!" said Madame Alvarez. "What's the meaning of this?"

"The meaning," said the girl, "is that Aunt Alicia wasn't in good form. But I've been out in Tonton's 'tuf-tuf.'"

Her lips parted in a bright smile.

"You know, Tonton, all the time I was in your automobile, I put on a martyred expression—like this—as if I was bored to death with every luxury under the sun. I had the time of my life."

She sent her hat flying across the room, and her hair fell tumbling over her forehead and cheeks. She perched herself on a rather high stool and tucked her knees up under her chin.

"Well, Tonton? You look as if you were dying of boredom. What about a game of piquet? It's Sunday, and Mama doesn't come back between the two performances. Who's been eating all my licorice? Oh, Tonton, you can't get away with that! The least you can do is to send me some more to make up for it."

"Gilberte, your manners!" scolded Madame Alvarez. "Lower your knees! Gaston hasn't the time to bother

about your licorice. Pull down your skirts. Gaston, would you like me to send her to her room?"

Young Lachaille, with one eye on the dirty pack of cards in Gilberte's hand, was longing simultaneously to give way to tears, to confide his sorrows, to go to sleep in the old armchair, and to play piquet.

"Let the child stay! In this room I can relax. It's restful. Gigi, I'll play you for twenty pounds of sugar."

"Your sugar's not very tempting. I much prefer sweets."

"It's the same thing. And sugar is better for you than sweets."

"You only say that because you make it."

"Gilberte, you forget yourself!"

A smile enlivened the mournful eyes of Gaston Lachaille.

"Let her say what she likes, Mamita. And if I lose, Gigi, what would you like? A pair of silk stockings?"

The corners of Gilberte's big childish mouth fell.

"Silk stockings make my legs itch. I would rather—"

She raised the snub-nosed face of an angel toward the ceiling, put her head on one side, and tossed her curls from one cheek to the other.

"I would rather have a Nile-green Persephone corset, with rococo roses embroidered on the garters. No, I'd rather have a music case."

"Are you studying music now?"

"No, but my older friends at school carry their notebooks in music cases because it makes them look like students at the Conservatoire."

"Gilberte, you're becoming indiscreet!" said Madame Alvarez.

"You shall have your case and your licorice. Cut, Gigi."

The next moment, the heir of Lachaille-Sugar was deep in the game. His prominent nose, large enough to appear false, and his slightly black eyes did not in the least intimidate his opponent. With her elbows on the table, her shoulders on a level with her ears, and her blue eyes and red cheeks at their most vivid, she looked like a tipsy page. They both played passionately, almost in silence, exchanging occasional insults under their breath. "You spindly spider! You sorrel run to seed!" Lachaille muttered. "You old crow's beak!" the girl countered. The March twilight deepened over the narrow street.

"Please don't think I want you to go, Gaston," said Madame Alvarez, "but it's half-past seven. Will you excuse me while I just see about our dinner?"

"Half-past seven!" cried Lachaille. "And I'm supposed to be dining at Larue's with De Dion, Feydeau, and one of the Barthous! This must be the last hand, Gigi."

"Why one of the Barthous?" asked Gilberte. "Are there several of them?"

"Two. One handsome and the other less so. The best known is the least handsome."

"That's not fair," said Gilberte. "And Feydeau, who's he?"

Lachaille plopped down his cards in amazement.

"Well, I must say! She doesn't know who Feydeau is! Don't you ever go to a play?"

"Hardly ever, Tonton."

"Don't you like the theater?"

"I'm not mad about it. And Grandmama and Aunt Alicia both say that going to plays prevents one from thinking about the serious side of life. Don't tell Grandmama I told you."

She lifted the weight of her hair away from her ears and let if fall forward again. "Phew!" she sighed. "This mane does make me hot!"

"And what do they mean by the serious side of life?"

"Oh, I don't know it all by heart, Uncle Gaston. And what's more, they don't always agree about it. Grandmama says: 'Don't read novels, they only depress you. Don't put on powder, it ruins the complexion. Don't wear a corset, it spoils the figure. Don't dawdle and gaze at shop windows when you're by yourself. Don't get to know the families of your school friends, especially not the fathers who wait at the gates to fetch their daughters home from school.'"

She spoke very rapidly, panting between words like a child who has been running.

"And on top of that, Aunt Alicia goes off on another tack! I've reached the age when I can wear a corset, and I should take lessons in dancing and deportment, and I should be aware of what's going on, and know the meaning of 'carat,' and not be taken in by the clothes that actresses wear. 'It's quite simple,' she tells me. 'Of all the dresses you see on the stage, nineteen out of twenty would look ridiculous in the paddock.' In fact, my head is ready to split with it all! What will you be eating at Larue's this evening, Tonton?"

"How should I know! *Filets de sole aux moules*, for a change. And of course, saddle of lamb with truffles. Get on with the game, Gigi! I've got a point of five."

"That won't get you anywhere. I've got all the cards in the pack. Here at home we're having the warmed-up remains of the *cassoulet*. I'm very fond of *cassoulet*."

"A plain dish of *cassoulet* with bacon rind," said Inez Alvarez modestly as she came in. "Goose was exorbitant this week."

"I'll have one sent to you from Bon-Abri," said Gaston.

"Thank you very much, Gaston. Gigi, help Monsieur Lachaille on with his overcoat. Fetch him his hat and stick!"

When Lachaille had gone, rather sulky after a regretful sniff at the warmed-up *cassoulet*, Madame Alvarez turned to her granddaughter.

"Will you please inform me, Gilberte, why it was you returned so early from Aunt Alicia's? I didn't ask you in front of Gaston. Family matters must never be discussed in front of a third person, remember that!"

"There's no mystery about it, Grandmama. Aunt Alicia was wearing her little lace cap to show me she had a headache. She said to me, 'I'm not very well.' I said to her, 'Oh! Then I mustn't tire you out. I'll go home again.' She said to me, 'Sit down and rest for five minutes.' 'Oh,' I said to her, 'I'm not tired. I drove here.' 'You drove here!' she said to me, raising her hands like this. As you may imagine, I had kept the motor car waiting a few minutes, to show Aunt Alicia. 'Yes,' I said to her, 'the four-seater-De-Dion-Bouton-with-the-collapsible-hood, which Tonton lent me while he was paying a call on us. He has had a fight with Liane.' 'Who do you think you're talking to?' she says to me. 'I don't have one foot in the grave yet! I'm still kept informed about public events when they're important. I know that he has had a fight with that great lampstand of a woman. Well, you'd better run along

home and not bother about a poor sick old woman like me.' She waved to me from the window as I got into the motor car."

Madame Alvarez pursed her lips.

"A poor sick old woman! She has never suffered so much as a cold in her life! I like that! What..."

"Grandmama, do you think he'll remember my licorice and the music case?"

Madame Alvarez slowly lifted her heavy eyes toward the ceiling.

"Perhaps, my child, perhaps."

"But, since he lost, he owes them to me, doesn't he?"

"Yes, yes, he owes them to you. Perhaps you'll get them after all. Slip on your smock and set the table. Put away your cards."

"Yes, Grandmama. Grandmama, what did he tell you about Madame Liane? Is it true she ran out on him with Sandomir and the rope of pearls?"

"In the first place, one doesn't say 'ran out on' anyone. In the second, come here and let me tighten your ribbon, so that your curls won't get soaked in the soup. And finally, the sayings and doings of a person who has broken the rules of etiquette are not for your ears. These happen to be Gaston's private affairs."

"But, Grandmama, they are no longer private since everyone's talking about them, and the whole thing came out in *Gil Blas*."

"Quiet! All you need to know is that the conduct of Madame Liane d'Exelmans has been the reverse of sensible. The ham for your mother is between two plates: you will put it in a cool place."

Gilberte was asleep when her mother—Andrée Alvar, in small type on the Opéra-Comique playbills—returned home. Madame Alvarez, the elder, seated at a game of patience, inquired from force of habit whether she was not too tired. Following polite family custom, Andrée reproached her mother for having waited up, and Madame Alvarez made her ritual reply: "I shouldn't sleep in peace unless I knew you were in. There is some ham and a little bowl of warm *cassoulet*. And some stewed prunes. The beer is on the windowsill."

"The child is in bed?"

"Of course."

Andrée Alvar ate a solid meal—pessimists have good appetites. She still looked pretty in theatrical makeup. Without it, the rims of her eyes were pink and her lips colorless. For this reason, Aunt Alicia declared, Andrée never met with the admiration in real life that she gained on the stage.

"Did you sing well, my child?"

"Yes, I sang well. But where does it get me? All the applause goes to Tiphaine, as you may well imagine. Oh dear, oh dear, I really don't think I can bear to go on with this sort of life."

"It was your own choice. But you would bear it much better," said Madame Alvarez sententiously, "if you had someone! It's your loneliness that gets on your nerves and makes you take such black views. You're behaving contrary to nature."

"Oh, Mother, don't start that all over again. I'm tired enough as it is. What news is there?"

"None. Everyone's talking of Gaston's break with Liane."

"Yes, they certainly are! Even in the green room at

the Opéra-Comique, which can hardly be called up-to-date."

"It's an event of worldwide interest," said Madame Alvarez.

"Is there talk of who's in the running?"

"I should think not! It's far too recent. He is in full mourning, so to speak. Can you believe it, at a quarter to eight he was sitting exactly where you are now, playing a game of piquet with Gigi? He says he has no wish to attend the Battle of Flowers."

"Not really!"

"Yes. If he doesn't go, it will cause a great deal of talk. I advised him to think twice before making such a decision."

"They were saying at the *Théâtre* that a certain music-hall artiste might stand a chance," said Andrée. "The one billed as the Cobra at the Olympia. It seems she does an acrobatic turn, and is brought on in a basket hardly big enough for a fox terrier, and from this she uncurls like a snake."

Madame Alvarez protruded her heavy lower lip in contempt.

"What an idea! Gaston Lachaille has not sunk to that level! A music-hall performer! Do him the justice to admit that, as befits a bachelor of his standing, he has always confined himself to the great ladies of the profession."

"A fine pack of bitches!" murmured Andrée.

"Be more careful how you express yourself, my child. Calling people and things by their names has never done anyone any good. Gaston's mistresses have all had an air about them. A liaison with a great professional lady is the only suitable way for him to wait for a great marriage, always supposing that some day he does marry. Whatever may happen, we're in the front row when anything fresh turns up. Gaston has such confidence in me! I wish you had seen him asking me for camomile! A boy, a regular boy! Indeed, he is only thirty-three. And all that wealth weighs so heavily on his shoulders."

Andrée's pink eyelids blinked ironically.

"Pity him, Mother, if you like. I'm not complaining, but all the time we've known Gaston, he has never given you anything except his confidence."

"He owes us nothing. And thanks to him we've always had sugar for our jams and, from time to time, for my *curaçao*; and birds from his farm, and odds and ends for the child."

"If you're satisfied with that!"

Madame Alvarez held high her majestic head.

"Perfectly satisfied. And even if I was not, what difference would it make?"

"In fact, as far as we're concerned, Gaston Lachaille, rich as he is, behaves as if he wasn't rich at all. Supposing we were in real straits! Would he come to our rescue, do you suppose?"

Madame Alvarez placed her hand on her heart.

"I'm convinced that he would," she said. And after a pause, she added, "But I would rather not have to ask him."

Andrée picked up the *Journal* again, in which there was a photograph of Liane, the ex-mistress. "When you take a good look at her, she's not so extraordinary."

"You're wrong," retorted Madame Alvarez, "she is

extraordinary. Otherwise she would not be so famous. Success and fame are not a matter of luck. You talk like those scatterbrains who say, 'Seven rows of pearls would look every bit as well on me as on Madame de Pougy. She certainly cuts a fine figure—but so could I.' Such nonsense makes me laugh. Take what's left of the camomile to bathe your eyes."

"Thank you, Mother. Did the child go to Aunt Alicia's?"

"She did indeed, and in Gaston's motorcar, what's more! He lent it to her. It can go forty miles an hour, I believe! She was in seventh heaven."

"Poor lamb, I wonder what she'll make of her life. She's quite capable of ending up as a mannequin or a salesgirl. She's so backward. At her age I—"

There was no indulgence in the glance Madame Alvarez gave her daughter.

"Don't boast too much about what you were doing when you were her age. If I remember rightly, at her age you were snapping your fingers at Monsieur Mennesson and all his flour mills, though he was perfectly ready to make you your fortune. Instead, you had to run off with a wretched music master."

Andrée Alvar kissed her mother's lustrous braids.

"My darling mother, don't curse me at this hour. I'm so sleepy. Good night, Mother. I've a rehearsal tomorrow at a quarter to one. I'll eat at the dairy during the entr'acte; don't bother about me."

She yawned and walked in the dark through the little room where her daughter was asleep. All she could see of Gilberte in the obscurity was a bush of hair and the Russian braid of her nightdress. She locked herself into the diminutive bathroom and, late though it was, lit the gas under a kettle. Madame Alvarez had instilled in her progeny, among other virutes, a respect for certain rites. One of her maxims was, "You can, at a pinch, leave the face till the morning when traveling or pressed for time. For a woman, attention to the lower parts is the first law of self-respect."

The last to go to bed, Madame Alvarez was the first to rise, and allowed the daily cleaning woman no hand in preparing the breakfast coffee. She slept in the dining-sitting room on a sofa bed, and at the stroke of half-past seven she opened the door to the papers, the quart of milk, and the daily maid—who was carrying the others. By eight o'clock she had taken out her curling pins, and her beautiful coils of hair were brushed and smooth. At ten minutes to nine, Gilberte left for school, clean and tidy, her hair well brushed. At ten o'clock Madame Alvarez was "thinking about" the midday meal, that is, she got into her waterproof, slipped her arm through the handle of her shopping bag, and set off to market.

Today, as on all other days, she made sure that her granddaughter would not be late; she placed the coffee pot and the jug of milk piping hot on the table and unfolded the newspaper while waiting for her. Gilberte came in fresh as a flower, smelling of lavender water, with some vestiges of sleep still clinging to her. A cry from Madame Alvarez made her fully wide awake.

"Call your mother, Gigi! Liane d'Exelmans has committed suicide."

The child replied with a long drawn-out "Oooh!" and asked, "Is she dead?"

"Of course not. She knows how to do things."

"How did she do it, Grandmama? A revolver?"

Madame Alvarez looked pityingly at her granddaughter.

"The idea! Laudanum, as usual. 'Doctors Morèze and Pelledoux, who have never left the heartbroken beauty's bedside, cannot yet answer for her life, but their diagnosis is reassuring....' My own diagnosis is that if Madame d'Exelmans goes on playing that game, she'll wind up ruining her stomach."

"The last time she killed herself, Grandmama, was for the sake of Prince Georgevitch, wasn't it?"

"Where are your brains, my darling? It was for Count Berthou de Sauveterre."

"Oh, so it was. And what will Tonton do now, do you think?"

A dreamy look passed across the huge eyes of Madame Alvarez.

"It's a toss-up, my child. We'll know everything in good time, even if he starts by refusing to give an interview to anybody. You must always start by refusing to give an interview to anybody. Then later you can fill the front page. Tell the concierge, by the way, to get us the evening papers. Have you had enough to eat? Did you have your second cup of milk and your two pieces of bread and butter? Put on your gloves before you go out. Don't dawdle on the way. I'm going to call your mother. What a story! Andrée, are you asleep? Oh, so you're out of bed! Andrée, Liane has committed suicide!"

"That's a nice change," muttered Andrée. "She has only one idea in her head, that woman, but she sticks to it."

"You haven't taken out your curlers yet, Andrée?"

"And have my hair go limp in the middle of rehearsal? No thank you!"

Madame Alvarez ran her eyes over her daughter, from the spiky tips of her curlers to the felt slippers. "It's plain that there's no man here for you to bother about, my child! A man in the house soon cures a woman of traipsing about in dressing gown and slippers. What excitement, this suicide! Unsuccessful, of course."

Andrée's pallid lips parted in a contemptuous smile: "It's getting too boring—the way she takes laudanum as if it was castor oil!"

"Anyhow, who cares about her? It's the Lachaille heir who matters. This is the first time such a thing has happened to him. He's already had—let me see. He's had Gentiane, who stole his private papers; then that foreigner, who tried to force him into marriage; but Liane is his first suicide. In such circumstances a man so much in the public eye has to be extremely careful about what sort of thing he says."

"Hm!" He'll be bursting with pride, you may be sure."

"And with good reason, too," said Madame Alvarez. "We shall be seeing great things before very long. I wonder what Alicia will have to say about the situation."

"She'll do her best to make a mountain of a molehill."

"Alicia is no angel. But I must confess that she is farsighted. And that without ever leaving her room!"

"She's no need to, since she has the telephone. Mother, won't you have one put in here?"

"It's expensive," said Madame Alvarez thoughtfully.

La Revue Blanche
by Pierre Bonnard
1894

"We only just mange to make both ends meet as it is. The telephone is of real use only to important business-men or to women who have something to hide. Now, if you were to change your mode of life—and I'm only putting it forward as a supposition—and if Gigi were to start on a life of her own, I would be the first to say, 'We'll have the telephone put in.' But we haven't reached that point yet, unfortunately."

She allowed herself a single sigh, pulled on her rubber gloves, and coolly set about her household chores. Thanks to her care, the modest flat was growing old without too many signs of deterioration. She retained, from her past life, the honorable habits of women who have lost their honor, and these she taught to her daughter and her daughter's daughter. Sheets never stayed on the beds longer than ten days, and the combination cleaning- and washer-woman told everyone that the chemises and drawers of the ladies of Madame Alvarez' were changed more often than she could count, and so were the table napkins. At any moment, at the cry of "Gigi, take off your shoes!" Gilberte had to remove shoes and stockings, exhibit white feet to the closest inspection, and announce the least suspicion of a corn.

During the week following Madame d'Exelmans' suicide, Lachaille's reactions were somewhat incoherent. He engaged the stars of the National Musical Academy to dance at a midnight fete held at his own house, and, wishing to give a supper party at the Pré-Catalan, he arranged for that restaurant to open a fortnight earlier than was their custom. The clowns Footit and Chocolat did a turn: Rita del Erido caracoled on horseback between the supper tables, wearing a divided skirt of white lace flounces, a white hat on her black hair with white ostrich feathers frothing around the relentless beauty of her face. Indeed, Paris mistakenly proclaimed, such was her beauty, that Gaston Lachaille was hoisting her astride a throne of sugar. Twenty-four hours later, Paris was undeceived. For in the false prophecies it had published, *Gil Blas* nearly lost the subsidy it received from Gaston Lachaille. A specialized weekly, *Paris en amour*, provided another red herring, under the headline: "Young Yankee millionairess makes no secret of weakness for French sugar."

Madame Alvarez' ample bust shook with incredulous laughter when she read the daily papers: she had received her information from none other than Gaston Lachaille in person. Twice in ten days he had found time to drop in for a cup of camomile, to sink into the depths of the now-sagging, conch-shaped armchair, and there forget his business worries and his dislike of being unattached. He even brought Gigi an absurd Russian leather music case with a silver-gilt clasp, and twenty boxes of licorice. Madame Alvarez was given a *pâté de foie gras* and six bottles of champagne, and of these bounties Tonton Lachaille partook by inviting himself to dinner. Throughout the meal Gilberte regaled them rather tipsily with tittle-tattle about her school, and later won Gaston's gold pencil at piquet. He lost with good grace, recovered his spirits, laughed, and, pointing to the child, said to Madame Alvarez, "There's my best pal!" Madame Alvarez' Spanish eyes moved with slow watchfulness from Gigi's reddened cheeks and white teeth to Lachaille, who was pulling

her hair by the fistful. "You little devil, you had the fourth king up your sleeve all the time!"

It was at this moment that Andrée, coming back from the Opéra-Comique, looked at Gigi's disheveled head rolling against Lachaille's sleeve and saw the tears of excited laughter in her lovely slate-blue eyes. She said nothing and accepted a glass of champagne, then another, and yet another. After her third glass, Gaston Lachaille was threatened with the Bell Song from *Lakmé*, at which point Andrée's mother led her away to bed.

The following day, no one spoke of this family party except Gilberte, who exclaimed, "Never, never in all my life, have I laughed so much! And the pencil is real gold!" Her unreserved chatter met with a strange silence, or rather with "Now then, Gigi, try to be a little more serious!" thrown out almost absentmindedly.

After that, Gaston Lachaille let two weeks go by without showing a sign of life, and the Alvarez family gathered its information from the papers only.

"Did you see, Andrée? In the gossip column it says that Monsieur Gaston Lachaille has left for Monte Carlo. 'The reason for this seems to be of a sentimental nature—a secret that we respect.' What next!"

"Would you believe it, Grandmama, Lydia Poret was saying at the dancing class that Liane traveled on the same train as Tonton, but in another compartment! Grandmama, do you think it can be true?"

Madame Alvarez shrugged her shoulders.

"If it was true, how on earth would those Porets know? Have they become friends with Monsieur Lachaille all of a sudden?"

"No, but Lydia Poret heard the story in her aunt's dressing room at the Comédie Française."

Madame Alvarez exchanged looks with her daugher.

"In her dressing room! That explains everything!" she exclaimed, for she held the theatrical profession in contempt, although Andrée worked so hard. When Madame Emilienne d'Alençon had decided to present performing rabbits, and Madame de Pougy—shyer on the stage than any young girl—had amused herself by pantomiming the part of Columbine in spangled black tulle, Madame Alvarez had stigmatized them both in a single phrase: "What! Have they sunk to that?"

"Grandmama, tell me, Grandmama, do you know him, this Prince Radziwill?" Gilberte went on again.

"What's come over the child today? Has she been bitten by a flea? Which Prince Radziwill, to begin with? There's more than one."

"I don't know," said Gigi. "The one who's getting married. Among the list of presents, it says here, '...are three writing sets in malachite.' What is malachite?"

"Oh, you're being tiresome, child. If he's getting married, he's no longer interesting."

"But if Tonton got married, wouldn't he be interesting either?"

"It all depends. It would be interesting if he were to marry his mistress. When Prince Cheniaguine married Valérie d'Aigreville, it was obvious that the life she had led him for the past fifteen years was all he wanted; scenes, plates flung across the room, and reconciliations in the middle of the restaurant Durand, Place de la Madeleine. Clearly, she was a woman who knew how to make herself valued. But all that is too complicated for you, my poor Gigi."

"And do you think it's to marry Liane that he's gone away with her?'"

Madame Alvarez pressed her forehead against the windowpane and seemed to be consulting the spring sunshine, which bestowed upon the street a sunny side and one with shade.

"No," she said, "not if I know anything about anything. I must have a word with Alicia. Gigi, come with me as far as her house; you can leave me there and find your way back along the quais. It will give you some fresh air, since, it would seem, one must have fresh air nowadays. I have never been in the habit of taking the air more than twice a year myself, at Cabourg, and at Monte Carlo. And I am none the worse for that."

That evening Madame Alvarez came in so late that the family dined off tepid soup, cold meat, and some cakes sent by Aunt Alicia. To Gilberte's "Well, what did she have to say?" she presented an icy front and answered in clarion tones: "She says that she is going to teach you how to eat ortolans."

"Lovely!" cried Gilberte. "And what did she say about the summer frock she promised me?"

"She said you would see. And that there's no reason why you should be displeased with the result."

"Oh!" said Gilberte gloomily.

"She also wants you to go to luncheon with her on Thursday, at twelve sharp."

"With you, too, Grandmama?"

Madame Alvarez looked at the willowy slip of a girl facing her across the table, at her high, rosy cheekbones beneath eyes as blue as an evening sky, at her strong, even teeth biting a fresh-colored but slightly chapped lip, and at the primitive splendor of her ash-gold hair.

"No," she said at last. "Without me."

Gilberte got up and wound an arm about her grandmother's neck.

"The way you said that, Grandmama, surely doesn't mean that you're going to send me to live with Aunt Alicia? I don't want to leave here, Grandmama!"

Madame Alvarez cleared her throat, gave a little cough, and smiled.

"Goodness gracious, what a foolish creature you are! Leave here! Why, my poor Gigi, I'm not scolding you, but you haven't reached the first stage toward leaving."

For a bellpull, Aunt Alicia had hung from her front door a length of bead-embroidered braid on a background of twining green vine leaves and purple grapes. The door itself, varnished and revarnished till it glistened, shone with the glow of a dark brown caramel. From the very threshold, where she was admitted by a "manservant," Gilberte enjoyed in her undiscriminating way an atmosphere of discreet luxury. The carpet, spread with Persian rugs, seemed to lend her wings. After hearing Madame Alvarez pronounce her sister's Louis XV little drawing room to be "boredom itself," Gilberte echoed her words by saying: "Aunt Alicia's drawing room is very pretty, but it's boredom itself!" reserving her admiration for the dining room, furnished in pale, almost golden, lemonwood dating from the Directoire, quite plain but for the grain of a wood as transparent as wax. "I shall buy myself a

set like that one day," Gigi had once said in all innocence.

"In the Faubourg Antoine, I dare say," Aunt Alicia had answered teasingly, with a smile of her cupid's bow mouth and a flash of small teeth.

She was seventy years old. Her fastidious taste was everywhere apparent: in her silver-gray bedroom with its red Chinese vases, in her narrow white bathroom as warm as a hothouse, and in her robust health, concealed by a pretense of delicacy. The men of her generation, when trying to describe Alicia de Saint-Efflam, fumbled for words and could only exclaim, "Ah, my dear fellow!" or "Nothing could give you the faintest idea..." Those who had known her intimately produced photographs that younger men found ordinary enough. "Was she really so lovely? You wouldn't think so from her photographs!" Looking at portraits of her, old admirers would pause for an instant, recollecting the turn of a wrist like a swan's neck, the tiny ear, the profile revealing a delicious kinship between the heart-shaped mouth and the wide-cut eyelids with their long lashes.

Gilberte kissed the pretty old lady, who was wearing a peak of black Chantilly lace on her white hair and, on her slightly dumpy figure, a tea gown of shot taffeta.

"You have one of your headaches, Aunt Alicia?"

"I'm not sure yet," replied Aunt Alicia. "It depends on the luncheon. Come quickly, the eggs are ready! Take off your coat! What on earth is that dress?"

"One of Mama's, altered to fit me. Are they difficult eggs today?"

"Not at all. *Oeufs brouilles aux croutons.* The ortolans are not difficult, either. And you shall have chocolate cream. So shall I."

With her young voice, a touch of pink on her amiable wrinkles, and lace on her white hair, Aunt Alicia was the perfect stage marquise. Gilberte had the greatest reverence for her aunt. In sitting down at the table in her presence, she would pull her skirt up behind, join her knees, hold her elbows close to her sides, straighten her shoulder blades, and to all appearances become the perfect young lady. She would remember what she had been taught, break her bread quickly, eat with her mouth shut, and take care when cutting her meat not to let her forefinger reach the blade of her knife.

Today her hair, severely tied back in a heavy knot at the nape of her neck, disclosed the fresh line of her forehead and ears, and a very powerful throat, rising from the rather ill-cut opening of her altered dress. This was a dingy blue, the bodice pleated about a let-in piece, and to cheer up this patchwork, three rows of mohair braid had been sewn around the hem of the skirt, and three times three rows of mohair braid around the sleeves, between the wrist and the elbow.

Aunt Alicia, sitting opposite her niece and examining her through fine dark eyes, could find no fault.

"How old are you?" she asked suddenly.

"The same as I was the other day, Aunt. Fifteen and a half. Aunt, what do you really think of this business of Tonton Gaston?"

"Why? Does it interest you?"

"Of course, Aunt. It worries me. If Tonton takes up with another lady, he won't come and play piquet with us any more or drink camomile tea—at least not for some time. That would be a shame."

"That's one way of looking at it, certainly."

Aunt Alicia examined her niece critically, through narrowed eyelids.

"Do you work hard, in class? Who are your friends? Ortolans should be cut in two with one quick stroke of the knife, and no grating of the blade on the plate. Bite up each half. The bones don't matter. Go on eating while you answer my question, but don't talk with your mouth full. You must manage it. If I can, you can. What friends have you made?"

"None, Aunt. Grandmama won't even let me have tea with the families of my school friends."

"She is quite right. Apart from that, there is no one who follows you, no little clerk hanging around your skirts? No schoolboy? No older man? I warn you, I shall know at once if you lie to me."

Gilberte gazed at the bright face of the imperious old lady who was questioning her so sharply.

"Why, no, Aunt, no one. Has somebody been telling you tales about me? I am always by myself. And why does Grandmama stop me from accepting invitations?"

"She is right, for once. You would be invited only by ordinary people, that is to say, useless people."

"And what about us? Aren't we ordinary people ourselves?"

"No."

"What makes these ordinary people inferior to us?"

"They have weak heads and dissolute bodies. Besides, they are married. But I don't think you understand."

"Yes, Aunt, I understand that we don't marry."

"Marriage is not forbidden to us. Instead of marrying 'at once,' it sometimes happens that we marry 'at last.'"

"But does that prevent me from seeing girls of my own age?"

"Yes. Are you bored at home? Well, be a little bored. It's not a bad thing. Boredom helps one to make decisions. What is the matter? Tears? The tears of a silly child who is backward for her age. Have another ortolan."

Aunt Alicia, with three glittering fingers, grasped the stem of her glass and raised it in a toast.

"To you and me, Gigi! You shall have an Egyptian cigarette with your coffee. On condition that you do not wet the end of your cigarette, and that you don't spit out specks of tobacco—going *ptu, ptu.* I shall also give you a note to the *première vendeuse* at Béchoff-David, an old friend of mine who was not a success. Your wardrobe is going to be changed. Nothing ventured, nothing gained."

The dark blue eyes gleamed. Gilberte stammered with joy.

"Aunt! Aunt! I'm going to—to Bé—"

"—choff-David. But I thought you weren't interested in clothes?"

Gilberte blushed.

"Aunt, I'm not interested in homemade clothes."

"I sympathize with you. Can it be that you have taste? When you think of looking your best, how do you see yourself dressed?"

"Oh, but I know just what would suit me, Aunt! I've seen—"

"Explain yourself without gestures. The moment you gesticulate you look common."

"I've seen a dress—oh, a dress created for Madame Lucy Gérard! Hundreds of tiny ruffles of pearl-gray silk muslin from top to bottom. And then a dress of lavender-blue cloth cut out on a black velvet foundation, the cutout design making a sort of peacock's tail on the train."

The small hand with its precious stones flashed through the air.

"Enough! Enough! I see your fancy is to be dressed like a leading *comédienne* at the Théâtre Français— and don't take that as a compliment! Come and pour out the coffee. And without jerking up the lip of the coffee pot to cut off the last drop. I'd rather have a footbath in my saucer than see you juggling like a waiter in a café."

The next hour passed very quickly for Gilberte: Aunt Alicia had unlocked a casket of jewels to use for a lesson that dazzled her.

"What is that, Gigi?"

"A marquise diamond."

"We say, a marquise-shaped brilliant. And that?"

"A topaz."

Aunt Alicia threw up her hands and the sunlight, glancing off her rings, set off a myriad scintillations.

"A topaz! I have sufferend many humiliations, but this surpasses them all. A topaz among my jewels! Why not an aquamarine or a chrysolite? It's a yellow diamond, little goose, and you won't often see it's like. And this?"

Gilberte half opened her mouth, as if in a dream.

"Oh! That's an emerald. Oh, how beautiful it is!"

Aunt Alicia slipped the large square-cut emerald on one of her thin fingers and was lost in silence.

"Do you see," she said in a hushed voice, "that almost blue flame darting about in the depths of the green light? Only the most beautiful emeralds contain that miracle of elusive blue."

"Who gave it to you, Aunt?" Gilberte dared to ask.

"A king," said Aunt Alicia simply.

"A great king?"

"No. A little one. Great kings do not give very fine stones."

"Why not?"

For a fleeting moment, Aunt Alicia proffered a glimpse of her tiny white teeth.

"If you want my opinion, it's because they don't want to. Between ourselves, the little ones don't either."

"Then who does give great big stones?"

"Who? The shy. The proud, too. And the boors, because they think that to give a monster jewel is a sign of good breeding. Sometimes a woman does, to humiliate a man. Never wear second-rate jewels. Wait till the really good ones come to you."

"And if they don't?"

"Well, then it can't be helped. Rather than a wretched little diamond full of flaws, wear a simple, plainly inexpensive ring. In that case you can say, 'It's a memento. I never part with it, day or night.' Don't ever wear artistic jewelry, it wrecks a woman's reputation."

"What is an artistic jewel?"

"It all depends. A mermaid in gold with eyes of chrysoprase. An Egyptian scarab. A large engraved amethyst. A not-very-heavy bracelet said to have been chased by a master-hand. A lyre or star mounted as a brooch. A studded tortoise. In a word, all of them, frightful. Never wear baroque pearls, not even as hatpins. Beware, above all things, of family jewels!"

"But Grandmama has a beautiful cameo, set as a medallion."

"There are no beautiful cameos," said Alicia with a toss of the head. "There are precious stones and pearls. There are white, yellow, blue, blue-white, or pink diamonds. We won't speak of black diamonds; they're not worth mentioning. Then there are rubies—when you can be sure of them; sapphires, when they come from Kashmir; emeralds, provided they have no fatal flaw or are not too light in color or have a yellowish tint."

"Aunt, I'm very fond of opals, too."

"I am very sorry, but you are not to wear them. I won't allow it."

Dumbfounded, Gilberte remained for a moment open-mouthed.

"Oh! Do you too, Aunt, really believe that they bring bad luck?"

"Why in the world not? You silly little creature," Alicia went bubbling on, "you must pretend to believe in such things. Believe in opals, believe—let's see, what can I suggest—in turquoises that die, in the evil eye..."

"But," said Gigi, haltingly, "those are—are superstitions!"

"Of course they are, child. They also go by the name of weaknesses. A pretty little collection of weaknesses and a terror of spiders are indispensable stock-in-trade with men."

"Why, Aunt?"

The old lady closed the casket and kept Gilberte kneeling before her.

"Because nine men out of ten are superstitious, nineteen out of twenty believe in the evil eye, and ninety-eight out of a hundred are afraid of spiders. They forgive us—oh, for many things, but not for the absence in us of their own failings," she said. "What makes you sigh?"

"I shall never remember all that!"

"The important thing is not for *you* to remember, but for me to know it."

"Aunt, what is a writing set in—in malachite?"

"Always a calamity. But where on earth did you pick up such terms?"

"From the list of presents at grand weddings, Aunt, printed in the papers."

"Nice reading! But at least you can gather from it what kind of presents you should never give or accept."

While speaking she began to touch here and there the young face on a level with her own, with the sharp pointed nail of her index finger. She lifted one slightly chapped lip, inspected the spotless enamel of the teeth.

"A fine jaw, my girl! With such teeth I should have gobbled up Paris and the rest of the world into the bargain. As it was, I had a good bite out of it. What's this you've got here? A small pimple? You shouldn't have a small pimple near your nose. And this? You've pinched a blackhead. You've no business to have such things or to pinch them. I'll give you some of my astringent lotion. You mustn't eat anything from the pork butcher's except cooked ham. You don't put on powder?"

"Grandmama won't let me."

"I should hope not. Do you go you-know-where regularly? Let me smell your breath. Not that it means anything at this hour. You've just had luncheon."

She laid her hands on Gigi's shoulders.

"Pay attention to what I'm going to say. You have it in your power to please. You have an impossible little nose, a nondescript mouth, cheeks rather like the wife of a muzhik—"

"Oh, Aunt!" sighed Gilberte.

"But, with your eyes and eyelashes, your teeth, and your hair, you can get away with it if you're not a perfect fool. As for the rest—"

She cupped her hands like conch shells over Gigi's bosom and smiled.

"A promise, but a pretty promise, neatly molded. Don't eat too many almonds, they add weight to the breasts. Ah, remind me to teach you how to choose cigars."

Gilberte opened her eyes so wide that the tips of her lashes touched her eyebrows.

"Why?"

She received a little tap on the cheek.

"Because—because I do nothing without good reason. If I take you in hand at all, I must do it thoroughly. Once a woman understands the tastes of a man, cigars included, and once a man knows what pleases a woman, they may be said to be well matched."

"And then they fight," concluded Gigi with a knowing air.

"What do you mean, they fight?"

The old lady looked at Gigi in consternation.

"Ah," she added, "you certainly never invented the triple mirror! Come, you little psychologist! Let me give you a note for Madame Henriette at Béchoff."

While her aunt was writing at a miniature rose-pink writing table Gilberte breathed in the scent of the fastidiously furnished room. Without wanting them for herself, she examined the objects she knew so well but hardly appreciated: Cupid, the Archer, pointing to the hours on the mantelpiece; two rather daring pictures; a bed like the basin of a fountain and its chinchilla coverlet; a rosary of small seed pearls and the New Testament on the bedside table; two red Chinese vases fitted as lamps—a happy note against the gray of the walls.

"Run along, my little one. I shall send for you again quite soon. Don't forget to ask Victor for the cake you're to take home. Gently—don't disarrange my hair! And remember, I shall have my eye on you as you leave the house. Woe betide you if you march like a guardsman or drag your feet behind you!"

The month of May fetched Gaston Lachaille back to Paris and brought to Gilberte two well-cut dresses and a lightweight coat—"a sack coat like Cléo de Mérode's" she called it—as well as hats and boots and shoes. To these she added, on her own account, a few curls over the forehead, which cheapened her apearance. She paraded in front of Gaston in a blue and white dress reaching almost to the ground. "A full seven and a half yards around, Tonton, my skirt measures!" She was more than proud of her slender waist, held in by a grosgrain sash with a silver buckle; but she tried every dodge to free her lovely strong neck from its whalebone collar of "imitation Venetian point," which matched the tucks of the bodice. The full sleeves and wide flounced skirt of blue and white striped silk rustled deliciously, and Gilberte delighted in picking at the sleeves, to puff them out just below the shoulder.

"You remind me of a performing monkey," Lachaille said to her. "I liked you much better in your old tartan dress. In that uncomfortable collar you look just like a hen with a full gullet. Take a look at yourself!"

Feeling a little ruffled, Gilberte turned around to face the looking glass. She had a lump in one of her cheeks caused by a large caramel, out of a box sent all the way from Nice at Gaston's order.

"I've heard a good deal about you, Tonton," she retorted, "but I've never heard it said that you had any taste in clothes."

He stared, almost choking, at this newly fledged young woman, then turned to Madame Alvarez. "Charming manners you've taught her! I congratulate you!"

Whereupon he left the house without drinking his camomile tea, and Madame Alvarez wrung her hands.

"Look what you've done to us now, my poor Gigi!"

"I know," said Gigi, "but then why does he fly at me? He must know by now, I should think, that I can give as good as I get!"

Her grandmother shook her by the arm.

"But think what you've done, you wretched child! Good heavens! When will you learn to think? You've mortally offended the man, as likely as not. Just when we are doing our utmost to—"

"To do what, Grandmama?"

"Why, to do everything, to make an elegant young lady of you, to show you off to advantage."

"For whose benefit, Grandmama? You must admit that one doesn't have to turn oneself inside out for an old friend like Tonton!"

But Madame Alvarez admitted nothing; not even to her astonishment, when, the following day, Gaston Lachaille arrived in the best of spirits, wearing a light-colored suit.

"Put on your hat, Gigi! I'm taking you out to tea."

"Where?" cried Gigi.

"To the *Réservoirs*, at Versailles!"

"Hurrah! Hurrah! Hurrah!" chanted Gilberte.

She turned toward the kitchen.

"Grandmama, I'm having tea at the *Réservoirs* with Tonton!"

Madame Alvarez appeared and, without stopping to untie the flowered satinette apron across her stomach, interposed her soft hand between Gilberte's arm and that of Gaston Lachaille.

"No, Gaston," she said simply.

"What do you mean, No?"

"Oh, Grandmama!" wailed Gigi.

Madame Alvarez seemed not to hear.

"Go to your room a minute, Gigi. I should like to talk to Monsieur Lachaille in private."

She watched Gilberte leave the room and close the door behind her; then, returning to Gaston, she met his dark, rather brutal, stare without flinching.

"What is the meaning of all this, Mamita? Ever since yesterday, I find quite a change here. What's going on?"

"I shall be glad if you will sit down, Gaston. I'm tired," said Madame Alvarez. "Oh, my poor legs!"

She sighed, waited for a response that did not come, and then untied her apron, under which she was wearing a black dress with a large cameo pinned upon it. She motioned her guest to a high-backed chair, keeping the armchair for herself. Then she sat down heavily, smoothed her graying black coils, and folded her hands on her lap. The unhurried movement of her large, dark, lambent eyes and the ease with which she remained motionless were sure sign of her self-control.

"Gaston, you cannot doubt my friendship for you!" Lachaille emitted a short, businesslike laugh and tugged at his mustache. "My friendship and my gratitude. Nevertheless, I must never forget that I have a soul entrusted to my care. Andrée, as you know, has neither the time nor the inclination to look after the girl. Our Gilberte doesn't have the gumption to make her own way in the world, like so many. She is just a child."

"Of sixteen," said Lachaille.

"Of nearly sixteen," consented Madame Alvarez. "For years you have been giving her sweets and playthings. She swears by Tonton, and by him alone. And now you want to take her out to tea, in your automobile, to the *Réservoirs*!"

Madame Alvarez placed a hand on her heart.

"Upon my soul and conscience, Gaston, if there were only you and me, I should say to you, 'Take Gilberte anywhere you like, I entrust her to you blindly.' But there are always the others. The eyes of the world are on you. To be seen tête-à-tête with you is, for a woman—"

Gaston Lachaille lost patience.

"All right, all right, I understand. You want me to believe that once she is seen having tea with me, Gilberte is compromised! A slip of a girl, a fledgling, a kid whom no one knows, whom no one notices!"

"Let us say, rather," interrupted Madame Alvarez gently, "that she will be labeled. No matter where you put in an appearance, Gaston, your presence is commented on. A young girl who goes out alone with you is no longer an ordinary girl, or even—to put it bluntly—a respectable girl. Now our little Gilberte must not, above all things, cease to be an ordinary young girl, at least not by that method. So far as it concerns you, it will simply end in one more story to be added to the long list already in existence, but personally, when I read of it in *Gil Blas*, I shall not be amused."

Gaston Lachaille rose, paced from the table to the door, then from the door to the window, before replying.

"Very good, Mamita, I have no wish to vex you. I won't argue," he said coldly. "Keep your precious child."

He turned around again to face Madame Alvarez, his chin held high.

"I can't help wondering, as a matter of interest, whom you are keeping her for! A clerk earning a hundred a year, who'll marry her and give her four children in three years?"

"I know the duty of a mother better than that," said Madame Alvarez composedly. "I shall do my best to entrust Gigi only to the care of a man capable of saying, 'I take charge of her and answer for her future.' May I have the pleasure of brewing you some camomile tea, Gaston?"

Woman with Gloves
by Toulouse-Lautrec

"No, thank you. I'm late already."

"Would you like Gigi to come and say good-bye?"

"Don't bother, I'll see her another time. I can't say when, I'm sure. I'm very much taken up these days."

"Never mind, Gaston, don't worry about her. Have a good time, Gaston."

Once alone, Madame Alvarez mopped her forehead and went to open the door of Gilberte's room.

"You were listening at the door, Gigi!"

"No, Grandmama."

"Yes, you had your ear to the keyhole. You must never listen at keyholes. You don't hear properly and so you get things all wrong. Monsieur Lachaille has gone."

"So I can see," said Gilberte.

"Now you must rub the new potatoes in a cloth. I'll sauté them when I come in."

"Are you going out, Grandmama?"

"I'm going around to see Alicia."

"Again?"

"Is it your place to object?" said Madame Alvarez severely. "You had better bathe your eyes in cold water, since you have been silly enough to cry."

"Grandmama!"

"What?"

"What difference could it make to you if you'd let me go out with Tonton Gaston in my new dress?"

"Silence! If you can't understand anything about anything, at least let those who are capable of using their reason do so for you. And put on my rubber gloves before you touch the potatoes!"

Throughout the whole of the following week, silence reigned over the Alvarez household, except for a surprise visit, one day, from Aunt Alicia. She arrived in a hired brougham, all black lace and dull silk with a rose at her shoulder, and carried on an anxious conversation, strictly between themselves, with her younger sister. As she was leaving she bestowed only a moment's attention on Gilberte, pecked at her cheek with a fleeting kiss, and was gone.

"What did she want?" Gilberte asked Madame Alvarez.

"Oh, nothing—the address of the heart specialist who treated Madame Buffetery."

Gilberte reflected for a moment.

"It was a long one," she said.

"What was long?"

"The address of the heart specialist. Grandmama, I should like a *cachet*. I have a headache."

"But you had one yesterday. A headache doesn't last forty-eight hours!"

"Presumably my headaches are different from other people's," said Gilberte, offended.

She was losing some of her sweetness and, on her return from school, would make some such remark as "My teacher has it in for me!" or complain of not being able to sleep. She was gradually slipping into a state of idleness, which her grandmother noticed but did nothing to overcome.

One day Gigi was busy applying liquid chalk to her white canvas button boots when Gaston Lachaille put in an appearance without ringing the bell. His hair was too long, his complexion suntanned, and he was wearing a broad check summer suit. He stopped short in front of Gilberte, who was perched high on a kitchen stool, her left hand shod with a boot.

"Oh! Grandmama left the key in the door. That's just like her!"

As Gaston Lachaille looked at her without saying a word she began to blush, put down the boot on the table, and pulled her skirt down over her knees.

"So, Tonton, you slip in like a burglar! I believe you're thinner. Aren't you fed properly by that famous chef of yours who used to be with the Prince of Wales? Being thinner makes your eyes look larger and at the same time makes your nose longer and—"

"I have something to say to your grandmother," interrupted Gaston Lachaille. "Run into your room, Gigi."

For a moment she remained open-mouthed; then she jumped off her stool. The strong column of her neck, like an archangel's, swelled with anger as she advanced on Lachaille.

"Run into your room! Run into your room! And suppose I said the same to you? Who do you think you are here, ordering me to run into my room? All right, I'm going to my room! And I can tell you one thing: as long as you're in the house, I won't come out of it!"

She slammed the door behind her, and there was a dramatic click of the bolt.

"Gaston," breathed Madame Alvarez, "I shall insist on the child's apologizing; yes, I shall insist; if necessary, I'll—"

Gaston was not listening to her, and stood staring at the closed door.

"Now, Mamita," said he, "let us talk briefly and to the point."

"Let us go over it all once again," said Aunt Alicia. "To begin with, you are quite sure he said, 'She will be spoiled, more than—'"

"Than any woman before her!"

"Yes, but that's the sort of vague phrase that every man comes out with. I like things cut and dried."

"Just what they were, Alicia, for he said that he would guarantee Gigi against every imaginable mishap, even against himself, by an insurance policy; and that he regarded himself more or less as her godfather."

"Yes, hmm . . . Not bad, not bad. But vague, vague as ever."

She was still in bed, her white hair arranged in curls against the pink pillow. She was absentmindedly tying and untying the ribbon of her nightdress. Madame Alvarez, as pale and wan under her morning hat as the moon behind passing clouds, was leaning cross-armed against the bedside.

"And he added, 'I don't wish to rush anything. Above all, I am Gigi's best pal. I shall give her all the time she wants to get used to me.' There were tears in his eyes. And he also said, 'After all, she won't have to deal with a savage.' A gentleman, in fact. A perfect gentleman."

"Yes, yes. Rather a vague gentleman. And the child, have you spoken frankly to her?"

"As was my duty, Alicia. This is no time for us to be treating her like a child from whom the cakes have to be hidden. Yes, I spoke frankly. I referred to Gaston as a miracle, as a god, as—"

Tut, tut, tut," criticized Alicia, "I should have stressed

the difficulties rather: the cards to be played, the fury of all those ladies, the conquest represented by so conspicuous a man."

Madame Alvarez wrung her hands.

"The difficulties! The cards to be played! Do you imagine she's like you? Don't you know her at all? She's very far from calculating, she's———"

"Thank you."

"I mean she has no ambition. I was even struck by the fact that she did not react either one way or the other. No cries of joy, no tears of emotion! All I got from her was, 'Oh, yes! Oh, it's very considerate of him.' Then, only at the very end, did she lay down, as her conditions—"

"Conditions, indeed!" murmured Alicia.

"—that she would answer Monsieur Lachaille's proposals herself and discuss the matter alone with him. In other words, it was her business, and hers only."

"Let us be prepared for the worst! You've brought a nitwit into the world. She will ask for the moon and, if I know him, she won't get it. He is coming at four o'clock?"

"Yes."

"Hasn't he sent anything? No flowers? No little present?"

"Nothing. Do you think that's a bad sign?"

"No. It's what one would expect. See that the child is nicely dressed. How is she looking?"

"Not too well, today. Poor little lamb—"

"Come, come!" said Alicia heartlessly. "You'll have time for tears another day—when she's succeeded in ruining the whole affair."

"You've eaten scarcely anything, Gigi."

"I wasn't too hungry, Grandmama. May I have a little more coffee?"

"Of course."

"And a drop of Combier?"

"Why, yes. There's nothing in the world better than Combier for settling the stomach."

Through the open window rose the noise and heat from the street below. Gigi let the tip of her tongue lick around the bottom of her liqueur glass.

"If Aunt Alicia could see you, Gigi!" said Madame Alvarez lightheartedly.

Gigi's only reply was a disillusioned little smile. Her old plaid dress was too tight across the breast, and under the table she stretched out her long legs well beyond the limits of her skirt.

"What can Mama be rehearsing today that's kept her from coming back to eat with us, Grandmama? Do you think there really is a rehearsal going on at her Opéra-Comique?"

"She said so, didn't she?"

"Personally, I don't think she wanted to eat here."

"What makes you think that?"

Without taking her eyes off the sunny window, Gigi simply shrugged her shoulders.

"Oh, nothing, Grandmama."

When she had drained the last drop of her Combier, she rose and began to clear the table.

"Leave all that, Gigi, I'll do it."

"Why, Grandmama? I do it as a rule."

She looked Madame Alvarez straight in the face with an expression the old lady could not meet.

"We began our meal late. It's almost three o'clock and you're not dressed yet; do pull yourself together, Gigi."

"It's never before taken me a whole hour to change my clothes."

"Won't you need my help? Are you satisfied your hair's all right?"

"It will do, Grandmama. When the doorbell rings, don't bother. I'll go and open it."

On the stroke of four, Gaston Lachaille rang three times. A childish, wistful face looked out from the bedroom door, listening. After three more impatient rings, Gilberte advanced as far as the middle of the hall. She still had on her old plaid dress and cotton stockings. She rubbed her cheeks with both fists, then ran up to open the door.

"Good afternoon, Uncle Gaston."

"Didn't you want to let me in, you bad girl?"

They bumped shoulders in passing through the door, said "Oh, sorry!" a little too self-consciously, then laughed awkwardly.

"Please sit down, Tonton. D'you know, I didn't have time to change. Not like you! That navy blue serge couldn't look better!"

"You don't know what you're talking about! It's tweed."

"Of course, How silly of me!"

She sat down facing him, pulled her skirt over her knees, and they stared at each other. Gilberte's tomboy assurance deserted her; a strange woebegone look made her blue eyes seem twice their natural size.

"What's the matter with you, Gigi?" asked Lachaille softly. "Tell me something! Do you know why I'm here?"

She assented with an exaggerated nod.

"Do you want to or don't you?" he asked, lowering his voice.

She pushed a curl behind her ear and swallowed bravely.

"I don't want to."

Lachaille twirled the tips of his mustache between two fingers and for a moment looked away from a pair of darkened blue eyes, a pink cheek with a single freckle, curved lashes, a mouth unaware of its power, a heavy mass of ash-gold hair, and a neck as straight as a column, strong, hardly feminine, all of a piece, innocent of jewelry.

"I don't want what you want," Gilberte began again. "You said to Grandmama—"

He put out his hand to stop her. His mouth was slightly twisted to one side, as if he had a toothache.

"I know what I said to your grandmother. It's not worth repeating. Just tell me what it is you don't want. You can then tell me what you do want. I shall give it to you."

"You mean that?" cried Gilberte.

He nodded, letting his shoulders droop, as if tired out. She watched, with surprise, these signs of exhaustion and torment.

"Tonton, you told Grandmama you wanted to make me my fortune."

"A very fine one," said Lachaille firmly.

"It will be fine if I like it," said Gilberte, no less

Young Woman in a Ball Gown
by Berthe Morisot
1879

firmly. "They've drummed into my ears that I am backward for my age, but all the same I know the meaning of words. 'Make me my fortune,' that means I should go away from here with you and that I should sleep in your bed."

"Gigi, I beg of you!"

She stopped because of the strong note of appeal in his voice.

"But, Tonton, why should I mind speaking of it to you? You didn't mind speaking of it to Grandmama. Neither did Grandmama mind speaking of it to me. Grandmama wanted me to see nothing but the bright side. But I know more than she told me. I know very well that if you make me my fortune, then I must have my photograph in the papers, go to the Battle of Flowers and to the races at Deauville. When we quarrel, *Gil Blas* and *Paris en amour* will tell the whole story. When you throw me over once and for all, as you did Gentiane des Cevennes when you'd had enough of her—"

"What! You've heard about that? They've bothered you with all those old stories?"

She gave a solemn little nod.

"Grandmama and Aunt Alicia. They've taught me that you're world famous. I know too that Maryse Chuquet stole your letters, and you brought a lawsuit against her. I know that Countess Pariewsky was angry with you because you didn't want to marry a *divorcée*, and she tried to shoot you. I know what all the world knows."

Lachaille put his hand on Gilberte's knee.

"Those are not the things we have to talk about together, Gigi. All that's in the past. All that's over and done with."

"Of course, Tonton, until it begins again. It's not your fault if you're world famous. But I haven't got a world-famous sort of nature. So it won't do for me."

In pulling at the hem of her skirt, she caused Lachaille's hand to slip off her knee.

"Aunt Alicia and Grandmama are on your side. But as it concerns me a little, after all, I think you must allow me to say a word on the subject. And my word is, that it won't do for me."

She got up and walked about the room. Gaston Lachaille's silence seemed to embarrass her. She punctuated her wanderings with, "After all, it's true, I suppose! No, it really won't do!"

"I would like to know," said Gaston at last, "whether you're not just trying to hide from me the fact that you dislike me. If you dislike me, you had better say so at once."

"Oh no, Tonton, I don't dislike you at all! I'm always delighted to see you! I'll prove it by making a suggestion in my turn. You could go on coming here as usual, even more often. No one would see any harm in it since you're a friend of the family. You could go on bringing me licorice, champagne on my birthdays, and on Sunday we could have an extra-special game of piquet. Wouldn't that be a pleasant little life? A life without all this business of sleeping in your bed and everybody knowing about it, losing strings of pearls, being photographed all the time, and having to be so careful."

She was absentmindedly twisting a strand of hair

around her nose and pulled it so tight that she snuffled, and the tip of her nose turned purple.

"A very pretty little life, as you say," interrupted Gaston Lachaille. "You're forgetting one thing only, Gigi, and that is, I'm in love with you."

"Oh," she cried, "you never told me that!"

"Well," he admitted uneasily, "I'm telling you now."

She remained standing before him silent and breathing fast. There was no concealing her embarrassment; the rise and fall of her bosom under the tight bodice, the hectic flush high on her cheeks, and the quivering of her closely pressed lips—albeit ready to open again and taste of life.

"That's quite another thing!" she cried at last. "But then you are a terrible man! You're in love with me, and you want to drag me into a life where I'll have nothing but worries, where everyone gossips about everyone else, where the papers print nasty stories. You're in love with me, and you don't care at all if you let me in for all sorts of horrible adventures, ending in separations, quarrels, Sandomirs, revolvers, and lau— and laudanum."

She burst into violent sobs, which made as much noise as a fit of coughing. Gaston put his arms around her to bend her toward him like a branch, but she escaped and took refuge between the wall and the piano.

"But listen, Gigi! Listen to me!"

"Never! I never want to see you again! I should never have believed it of you. You're not in love with me. You're a wicked man! Go away from here!"

She shut him out from sight by rubbing her eyes with closed fists. Gaston had moved over to her and was trying to discover some place on her well-guarded face where he could kiss her. But his lips found only the point of a small chin wet with tears. At the sound of sobbing, Madame Alvarez had hurried in. Pale and circumspect, she had stopped in hesitation at the kitchen door.

"Good gracious, Gaston!" she said. "What on earth's the matter with her?"

"The matter!" said Lachaille. "The matter is that she doesn't want to."

"She doesn't want to!" repeated Madame Alvarez. "What do you mean, she doesn't want to?"

"No, she doesn't want to. I speak plainly enough, don't I?"

"No. I don't want to," whimpered Gigi.

Madame Alvarez looked at her granddaughter in a sort of terror.

"Gigi! It's enough to drive one mad! But I told you, Gigi. Gaston, as God is my witness, I told her—"

"You have told her too much!" cried Lachaille.

He turned his face toward the child, the face of a poor, sad, love-sick creature, but all he saw of her was a slim back shaken by sobs and a disheveled head of hair.

"Oh," he exclaimed hoarsely, "I've had enough of this!" and he went out, banging the door.

The next day, at three o'clock, Aunt Alicia, summoned by *pneumatique*, stepped out of her hired brougham. She climbed the stairs up to Alvarez' floor—pretending to the shortness of breath proper to someone with a weak heart—and noiselessly pushed open the door,

which her sister had left slightly ajar.

"Where's the child?"

"In her room. Do you want to see her?"

"There's plenty of time. How is she?"

"Very calm."

Alicia shook two angry little fists.

"Very calm! She has pulled the roof down about our heads, and she is very calm! These young people of today!"

Once again she raised her dotted veil and withered her sister with a single glance.

"And you, standing there, what do you propose doing?"

With a face like a crumpled rose, she sternly confronted the large pallid face of her sister, whose retort was extremely mild.

"What do I propose doing? How do you mean? I can't, after all, tie the child up!" Her burdened shoulders rose on a long sigh. "I surely have not deserved such children as these!"

"While you stand there wringing your hands Lachaille has rushed away from here and in such a state that he may do something idiotic!"

"And even without his straw hat," said Madame Alvarez. "He got into his car bareheaded! The whole street could have seen him!"

"If I were to be told that by this time he's already become engaged or is busy making it up with Liane, it would not surprise me in the least!"

"It is a moment fraught with destiny," said Madame Alvarez lugubriously.

"And afterward, how did you speak to that little brat?"

Madame Alvarez pursed her lips.

"Gigi may be a bit scatterbrained in certain things and backward for her age, but she's not what you say. A young girl who has held the attention of Monsieur Lachaille is not a little brat."

A furious shrug of the shoulders set Alicia's black lace quivering.

"All right, all right! With all due respect, then, how did you handle your precious princess?"

"I talked sense to her. I spoke to her of the family. I tried to make her understand that we sink or swim together. I enumerated all the things she could do for herself and for us."

"And what about nonsense? Did you talk nonsense to her? Didn't you talk to her of love, travel, moonlight, Italy? You must know how to harp on every string. Didn't you tell her that on the other side of the world the sea is phosphorescent, that there are hummingbirds in all the flowers, and that you make love under gardenias in full bloom beside a moonlit fountain?"

Madame Alvarez looked at her spirited elder sister with sadness in her eyes.

"I couldn't tell her all that, Alicia, because I know nothing about it. I've never been farther afield than Cabourg and Monte Carlo."

"Aren't you capable of inventing it?"

"No, Alicia."

Both fell silent. Alicia, with a gesture, made up her mind.

"Call the kid in to me. We shall see."

When Gilberte came in, Aunt Alicia had resumed all

the airs and graces of a frivolous old lady and was smelling the tea rose pinned near her chin.

"Good afternoon, my little Gigi."

"Good afternoon, Aunt Alicia."

"What is this Inez has been telling me? You have an admirer? And *what* an admirer! For your first attempt, it's a masterstroke!"

Gilberte acquiesced with a guarded, resigned little smile. She offered to Alicia's darting curiosity a fresh young face, to which the violet-blue shadow on her eyelids and the high color of her mouth gave an almost artificial effect. For coolness' sake, she had dragged back the hair off her temples with the help of two combs, and this drew up the corners of her eyes.

"And it seems you have been playing the naughty girl and tried your claws on Monsieur Lachaille! Bravo, my brave little girl!"

Gilberte raised incredulous eyes to her aunt.

"Yes, indeed! Bravo! It will only make him all the happier when you are nice to him again."

"But I am nice to him, Aunt. Only, I don't want to, that's all."

"Yes, yes, we know. You've sent him packing to his sugar refinery, that's perfect. But don't send him to the Devil: he's quite capable of going. The fact is, you don't love him."

Gilberte gave a little childish shrug.

"Yes, Aunt, I'm very fond of him."

"Just what I said, you don't love him. Mind you, there's no harm in that—it leaves you free to act as you please. Ah, if you'd been head over heels in love with him, then I should have been a little anxious. Lachaille is a fine figure of a man. Well built—you've only to look at the photographs of him taken at Deauville in his bathing suit. He's famous for that. Yes, I would feel sorry for you, my poor Gigi. To start by having a passionate love affair—to go away all by your two selves to the other side of the world, forgetting everything in the arms of the man who adores you, listening to the song of love in an eternal spring—surely things of that sort must touch your heart! What does all that say to you?"

"It says to me that when the eternal spring is over, Monsieur Lachaille will go off with another lady. Or else that the lady—me, if you like—will leave Monsieur Lachaille, and Monsieur Lachaille will hurry off to blab the whole story. And then the lady—still me, if you like—will have nothing else to do but get into another gentleman's bed. I don't want that. I'm not changeable by nature, indeed I'm not."

She crossed her arms over her breasts and shivered slightly.

"Grandmama, may I have a *cachet faivre*? I want to go to bed. I feel cold."

"You great goose!" burst out Aunt Alicia. "A silly little milliner's shop is all you deserve! Go! Go marry a bank clerk!"

"If you wish it, Aunt. But right now, I want to go to bed."

Madame Alvarez put her hand on Gigi's forehead.

"Don't you feel well?"

"I'm all right, Grandmama. Only, I'm sad."

She leaned her head on Madame Alvarez' shoulder and, for the first time in her life, closed her eyes pathetically like a grown woman. The two sisters exchanged glances.

"You must know, my Gigi," said Madame Alvarez, "that we won't torment you to that extent. If you say you really don't want to—"

"A failure is a failure," said Alicia caustically. "We can't go on discussing it forever."

"You'll never be able to say you didn't have good advice, and the very best at that," said Madame Alvarez.

"I know, Grandmama, but I'm sad all the same."

"Why?"

A tear trickled over Gilberte's downy cheek without wetting it, but she did not answer. A brisk ring of the doorbell made her jump where she stood.

"Oh, it must be him," she said. "It is him! Grandmama, I don't want to see him! Hide me, Grandmama!"

At the low, passionate tone of her voice, Aunt Alicia raised an attentive head and pricked an expert ear. Then she ran to open the door and came back a moment later. Gaston Lachaille, haggard, his eyes bloodshot, followed close behind her.

"Good afternoon, Mamita. Good afternoon, Gigi!" he said airily. "Please don't move. I've come to pick up my straw hat."

None of the three women replied, and his assurance left him.

"Well, you might at least say a word to me, even if it's only How-d'you-do?"

Gilberte took a step toward him.

"No," she said, "You haven't come to pick up your straw hat. You have another one in your hand. And you would never bother about a hat. You've come to make me more miserable than ever."

"Really!" burst out Madame Alvarez. "This is more than I can take. How can you, Gigi! Here is a man who, out of the goodness of his generous heart—"

"If you please, Grandmama, just a moment, and I'll be through."

Instinctively she straightened her dress, adjusted the buckle of her sash, and marched up to Gaston.

"I've been thinking, Gaston. In fact, I've been thinking a great deal—"

He interrupted her, to stop her saying what he was afraid to hear.

"I swear to you, my darling—"

"No, don't swear to me. I've been thinking I would rather be miserable with you than without you. So..."

She tried twice to go on.

"So... There you are. How d'you do, Gaston, how d'you do?"

She offered him her cheek in her usual way. He held her, a little longer than usual, until he felt her relax and become calm and gentle in his arms. Madame Alvarez seemed about to hurry forward, but Alicia's impatient little hand restrained her.

"Leave well enough alone. Don't meddle any more. Can't you see she is way beyond us?"

She pointed to Gigi, who was resting a trusting head and the rich abundance of her hair on Lachaille's shoulder.

The happy man turned to Madame Alvarez.

"Mamita," he said, "will you do me the honor, the favor, give me the infinite joy, of bestowing on me the hand..."

BE MINE

Illustration
by W. Steig
1980

The Passionate Shepherd
to His Love
by Christopher Marlowe

Come live with me and be my Love,
And we will all the pleasures prove
That hills and valleys, dales and fields,
Or woods or steepy mountain yields.

And we will sit upon the rocks,
And see the shepherds feed their flocks
By shallow rivers, to whose falls
Melodious birds sing madrigals.

And I will make thee beds of roses
And a thousand fragrant posies;
A cap of flowers, and a kirtle
Embroidered all with leaves of myrtle;

A gown made of the finest wool
Which from our pretty lambs we pull;
Fair-linéd slippers for the cold,
With buckles of the purest gold;

A belt of straw and ivy buds
With coral clasps and amber studs—
And if these pleasures may thee move,
Come live with me and be my Love.

The shepherd swains shall dance and sing
For thy delight each May morning—
If these delights thy mind may move,
Then live with me and be my Love.

The Proposal
by Adolphe William Bouguereau
1872

Jimmie's got a goil

by e. e. cummings

Jimmie's got a goil
                    goil
                         goil,
                              Jimmie
's got a goil and
she coitnly can shimmie

when you see her shake
                      shake
                           shake,
                                 when
you see her shake a
shimmie how you wish that you was Jimmie.

Oh for such a gurl
                  gurl
                      gurl,
                           oh
for such a gurl to
be a fellow's twistandtwirl

talk about your Sal-
                    Sal-
                        Sal-,
                             talk
about your Salo
-mes but gimmie Jimmie's gal.

Illustration

by Elwood H. Smith

1982

Long Walk to Forever
by Kurt Vonnegut, Jr.

They had grown up next door to each other, on the fringe of a city, near fields and woods and orchards, within sight of a lovely bell tower that belonged to a school for the blind.

Now they were twenty, had not seen each other for nearly a year. There had always been playful, comfortable warmth between them, but never any talk of love.

His name was Newt. Her name was Catharine. In the early afternoon, Newt knocked on Catharine's front door.

Catharine came to the door. She was carrying a fat, glossy magazine she had been reading. The magazine was devoted entirely to brides. "Newt!" she said. She was surprised to see him.

"Could you come for a walk?" he said. He was a shy person, even with Catharine. He covered his shyness by speaking absently, as though what really concerned him were far away—as though he were a secret agent pausing briefly on a mission between beautiful, distant, and sinister points. This manner of speaking had always been Newt's style, even in matters that concerned him desperately.

"A walk?" said Catharine.

"One foot in front of the other," said Newt, "through leaves, over bridges—"

"I had no idea you were in town," she said.

"Just this minute got in," he said.

"Still in the Army, I see," she said.

"Seven more months to go," he said. He was a private first class in the Artillery. His uniform was rumpled. His shoes were dusty. He needed a shave. He held out his hand for the magazine. "Let's see the pretty book," he said.

She gave it to him. "I'm getting married, Newt," she said.

"I know," he said. "Let's go for a walk."

"I'm awfully busy, Newt," she said. "The wedding is only a week away."

"If we go for a walk," he said, "it will make you rosy. It will make you a rosy bride." He turned the pages of the magazine. "A rosy bride like her—like her—like her," he said, showing her rosy brides.

Catharine turned rosy, thinking about rosy brides.

"That will be my present to Henry Stewart Chasens," said Newt. "By taking you for a walk, I'll be giving him a rosy bride."

"You know his name?" said Catharine.

"Mother wrote," he said. "From Pittsburgh?"

"Yes," she said. "You'd like him."

"Maybe," he said.

"Can—can you come to the wedding, Newt?" she said.

"That I doubt," he said.

"Your furlough isn't for long enough?" she said.

"Furlough?" said Newt. He was studying a two-page ad for flat silver. "I'm not on furlough," he said.

"Oh?" she said.

"I'm what they call A.W.O.L.," said Newt.

"Oh, Newt! You're not!" she said.

"Sure I am," he said, still looking at the magazine.

"Why, Newt?" she said.

"I had to find out what your silver pattern is," he said. He read names of silver patterns from the magazine. "Albemarle? Heather?" he said. "Legend? Rambler Rose?" He looked up, smiled. "I plan to give you and your husband a spoon," he said.

"Newt, Newt—tell me really," she said.

"I want to go for a walk," he said.

She wrung her hands in sisterly anguish. "Oh, Newt—you're fooling me about being A.W.O.L.," she said.

Newt imitated a police siren softly, raised his eyebrows.

"Where—where from?" she said.

"Fort Bragg," he said.

"North Carolina?" she said.

"That's right," he said. "Near Fayetteville—where Scarlett O'Hara went to school."

"How did you get here, Newt?" she said.

He raised his thumb, jerked it in a hitchhike gesture. "Two days," he said.

"Does your mother know?" she said.

"I didn't come to see my mother," he told her.

Spring in Central Park
by William Zorach
1914

"Who did you come to see?" she said.

"You," he said.

"Why me?" she said.

"Because I love you," he said. "Now can we take a walk?" he said. "One foot in front of the other—through leaves, over bridges—"

They were taking the walk now, were in a woods with a brown-leaf floor.

Catharine was angry and rattled, close to tears. "Newt," she said, "this is absolutely crazy."

"How so?" said Newt.

"What a crazy time to tell me you love me," she said. "You never talked that way before." She stopped walking.

"Let's keep walking," he said.

"No," she said. "So far, no farther. I shouldn't have come out with you at all," she said.

"You did," he said.

"To get you out of the house," she said. "If somebody walked in and heard you talking to me that way, a week before the wedding—"

"What would they think?" he said.

"They'd think you were crazy," she said.

"Why?" he said.

Catharine took a deep breath, made a speech. "Let me say that I'm deeply honored by this crazy thing you've done," she said. "I can't believe you're really A.W.O.L., but maybe you are. I can't believe you really love me, but maybe you do. But—"

"I do," said Newt.

"Well, I'm deeply honored," said Catharine, "and I'm very fond of you as a friend, Newt, extremely fond —but it's just too late." She took a step away from him. "You've never even kissed me," she said, and she protected herself with her hands. "I don't mean you should do it now. I just mean this is all so unexpected. I haven't got the remotest idea of how to respond."

"Just walk some more," he said. "Have a nice time."

They started walking again.

"How did you expect me to react?" she said.

"How would I know what to expect?" he said. "I've never done anything like this before."

"Did you think I would throw myself into your arms?" she said.

"Maybe," he said.

"I'm sorry to disappoint you," she said.

"I'm not disappointed," he said. "I wasn't counting on it. This is very nice, just walking."

Catharine stopped again. "You know what happens next?" she said.

"Nope," he said.

"We shake hands," she said. "We shake hands and part friends," she said. "That's what happens next."

Newt nodded. "All right," he said. "Remember me from time to time. Remember how much I loved you."

Involuntarily, Catharine burst into tears. She turned her back to Newt, looked into the infinite colonnade of the woods.

"What does that mean?" said Newt.

"Rage!" said Catharine. She clenched her hands. "You have no right—"

"I had to find out," he said.

"If I'd loved you," she said, "I would have let you know before now."

"You would?" he said.

"Yes," she said. She faced him, looked up at him, her face quite red. "You would have known," she said.

"How?" he said.

"You would have seen it," she said. "Women aren't very clever at hiding it."

Newt looked closely at Catharine's face now. To her consternation, she realized that what she had said was true, that a woman couldn't hide love.

Newt was seeing love now.

And he did what he had to do. He kissed her.

"You're hell to get along with!" she said when Newt let her go.

"I am?" said Newt.

"You shouldn't have done that," she said.

"You didn't like it?" he said.

"What did you expect," she said—"wild, abandoned passion?"

"I keep telling you," he said, "I never know what's going to happen next."

"We say good-by," she said.

He frowned slightly. "All right," he said.

She made another speech. "I'm not sorry we kissed," she said. "That was sweet. We should have kissed, we've been so close. I'll always remember you, Newt, and good luck."

"You too," he said.

"Thank you, Newt," she said.

"Thirty days," he said.

"What?" she said.

"Thirty days in the stockade," he said—"that's what one kiss will cost me."

"I—I'm sorry," she said, "but I didn't ask you to go A.W.O.L."

"I know," he said.

"You certainly don't deserve any hero's reward for doing something as foolish as that," she said.

"Must be nice to be a hero," said Newt. "Is Henry Stewart Chasens a hero?"

"He might be, if he got the chance," said Catharine. She noted uneasily that they had begun to walk again. The farewell had been forgotten.

"You really love him?" he said.

"Certainly I love him!" she said hotly. "I wouldn't marry him if I didn't love him!"

"What's good about him?" said Newt.

"Honestly!" she cried, stopping again. "Do you have any idea how offensive you're being? Many, many, many things are good about Henry! Yes," she said, "and many, many, many things are probably bad too. But that isn't any of your business. I love Henry, and I don't have to argue his merits with you!"

"Sorry," said Newt.

"Honestly!" said Catharine.

Newt kissed her again. He kissed her again because she wanted him to.

They were now in a large orchard.

"How did we get so far from home, Newt?" said Catharine.

"One foot in front of the other—through leaves, over bridges," said Newt.

"They add up—the steps," she said.

Bells rang in the tower of the school for the blind nearby.

"School for the blind," said Newt.

"School for the blind," said Catharine. She shook her head in drowsy wonder. "I've got to go back now," she said.

"Say good-by," said Newt.

"Every time I do," said Catharine, "I seem to get kissed."

Newt sat down on the close-cropped grass under an apple tree. "Sit down," he said.

"No," she said.

"I won't touch you," he said.

"I don't believe you," she said.

She sat down under another tree, twenty feet away from him. She closed her eyes.

"Dream of Henry Stewart Chasens," he said.

"What?" she said.

"Dream of your wonderful husband-to-be," he said.

"All right, I will," she said. She closed her eyes tighter, caught glimpses of her husband-to-be.

Newt yawned.

The bees were humming in the trees, and Catharine almost fell asleep. When she opened her eyes she saw that Newt really was asleep.

He began to snore softly.

Catharine let Newt sleep for an hour, and while he slept she adored him with all her heart.

The shadows of the apple trees grew to the east. The bells in the tower of the school for the blind rang again.

"*Chick-a-dee-dee-dee*," went a chickadee.

Somewhere far away an automobile starter nagged and failed, nagged and failed, fell still.

Catharine came out from under her tree, knelt by Newt.

"Newt?" she said.

"H'm?" he said. He opened his eyes.

"Late," she said.

"Hello, Catharine," he said.

"Hello, Newt," she said.

"I love you," he said.

"I know," she said.

"Too late," he said.

"Too late," she said.

He stood, stretched groaningly. "A very nice walk," he said.

"I thought so," she said.

"Part company here?" he said.

"Where will you go?" she said.

"Hitch into town, turn myself in," he said.

"Good luck," she said.

"You, too," he said. "Marry me, Catharine?"

"No," she said.

He smiled, stared at her hard for a moment, then walked away quickly.

Catharine watched him grow smaller in the long perspective of shadows and trees, knew that if he stopped and turned now, if he called to her, she would run to him. She would have no choice.

Newt did stop. He did turn. He did call. "Catharine," he called.

She ran to him, put her arms around him, could not speak.

73

The Owl and the Pussy-Cat
by Edward Lear

The Owl and the Pussy-Cat went to sea
   In a beautiful pea-green boat;
They took some honey, and plenty of money
   Wrapped up in a five-pound note.
The Owl looked up to the stars above,
   And sang to a small guitar,
"O lovely Pussy, O Pussy, my love,
   What a beautiful Pussy you are,
         You are,
         You are!
   What a beautiful Pussy you are!"

Pussy said to the Owl, "You elegant fowl,
   How charmingly sweet you sing!
Oh! let us be married; too long we have tarried;
   But what shall we do for a ring?"
They sailed away, for a year and a day,
   To the land where the bong-tree grows;
And there in a wood a Piggy-wig stood,
   With a ring at the end of his nose,
         His nose,
         His nose,
   With a ring at the end of his nose.

"Dear Pig, are you willing to sell for one shilling
   Your ring?" Said the Piggy, "I will."
So they took it away, and were married next day
   By the Turkey who lives on the hill.
They dined on mince and slices of quince,
   Which they ate with a runcible spoon;
And hand in hand, on the edge of the sand,
   They danced by the light of the moon,
         The moon,
         The moon,
   They danced by the light of the moon.

Illustrations
by Walt Lee
1982

But Beautiful
Lyrics by Johnny Burke

Who can say what love is?
Does it start in the mind or the heart?
When I hear discussions on what love is,
Everybody speaks a different part.

Love is funny or it's sad
Or it's quiet or it's mad;
It's a good thing or it's bad,
But beautiful!

Beautiful to take a chance
And if you fall, you fall,
And I'm thinking
I wouldn't mind at all.

Love is tearful or it's gay;
It's a problem or it's play;
It's a heartache either way,
But beautiful!

And I'm thinking
If you were mine I'd never let you go,
And that would be
But beautiful I know.

The White Window
by Marc Chagall
1955

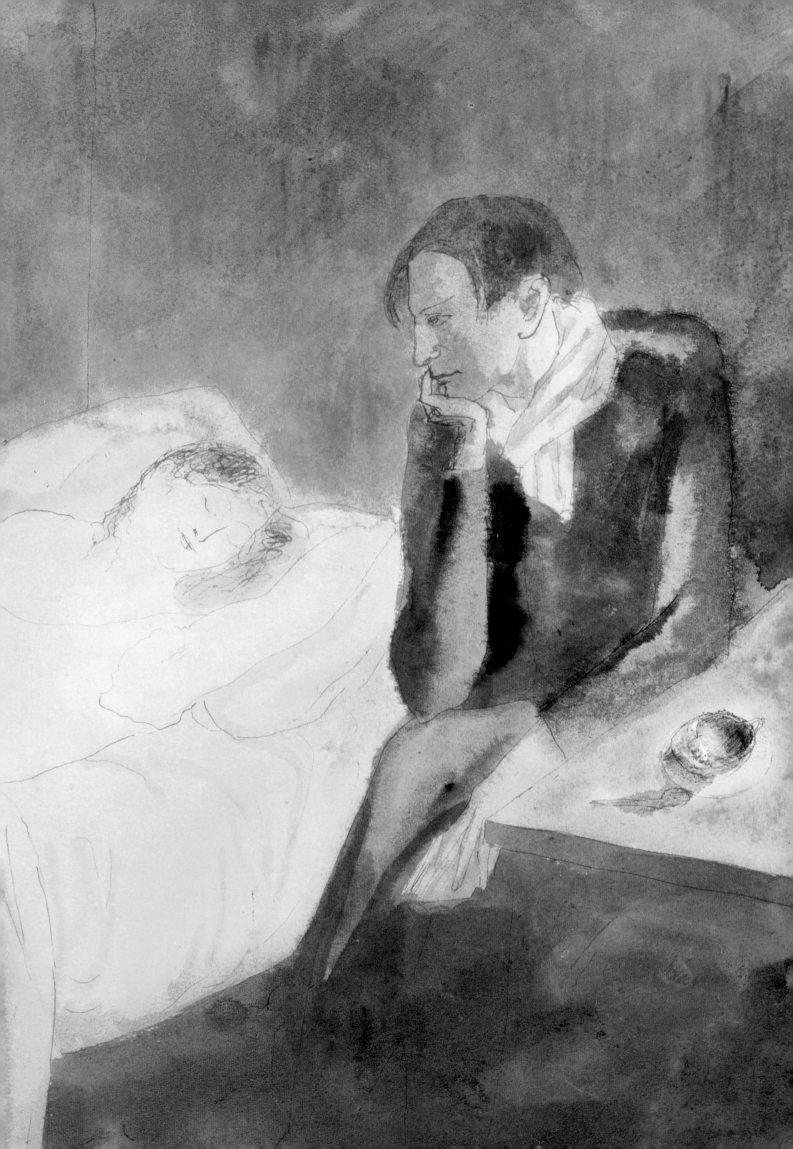

Coming, Aphrodite!
by Willa Cather

Don Hedger had lived for four years on the top floor of an old house on the south side of Washington Square, and nobody had ever disturbed him. He occupied one big room with no outside exposure except on the north, where he had built in a many-paned studio window that looked upon a court and upon the roofs and walls of other buildings. His room was very cheerless, since he never got a ray of direct sunlight; the south corners were always in shadow. In one of the corners was a clothes closet, built against the partition, in another a wide divan, serving as a seat by day and a bed by night. In the front corner, the one farther from the window, was a sink, and a table with two gas burners where he sometimes cooked his food. There, too, in the perpetual dusk, was the dog's bed, and often a bone or two for his comfort.

The dog was a Boston bull terrier, and Hedger explained his surly disposition by the fact that he had been bred to the point where it told on his nerves. His name was Caesar III, and he had taken prizes at very exclusive dog shows. When he and his master went out to prowl about University Place or to promenade along West Street, Caesar III was invariably fresh and shining. His pink skin showed through his mottled coat, which glistened as if it had just been rubbed with olive oil, and he wore a brass-studded collar, bought at the smartest saddler's. Hedger, as often as not, was hunched up in an old striped blanket coat, with a shapeless felt hat pulled over his bushy hair, wearing black shoes that had become grey, or brown ones that had become black, and he never put on gloves unless the day was biting cold.

Early in May, Hedger learned that he was to have a new neighbour in the rear apartment—two rooms, one large and one small, that faced the west. His studio was shut off from the larger of these rooms by double doors, which, though they were fairly tight, left him a good deal at the mercy of the occupant. The rooms had been leased, long before he came there, by a trained nurse who considered herself knowing in old furniture. She went to auction sales and bought up mahogany and dirty brass and stored it away here, where she meant to live when she retired from nursing. Meanwhile, she sub-let her rooms, with their precious furniture, to young people who came to New York to "write"

or to "paint"—who proposed to live by the sweat of the brow rather than of the hand, and who desired artistic surroundings. When Hedger first moved in, these rooms were occupied by a young man who tried to write plays,—and who kept on trying until a week ago, when the nurse had put him out for unpaid rent.

A few days after the playwright left, Hedger heard an ominous murmur of voices through the bolted double doors: the lady-like intonation of the nurse—doubtless exhibiting her treasures—and another voice, also a woman's, but very different; young, fresh, unguarded, confident. All the same, it would be very annoying to have a woman in there. The only bath-room on the floor was at the top of the stairs in the front hall, and he would always be running into her as he came or went from his bath. He would have to be more careful to see that Caesar didn't leave bones about the hall, too; and she might object when he cooked steak and onions on his gas burner.

As soon as the talking ceased and the women left, he forgot them. He was absorbed in a study of paradise fish at the Aquarium, staring out at people through the glass and green water of their tank. It was a highly gratifying idea; the incommunicability of one stratum of animal life with another,—though Hedger pretended it was only an experiment in unusual lighting. When he heard trunks knocking against the sides of the narrow hall, then he realized that she was moving in at once. Toward noon, groans and deep gasps and the creaking of ropes, made him aware that a piano was arriving. After the tramp of the movers died away down the stairs, somebody touched off a few scales and chords on the instrument, and then there was peace. Presently he heard her lock her door and go down the hall humming something; going out to lunch, probably. He stuck his brushes in a can of turpentine and put on his hat, not stopping to wash his hands. Caesar was smelling along the crack under the bolted doors; his bony tail stuck out hard as a hickory withe, and the hair was standing up about his elegant collar.

Hedger encouraged him. "Come along, Caesar. You'll soon get used to a new smell."

In the hall stood an enormous trunk, behind the ladder that led to the roof, just opposite Hedger's door. The dog flew at it with a growl of hurt amazement.

Meditation (Contemplation)
by Pablo Picasso
1904

They went down three flights of stairs and out into the brilliant May afternoon.

Behind the Square, Hedger and his dog descended into a basement oyster house where there were no tablecloths on the tables and no handles on the coffee cups, and the floor was covered with sawdust, and Caesar was always welcome,—not that he needed any such precautionary flooring. All the carpets of Persia would have been safe for him. Hedger ordered steak and onions absentmindedly, not realizing why he had an apprehension that this dish might be less readily at hand hereafter. While he ate, Caesar sat beside his chair, gravely disturbing the sawdust with his tail.

After lunch Hedger strolled about the Square for the dog's health and watched the stages pull out;—that was almost the very last summer of the old horse stages on Fifth Avenue. The fountain had but lately begun operations for the season and was throwing up a mist of rainbow water which now and then blew south and sprayed a bunch of Italian babies that were being supported on the outer rim by older, very little older, brothers and sisters. Plump robins were hopping about on the soil; the grass was newly cut and blindingly green. Looking up the Avenue through the Arch, one could see the young poplars with their bright, sticky leaves, and the Brevoort glistening in its spring coat of paint, and shining horses and carriages,—occasionally an automobile, mis-shapen and sullen, like an ugly threat in a stream of things that were bright and beautiful and alive.

While Caesar and his master were standing by the fountain, a girl approached them, crossing the Square. Hedger noticed her because she wore a lavender cloth suit and carried in her arms a big bunch of fresh lilacs. He saw that she was young and handsome,—beautiful, in fact, with a splendid figure and good action. She, too, paused by the fountain and looked back through the Arch up the Avenue. She smiled rather patronizingly as she looked, and at the same time seemed delighted. Her slowly curving upper lip and half-closed eyes seemed to say: "You're gay, you're exciting, you are quite the right sort of thing; but you're none too fine for me!"

In the moment she tarried, Caesar stealthily approached her and sniffed at the hem of her lavender skirt, then, when she went south like an arrow, he ran back to his master and lifted a face full of emotion and alarm, his lower lip twitching under his sharp white teeth and his hazel eyes pointed with a very definite discovery. He stood thus, motionless, while Hedger watched the lavender girl go up the steps and through the door of the house in which he lived.

"You're right, my boy, it's she! She might be worse looking, you know."

When they mounted to the studio, the new lodger's door, at the back of the hall, was a little ajar, and Hedger caught the warm perfume of lilacs just brought in out of the sun. He was used to the musty smell of the old hall carpet. (The nurse-lessee had once knocked at his studio door and complained that Caesar must be somewhat responsible for the particular flavour of that mustiness, and Hedger had never spoken to her since.) He was used to the old smell, and he preferred it to that of the lilacs, and so did his companion, whose nose was so much more discriminating. Hedger shut his door vehemently, and fell to work.

Most young men who dwell in obsure studios in New York have had a beginning, come out of something, have somewhere a home town, a family, a paternal roof. But Don Hedger had no such background. He was a foundling, and had grown up in a school for homeless boys, where book-learning was a negligible part of the curriculum. When he was sixteen, a Catholic priest took him to Greensburg, Pennsylvania, to keep house for him. The priest did something to fill in the large gaps in the boy's education,—taught him to like "Don Quixote" and "The Golden Legend," and encouraged him to mess with paints and crayons in his room up under the slope of the mansard. When Don wanted to go to New York to study at the Art League, the priest got him a night job as packer in one of the big department stores. Since then, Hedger had taken care of himself; that was his only responsibility. He was singularly unencumbered; had no family duties, no social ties, no obligations toward any one but his landlord. Since he travelled light, he had travelled rather far. He had got over a good deal of the earth's surface, in spite of the fact that he never in his life had more than three hundred dollars ahead at any one time, and he had already outlived a succession of convictions and revelations about his art.

Though he was not but twenty-six years old, he had twice been on the verge of becoming a marketable product; once through some studies of New York streets he did for a magazine, and once through a collection of pastels he brought home from New Mexico, which Remington, then at the height of his popularity, happened to see, and generously tried to push. But on both occasions Hedger decided that this was something he didn't wish to carry further,—simply the old thing over again and got nowhere,—so he took enquiring dealers experiments in a "later manner," that made them put him out of the shop. When he ran short of money, he could always get any amount of commercial work; he was an expert draughtsman and worked with lightning speed. The rest of his time he spent in groping his way from one kind of painting into another, or travelling about without luggage, like a tramp, and he was chiefly occupied with getting rid of ideas he had once thought very fine.

Hedger's circumstances, since he had moved to Washington Square, were affluent compared to anything he had ever known before. He was now able to pay advance rent and turn the key on his studio when he went away for four months at a stretch. It didn't occur to him to wish to be richer than this. To be sure, he did without a great many things other people think necessary, but he didn't miss them, because he had never had them. He belonged to no clubs, visited no houses, had no studio friends, and he ate his dinner alone in some decent little restaurant, even on Christmas and New Year's. For days together he talked to nobody but his dog and the janitress and the lame oysterman.

After he shut the door and settled down to his paradise fish on that first Tuesday in May, Hedger forgot all about his new neighbour. When the light failed, he took Caesar out for a walk. On the way home he did his marketing on West Houston Street, with a one-eyed Italian woman who always cheated him. After he had cooked his beans and scallopini, and drunk half a bottle of Chianti, he put his dishes in the sink and went up on the roof to smoke. He was the only person in the house who ever went to the roof, and he had a secret understanding with the janitress about it. He was to have "the privilege of the roof," as she said, if he opened the heavy trapdoor on sunny days to air out the upper hall, and was watchful to close it when rain threatened. Mrs. Foley was fat and dirty and hated to climb stairs,—besides, the roof was reached by a perpendicular iron ladder, definitely inaccessible to a woman of her bulk, and the iron door at the top of it was too heavy for any but Hedger's strong arm to lift. Hedger was not above medium height, but he practised with weights and dumb-bells, and in the shoulders he was as strong as a gorilla.

So Hedger had the roof to himself. He and Caesar often slept up there on hot nights, rolled in blankets he had brought home from Arizona. He mounted with Caesar under his left arm. The dog had never learned to climb a perpendicular ladder, and never did he feel so much his master's greatness and his own dependence upon him, as when he crept under his arm for this perilous ascent. Up there was even gravel to scratch in, and a dog could do whatever he liked, so long as he did not bark. It was a kind of Heaven, which no one was strong enough to reach but his great, paint-smelling master.

On this blue May night there was a slender, girlish looking young moon in the west, playing with a whole company of silver stars. Now and then one of them darted away from the group and shot off into the gauzy blue with a soft little trail of light, like laughter. Hedger and his dog were delighted when a star did this. They were quite lost in watching the glittering game, when they were suddenly diverted by a sound,—not from the stars, though it was music. It was not the Prologue to Pagliacci, which rose ever and anon on hot evenings from an Italian tenement on Thompson Street, with the gasps of the corpulent baritone who got behind it; nor was it the hurdy-gurdy man, who often played at the corner in the balmy twilight. No, this was a woman's voice, singing the tempestuous, over-lapping phrases of Signor Puccini, then comparatively new in the world, but already so popular that even Hedger recognized his unmistakable gusts of breath. He looked about over the roofs; all was blue and still, with the well-built chimneys that were never used now standing up dark and mournful. He moved softly toward the yellow quadrangle where the gas from the hall shone up through the half-lifted trapdoor. Oh yes! It came up through the hole like a strong draught, a big, beautiful voice, and it sounded rather like a professional's. A piano had arrived in the morning, Hedger remembered. This might be a very great nuisance. It would be pleasant enough to listen to, if you could turn it on and off as you wished; but you couldn't. Caesar, with the gas light shining on his collar and his ugly but sensitive face, panted and looked up for information. Hedger put down a reassuring hand.

"I don't know. We can't tell yet. It may not be so bad."

He stayed on the roof until all was still below, and finally descended, with quite a new feeling about his neighbour. Her voice, like her figure, inspired respect, —if one did not choose to call it admiration. Her door was shut, the transom was dark; nothing remained of her but the obtrusive trunk, unrightfully taking up room in the narrow hall.

II

For two days Hedger didn't see her. He was painting eight hours a day just then, and only went out to hunt for food. He noticed that she practised scales and exercises for about an hour in the morning; then she locked her door, went humming down the hall, and left him in peace. He heard her getting her coffee ready at about the same time he got his. Earlier still, she passed his room on her way to her bath. In the evening she sometimes sang, but on the whole she didn't bother him. When he was working well he did not notice anything much. The morning paper lay before his door until he reached out for his milk bottle, then he kicked the sheet inside and it lay on the floor until evening. Sometimes he read it and sometimes he did not. He forgot there was anything of importance going on in the world outside of his third floor studio. Nobody had ever taught him that he ought to be interested in other people; in the Pittsburgh steel strike, in the Fresh Air Fund, in the scandal about the Babies' Hospital. A grey wolf, living in a Wyoming canyon, would hardly have been less concerned about these things than was Don Hedger.

One morning he was coming out of the bath-room at the front end of the hall, having just given Caesar his bath and rubbed him into a glow with a heavy towel. Before the door, lying in wait for him, as it were, stood a tall figure in a flowing blue silk dressing gown that fell away from her marble arms. In her hands she carried various accessories of the bath.

Her name, Hedger discovered from her letters, which the postman left on the table in the lower hall, was Eden Bower.

III

In the closet that was built against the partition separating his room from Miss Bower's, Hedger kept all his wearing apparel, some of it on hooks and hangers, some of it on the floor. When he opened his closet door now-a-days, little dust-coloured insects flew out on downy wing, and he suspected that a brood of moths were hatching in his winter overcoat. Mrs. Foley, the janitress, told him to bring down all his heavy clothes and she would give them a beating and hang them in the court. The closet was in such disorder that he shunned the encounter, but one hot afternoon he set himself to the task. First he threw out a pile of forgotten laundry and tied it up in a sheet. The bundle stood as high as his middle when he had knotted the corners. Then he got his shoes and overshoes together. When he took his overcoat from its place against the partition, a long ray of yellow light shot across the dark enclosure, —a knot hole, evidently, in the high wainscoating of the west room. He had never noticed it before, and without realizing what he was doing, he stooped and squinted through it.

Yonder, in a pool of sunlight, stood his new neighbour, wholly unclad, doing exercises of some sort before a long gilt mirror. Hedger did not happen to think how unpardonable it was of him to watch her. Nudity was not improper to any one who had worked so much from the figure, and he continued to look, simply because he had never seen a woman's body so beautiful as this one,—positively glorious in action. As she swung her arms and changed from one pivot of motion to another, muscular energy seemed to flow through her from her toes to her finger-tips. The soft flush of exercise and the gold of afternoon sun played over her flesh together, enveloped her in a luminous mist which, as she turned and twisted, made now an arm, now a shoulder, now a thigh, dissolve in pure light and instantly recover its outline with the next gesture. Hedger's fingers curved as if he were holding a crayon; mentally he was doing the whole figure in a single running line, and the charcoal seemed to explode in his hand at the point where the energy of each gesture was discharged into the whirling disc of light, from a foot or shoulder, from the up-thrust chin or the lifted breasts.

He could not have told whether he watched her for six minutes or sixteen. When her gymnastics were over, she paused to catch up a lock of hair that had come down, and examined with solicitude a little reddish mole that grew under her left arm-pit. Then, with her hand on her hip, she walked unconcernedly across the room and disappeared through the door into her bedchamber.

Disappeared—Don Hedger was crouching on his knees, staring at the golden shower which poured in through the west windows, at the lake of gold sleeping on the faded Turkish carpet. The spot was enchanted; a vision out of Alexandria, out of the remote pagan past, had bathed itself there in Helianthine fire.

When he crawled out of his closet, he stood blinking at the grey sheet stuffed with laundry, not knowing what had happened to him. He felt a little sick as he contemplated the bundle. Everything here was different; he hated the disorder of the place, the grey prison light, his old shoes and himself and all his slovenly habits. The black calico curtains that ran on wires over his big window were white with dust. There were three greasy frying pans in the sink, and the sink itself—He felt desperate. He couldn't stand this another minute. He took up an armful of winter clothes and ran down four flights into the basement.

"Mrs. Foley," he began, "I want my room cleaned this afternoon, thoroughly cleaned. Can you get a woman for me right away?"

"Is it company you're having?" the fat, dirty janitress enquired. Mrs. Foley was the widow of a useful Tammany man, and she owned real estate in Flatbush. She was huge and soft as a feather bed. Her face and arms were permanently coated with dust, grained like wood where the sweat had trickled.

"Yes, company. That's it."

"Well, this is a queer time of the day to be asking for a cleaning woman. It's likely I can get you old Lizzie, if she's not drunk. I'll send Willy round to see."

Willy, the son of fourteen, roused from the stupor and stain of his fifth box of cigarettes by the gleam of a quarter, went out. In five minutes he returned with old Lizzie,—she smelling strong of spirits and wearing several jackets which she had put on one over the other, and a number of skirts, long and short, which made her resemble an animated dish-clout. She had, of course, to borrow her equipment from Mrs. Foley, and toiled up the long flights, dragging mop and pail and broom. She told Hedger to be of good cheer, for he had got the right woman for the job, and showed him a great leather strap she wore about her wrist to prevent dislocation of tendons. She swished about the place, scattering dust and splashing soapsuds, while he watched her in nervous despair. He stood over Lizzie and made her scour the sink, directing her roughly, then paid her and got rid of her. Shutting the door on his failure, he hurried off with his dog to lose himself among the stevedores and dock labourers on West Street.

A strange chapter began for Don Hedger. Day after day, at that hour in the afternoon, the hour before his neighbour dressed for dinner, he crouched down in his closet to watch her go through her mysterious exercises. It did not occur to him that his conduct was detestable; there was nothing shy or retreating about this unclad girl,—a bold body, studying itself quite coolly and evidently well pleased with itself, doing all this for a purpose. Hedger scarcely regarded his action as conduct at all; it was something that had happened to him. More than once he went out and tried to stay away for the whole afternoon, but at about five o'clock he was sure to find himself among his old shoes in the dark. The pull of that aperture was stronger than his will,—and he had always considered his will the strongest thing about him. When she threw herself upon the divan and lay resting, he still stared, holding his breath. His nerves were so on edge that a sudden noise made him start and brought out the sweat on his forehead. The dog would come and tug at his sleeve, knowing that something was wrong with his master. If he attempted a mournful whine, those strong hands closed about his throat.

When Hedger came slinking out of his closet, he sat down on the edge of the couch, sat for hours without moving. He was not painting at all now. This thing, whatever it was, drank him up as ideas had sometimes done, and he sank into a stupor of idleness as deep and dark as the stupor of work. He could not understand it; he was no boy, he had worked from models for years, and a woman's body was no mystery to him. Yet now he did nothing but sit and think about one. He slept very little, and with the first light of morning he awoke as completety possessed by this woman as if he had been with her all the night before. The unconscious operations of life went on in him only to perpetuate this excitement. His brain held but one image now—vibrated, burned with it. It was a heathenish feeling; without friendliness, almost without tenderness.

Women had come and gone in Hedger's life. Not having had a mother to begin with, his relations with them, whether amorous or friendly, had been casual.

He got on well with janitresses and wash-women, with Indians and with the peasant women of foreign countries. He had friends among the silk-skirt factory girls who came to eat their lunch in Washington Square, and he sometimes took a model for a day in the country. He felt an unreasoning antipathy toward the well-dressed women he saw coming out of big shops, or driving in the Park. If, on his way to the Art Museum, he noticed a pretty girl standing on the steps of one of the houses on upper Fifth Avenue, he frowned at her and went by with his shoulders hunched up as if he were cold. He had never known such girls, or heard them talk, or seen the inside of the houses in which they lived; but he believed them all to be artificial and, in an aesthetic sense, perverted. He saw them enslaved by desire of merchandise and manufactured articles, effective only in making life complicated and insincere and in embroidering it with ugly and meaningless trivialities. They were enough, he thought, to make one almost forget woman as she existed in art, in thought, and in the universe.

He had no desire to know the woman who had, for the time at least, so broken up his life,—no curiosity about her every-day personality. He shunned any revelation of it, and he listened for Miss Bower's coming and going, not to encounter, but to avoid her. He wished that the girl who wore shirt-waists and got letters from Chicago would keep out of his way, that she did not exist. With her he had naught to make. But in a room full of sun, before an old mirror, on a little enchanted rug of sleeping colours, he had seen a woman who emerged naked through a door, and disappeared naked. He thought of that body as never having been clad, or as having worn the stuffs and dyes of all the centuries but his own. And for him she had no geographical associations; unless with Crete, or Alexandria, or Veronese's Venice. She was the immortal conception, the perennial theme.

The first break in Hedger's lethargy occurred one afternoon when two young men came to take Eden Bower out to dine. They went into her music room, laughed and talked for a few minutes, and then took her away with them. They were gone a long while, but he did not go out for food himself; he waited for them to come back. At last he heard them coming down the hall, gayer and more talkative than when they left. One of them sat down at the piano, and they all began to sing. This Hedger found absolutely unendurable. He snatched up his hat and went running down the stairs. Caesar leaped beside him, hoping that old times were coming back. They had supper in the oysterman's basement and then sat down in front of their own doorway. The moon stood full over the Square, a thing of regal glory; but Hedger did not see the moon; he was looking, murderously, for men. Presently two, wearing straw hats and white trousers and carrying canes, came down the steps from his house. He rose and dogged them across the Square. They were laughing and seemed very elated about something. As one stopped to light a cigarette, Hedger caught from the other:

"Don't you think she has a beautiful talent?"

His companion threw away his match. "She has a beautiful figure." They both ran to catch the stage.

Hedger went back to his studio. The light was shining from her transom. For the first time he violated her privacy at night, and peered through that fatal aperture. She was sitting, fully dressed, in the window, smoking a cigarette and looking out over the house-tops. He watched her until she rose, looked about her with a disdainful, crafty smile, and turned out the light.

The next morning, when Miss Bower went out, Hedger followed her. Her white skirt gleamed ahead of him as she sauntered about the Square. She sat down behind the Caribaldi statue and opened a music book she carried. She turned the leaves carelessly, and several times glanced in his direction. He was on the point of going over to her, when she rose quickly and looked up at the sky. A flock of pigeons had risen from somewhere in the crowded Italian quarter to the south, and were wheeling rapidly up through the morning air, soaring and dropping, scattering and coming together, now grey, now white as silver, as they caught or intercepted the sunlight. She put up her hand to shade her eyes and followed them with a kind of defiant delight in her face.

Hedger came and stood beside her. "You've surely seen them before?"

"Oh, yes," she replied, still looking up. "I see them every day from my windows. They always come home about five o'clock. Where do they live?"

"I don't know. Probably some Italiana raises them for the market. They were here long before I came, and I've been here four years."

"In that same gloomy room? Why didn't you take mine when it was vacant?"

"It isn't gloomy. That's the best light for painting."

"Oh, is it? I don't know anything about painting. I'd like to see your pictures sometime. You have such a lot in there. Don't they get dusty, piled up against the wall like that?"

"Not very. I'd be glad to show them to you. Is your name really Eden Bower? I've seen your letters on the table."

"Well, it's the name I'm going to sing under. My father's name is Bowers, but my friend Mr. Jones, a Chicago newspaper man who writes about music, told me to drop the 's.' He's crazy about my voice."

Miss Bower didn't usually tell the whole story,—about anything. Her first name, when she lived in Huntington, Illinois, was Edna, but Mr. Jones had persuaded her to change it to one which he felt would be worthy of her future. She was quick to take suggestions, though she told him she "didn't see what was the matter with 'Edna.'"

She explained to Hedger that she was going to Paris to study. She was waiting in New York for Chicago friends who were to take her over, but who had been detained. "Did you study in Paris?" she asked.

"No, I've never been in Paris. But I was in the south of France all last summer, studying with C——. He's the biggest man among the moderns,—at least I think so."

Miss Bower sat down and made room for him on the bench. "Do tell me about it. I expected to be there by this time, and I can't wait to find out what it's like."

Hedger began to relate how he had seen some of this Frenchman's work in an exhibition, and deciding at once that this was the man for him, he had taken a boat for Marseilles the next week, going over steerage. He proceeded at once to the little town on the coast where his painter lived, and presented himself. The man never took pupils, but because Hedger had come so far, he let him stay. Hedger lived at the master's house and every day they went out together to paint, sometimes on the blazing rocks down by the sea. They wrapped themselves in light woollen blankets and didn't feel the heat. Being there and working with C——was being in Paradise, Hedger concluded; he learned more in three months than in all his life before.

Eden Bower laughed. "You're a funny fellow. Didn't you do anything but work? Are the women very beautiful? Did you have awfully good things to eat and drink?"

Hedger said some of the women were fine looking, especially one girl who went about selling fish and lobsters. About the food there was nothing remarkable, —except the ripe figs, he liked those. They drank sour wine, and used goat-butter, which was strong and full of hair, as it was churned in a goat skin.

"But don't they have parties or banquets? Aren't there any fine hotels down there?"

"Yes, but they are all closed in summer, and the country people are poor. It's a beautiful country, though."

"How, beautiful?" she persisted.

"If you want to go in, I'll show you some sketches, and you'll see."

Miss Bower rose. "All right. I won't go to my fencing lesson this morning. Do you fence? Here comes your dog. You can't move but he's after you. He always makes a face at me when I meet him in the hall, and shows his nasty little teeth as if he wanted to bite me."

In the studio Hedger got out his sketches, but to Miss Bower, whose favourite pictures were Christ Before Pilate and a redhaired Magdalen of Henner, these landscapes were not at all beautiful, and they gave her no idea of any country whatsoever. She was careful not to commit herself, however. Her vocal teacher had already convinced her that she had a great deal to learn about many things.

"Why don't we go out to lunch somewhere?" Hedger asked, and began to dust his fingers with a handkerchief —which he got out of sight as swiftly as possible.

"All right, the Brevoort," she said carelessly. "I think that's a good place, and they have good wine. I don't care for cocktails."

Hedger felt his chin uneasily. "I'm afraid I haven't shaved this morning. If you could wait for me in the Square? It won't take me ten minutes."

Left alone, he found a clean collar and handkerchief, brushed his coat and blacked his shoes, and last of all dug up ten dollars from the bottom of an old copper kettle he had brought from Spain. His winter hat was of such a complexion that the Brevoort hall boy winked at the porter as he took it and placed it on the rack in a row of fresh straw ones.

IV

That afternoon Eden Bower was lying on the couch

The East Window
by Childe Hassam
1913

in her music room, her face turned to the window, watching the pigeons. Reclining thus she could see none of the neighbouring roofs, only the sky itself and the birds that crossed and recrossed her field of vision, white as scraps of paper blowing in the wind. She was thinking that she was young and handsome and had had a good lunch, that a very easy-going, light-hearted city lay in the streets below her; and she was wondering why she found this queer painter chap, with his lean, bluish cheeks and heavy black eyebrows, more interesting than the smart young men she met at her teacher's studio.

Eden Bower was, at twenty, very much the same person that we all know her to be at forty, except that she knew a great deal less. But one thing she knew: that she was to be Eden Bower. She was like some one standing before a great show window full of beautiful and costly things, deciding which she will order. She understands that they will not all be delivered immediately, but one by one they will arrive at her door. She already knew some of the many things that were to happen to her; for instance, that the Chicago millionaire who was going to take her abroad with his sister as chaperone, would eventually press his claim in quite another manner. He was the most circumspect of bachelors, afraid of everything obvious, even of women who were too flagrantly handsome. He was a nervous collector of pictures and furniture, a nervous patron of music, and a nervous host; very cautious about his health, and about any course of conduct that might make him ridiculous. But she knew that he would at last throw all his precautions to the winds.

People like Eden Bower are inexplicable. Her father sold farming machinery in Huntington, Illinois, and she had grown up with no acquaintances or experiences outside of that prairie town. Yet from her earliest childhood she had not one conviction or opinion in common with the people about her,—the only people she knew. Before she was out of short dresses she had made up her mind that she was going to be an actress, that she would live far away in great cities, that she would be much admired by men and would have everything she wanted. When she was thirteen, and was already singing and reciting for church entertainments, she read in some illustrated magazine a long article about the late Czar of Russia, then just come to the throne or about to come to it. After that, lying in the hammock on the front porch on summer evenings, or sitting through a long sermon in the family pew, she amused herself by trying to make up her mind whether she would or would not be the Czar's mistress when she played in his Capital. Now Eden had met this fascinating world only in the novels of Ouida,—her hard-worked little mother kept a long row of them in the upstairs storeroom, behind the linen chest. In Huntington, women who bore that relation to men were called by a very different name, and their lot was not an enviable one; of all the shabby and poor, they were the shabbiest. But then, Eden had never lived in Huntington, not even before she began to find books like "Sappho" and "Mademoiselle de Maupin," secretly sold in paper covers throughout Illinois. It was as if she had come into Huntington, into the Bowers family, on one of the trains that puffed over the marshes behind their back fence all day long, and was waiting for another train to take her out.

As she grew older and handsomer, she had many beaux, but these small-town boys didn't interest her. If a lad kissed her when he brought her home from a dance, she was indulgent and she rather liked it. But if he pressed her further, she slipped away from him laughing. After she began to sing in Chicago, she was consistently discreet. She stayed as a guest in rich people's houses, and she knew that she was being watched like a rabbit in a laboratory. Covered up in bed, with the lights out, she thought her own thoughts, and laughed.

This summer in New York was her first taste of freedom. The Chicago capitalist, after all his arrangements were made for sailing, had been compelled to go to Mexico to look after oil interests. His sister knew an excellent singing master in New York. Why should not a discreet, well-balanced girl like Miss Bower spend the summer there, studying quietly? The capitalist suggested that his sister might enjoy a summer on Long Island; he would rent the Griffith's place for her, with all the servants, and Eden could stay there. But his sister met this proposal with a cold stare. So it fell out, that between selfishness and greed, Eden got a summer all her own—which really did a great deal toward making her an artist and whatever else she was afterward to become. She had time to look about, to watch without being watched; to select diamonds in one window and furs in another, to select shoulders and moustaches in the big hotels where she went to lunch. She had the easy freedom of obscurity and the consciousness of power. She enjoyed both. She was in no hurry.

While Eden Bower watched the pigeons, Don Hedger sat on the other side of the bolted doors, looking into a pool of dark turpentine, at his idle brushes, wondering why a woman could do this to him. He, too, was sure of his future and knew that he was a chosen man. He could not know, of course, that he was merely the first to fall under a fascination which was to be disastrous to a few men and pleasantly stimulating to many thousands. Each of these two young people sensed the future, but not completely. Don Hedger knew that nothing much would ever happen to him. Eden Bower understood that to her a great deal would happen. But she did not guess that her neighbour would have more tempestuous adventures sitting in his dark studio than she would find in all the capitals of Europe, or in all the latitude of conduct she was prepared to permit herself.

V

One Sunday morning Eden was crossing the Square with a spruce young man in a white flannel suit and a panama hat. They had been breakfasting at the Brevoort and he was coaxing her to let him come up to her rooms and sing for an hour.

"No, I've got to write letters. You must run along now. I see a friend of mine over there, and I want to ask him about something before I go up."

"That fellow with the dog? Where did you pick him

up?" the young man glanced toward the seat under a sycamore where Hedger was reading the morning paper.

"Oh, he's an old friend from the West," said Eden easily. "I won't introduce you, because he doesn't like people. He's a recluse. Good-bye. I can't be sure about Tuesday. I'll go with you if I have time after my lesson." She nodded, left him, and went over to the seat littered with newspapers. The young man went up the Avenue without looking back.

"Well, what are you going to do today? Shampoo this animal all morning?" Eden enquired teasingly.

Hedger made room for her on the seat. "No, at twelve o'clock I'm going out to Coney Island. One of my models is going up in a balloon this afternoon. I've often promised to go and see her, and now I'm going."

Eden asked if models usually did such stunts. No, Hedger told her, but Molly Welch added to her earnings in that way. "I believe," he added, "she likes the excitement of it. She's got a good deal of spirit. That's why I like to paint her. So many models have flaccid bodies."

"And she hasn't, eh? Is she the one who comes to see you? I can't help hearing her, she talks so loud."

"Yes, she has a rough voice, but she's a fine girl. I don't suppose you'd be interested in going?"

"I don't know," Eden sat tracing patterns on the asphalt with the end of her parasol. "Is it any fun? I got up feeling I'd like to do something different today. It's the first Sunday I've not had to sing in church. I had that engagement for breakfast at the Brevoort, but it wasn't very exciting. That chap can't talk about anything but himself."

Hedger warmed a little. "If you've never been to Coney Island, you ought to go. It's nice to see all the people; tailors and bar-tenders and prize-fighters with their best girls, and all sorts of folks taking a holiday."

Eden looked sidewise at him. So one ought to be interested in people of that kind, ought one? He was certainly a funny fellow. Yet he was never, somehow, tiresome. She had seen a good deal of him lately, but she kept wanting to know him better, to find out what made him different from men like the one she had just left—whether he really was as different as he seemed. "I'll go with you," she said at last, "if you'll leave that at home." She pointed to Caesar's flickering ears with her sunshade.

"But he's half the fun. You'd like to hear him bark at the waves when they come in."

"No, I wouldn't. He's jealous and disagreeable if he sees you talking to any one else. Look at him now."

"Of course, if you make a face at him. He knows what that means, and he makes a worse face. He likes Molly Welch, and she'll be disappointed if I don't bring him."

Eden said decidedly that he couldn't take both of them. So at twelve o'clock when she and Hedger got on the boat at Desbrosses street, Caesar was lying on his pallet, with a bone.

Eden enjoyed the boat-ride. It was the first time she had been on the water, and she felt as if she were embarking for France. The light warm breeze and the plunge of the waves made her very wide awake, and she liked crowds of any kind. They went to the balcony of a big, noisy restaurant and had a shore dinner, with

tall steins of beer. Hedger had got a big advance from his advertising firm since he first lunched with Miss Bower ten days ago, and he was ready for anything.

After dinner they went to the tent behind the bathing beach, where the tops of two balloons bulged out over the canvas. A red-faced man in a linen suit stood in front of the tent, shouting in a hoarse voice and telling the people that if the crowd was good for five dollars more, a beautiful young woman would risk her life for their entertainment. Four little boys in dirty red uniforms ran about taking contributions in their pill-box hats. One of the balloons was bobbing up and down in its tether and people were shoving forward to get nearer the tent.

"Is it dangerous, as he pretends?" Eden asked.

"Molly says it's simple enough if nothing goes wrong with the balloon. Then it would be all over, I suppose."

"Wouldn't you like to go up with her?"

"I? Of course not. I'm not fond of taking foolish risks."

Eden sniffed. "I shouldn't think sensible risks would be very much fun."

Hedger did not answer, for just then every one began to shove the other way and shout, "Look out. There she goes!" and a band of six pieces commenced playing furiously.

As the balloon rose from its tent enclosure, they saw a girl in green tights standing in the basket, holding carelessly to one of the ropes with one hand and with the other waving to the spectators. A long rope trailed behind to keep the balloon from blowing out to sea.

As it soared, the figure in green tights in the basket diminished to a mere spot, and the balloon itself, in the brilliant light, looked like a big silver-grey bat, with its wings folded. When it began to sink, the girl stepped through the hole in the basket to a trapeze that hung below, and gracefully descended through the air, holding to the rod with both hands, keeping her body taut and her feet close together. The crowd, which had grown very large by this time, cheered vociferously. The men took off their hats and waved, little boys shouted, and fat old women, shining with the heat and a beer lunch, murmured admiring comments upon the balloonist's figure. "Beautiful legs, she has!"

"That's so," Hedger whispered. "Not many girls would look well in that position." Then, for some reason, he blushed a slow, dark, painful crimson.

The balloon descended slowly, a little way from the tent, and the red-faced man in the linen suit caught Molly Welch before her feet touched the ground, and pulled her to one side. The band struck up "Blue Bell" by way of welcome, and one of the sweaty pages ran forward and presented the balloonist with a large bouquet of artificial flowers. She smiled and thanked him, and ran back across the sand to the tent.

"Can't we go inside and see her?" Eden asked. "You can explain to the door man. I want to meet her." Edging forward, she herself addressed the man in the linen suit and slipped something from her purse into his hand.

They found Molly seated before a trunk that had a mirror in the lid and a "make-up" outfit spread upon the tray. She was wiping the cold cream and powder from her neck with a discarded chemise.

"Hello, Don," she said cordially. "Brought a friend?"

Eden liked her. She had an easy, friendly manner, and there was something boyish and devil-may-care about her.

"Yes, it's fun. I'm mad about it," she said in reply to Eden's questions. "I always want to let go, when I come down on the bar. You don't feel your weight at all, as you would on a stationary trapeze."

The big drum boomed outside, and the publicity man began shouting to newly arrived boatloads. Miss Welch took a last pull at her cigarette. "Now you'll have to get out, Don. I change for the next act. This time I go up in a black evening dress, and lose the skirt in the basket before I start down."

"Yes, go along," said Eden. "Wait for me outside the door. I'll stay and help her dress."

Hedger waited and waited, while women of every build bumped into him and begged his pardon, and the red pages ran about holding out their caps for coins, and the people ate and perspired and shifted parasols against the sun. When the band began to play a two-step, all the bathers ran up out of the surf to watch the ascent. The second balloon bumped and rose, and the crowd began shouting to the girl in a black evening dress who stood leaning against the ropes and smiling. "It's a new girl," they called. "It ain't the Countess this time. You're a peach, girlie!"

The balloonist acknowledged these compliments, bowing and looking down over the sea of upturned faces,—but Hedger was determined she should not see him, and he darted behind the tent-fly. He was suddenly dripping with cold sweat, his mouth was full of the bitter taste of anger and his tongue felt stiff behind his teeth. Molly Welch, in a shirt-waist and a white tam-o'-shanter cap, slipped out from the tent under his arm and laughed up in his face. "She's a crazy one you brought along. She'll get what she wants!"

"Oh, I'll settle with you, all right!" Hedger brought out with difficulty.

"It's not my fault, Donnie. I couldn't do anything with her. She bought me off. What's the matter with you? Are you soft on her? She's safe enough. It's as easy as rolling off a log, if you keep cool." Molly Welch was rather excited herself, and she was chewing gum at a high speed as she stood beside him, looking up at the floating silver cone. "Now watch," she exclaimed suddenly. "She's coming down on the bar. I advised her to cut that out, but you see she does it first-rate. And she got rid of the skirt, too. Those black tights show off her legs very well. She keeps her feet together like I told her, and makes a good line along the back. See the light on those silver slippers,—that was a good idea I had. Come along to meet her. Don't be a grouch; she's done it fine!"

Molly tweaked his elbow, and then left him standing like a stump, while she ran down the beach with the crowd.

Though Hedger was sulking, his eye could not help seeing the low blue welter of the sea, the arrested bathers, standing in the surf, their arms and legs stained red by the dropping sun, all shading their eyes and gazing upward at the slowly falling silver star.

Molly Welch and the manager caught Eden under the arms and lifted her aside, a red page dashed up with a bouquet, and the band struck up "Blue Bell." Eden laughed and bowed, took Molly's arm, and ran up the sand in her black tights and silver slippers, dodging the friendly old women, and the gallant sports who wanted to offer their homage on the spot.

When she emerged from the tent, dressed in her own clothes, that part of the beach was almost deserted. She stepped to her companion's side and said carelessly: "Hadn't we better try to catch this boat? I hope you're not sore at me. Really, it was lots of fun."

Hedger looked at his watch. "Yes, we have fifteen minutes to get to the boat," he said politely.

As they walked toward the pier, one of the pages ran up panting. "Lady, you're carrying off the bouquet," he said, aggrievedly.

Eden stopped and looked at the bunch of spotty cotton roses in her hand. "Of course. I want them for a souvenir. You gave them to me yourself."

"I give 'em to you for looks, but you can't take 'em away. They belong to the show."

"Oh, you always use the same bunch?"

"Sure we do. There ain't too much money in this business."

She laughed and tossed them back to him. "Why are you angry?" she asked Hedger. "I wouldn't have done it if I'd been with some fellows, but I thought you were the sort who wouldn't mind. Molly didn't for a minute think you would."

"What possessed you to do such a fool thing?" he asked roughly.

"I don't know. When I saw her coming down, I wanted to try it. It looked exciting. Didn't I hold myself as well as she did?"

Hedger shrugged his shoulders, but in his heart he forgave her.

The return boat was not crowded, though the boats that passed them, going out, were packed to the rails. The sun was setting. Boys and girls sat on the long benches with their arms about each other, singing. Eden felt a strong wish to propitiate her companion, to be alone with him. She had been curiously wrought up by her balloon trip; it was a lark, but not very satisfying unless one came back to something after the flight. She wanted to be admired and adored. Though Eden said nothing, and sat with her arms limp on the rail in front of her, looking languidly at the rising silhouette of the city and the bright path of the sun, Hedger felt a strange drawing near to her. If he but brushed her white skirt with his knee, there was an instant communication between them, such as there had never been before. They did not talk at all, but when they went over the gangplank she took his arm and kept her shoulder close to his. He felt as if they were enveloped in a highly charged atmosphere, an invisible network of subtle, almost painful sensibility. They had somehow taken hold of each other.

An hour later, they were dining in the back garden of a little French hotel on Ninth Street, long since passed away. It was cool and leafy there, and the mosquitoes were not very numerous. A party of South Americans at another table were drinking champagne, and Eden murmured that she thought she would like some, if it were not too expensive. "Perhaps it will make me think I am in the balloon again. That was a very nice feeling.

You've forgiven me, haven't you?"

Hedger gave her a quick straight look from under his black eyebrows, and something went over her that was like a chill, except that it was warm and feathery. She drank most of the wine; her companion was indifferent to it. He was talking more to her tonight than he had ever done before. She asked him about a new picture she had seen in his room; a queer thing full of stiff, supplicating female figures. "It's Indian, isn't it?"

"Yes. I call it Rain Spirits, or maybe, Indian Rain. In the Southwest, where I've been a good deal, the Indian traditions make women have to do with the rain-fall. They were supposed to control it, somehow, and to be able to find springs, and make moisture come out of the earth. You see I'm trying to learn to paint what people think and feel; to get away from all that photographic stuff. When I look at you, I don't see what a camera would see, do I?"

"How can I tell?"

"Well, if I should paint you, I could make you understand what I see." For the second time that day Hedger crimsoned unexpectedly, and his eyes fell and steadily contemplated a dish of little radishes. "That particular picture I got from a story a Mexican priest told me; he said he found it in an old manuscript book in a monastery down there, written by some Spanish Missionary, who got his stories from the Aztecs. This one he called 'The Forty Lovers of the Queen,' and it was more or less about rain-making."

"Aren't you going to tell it to me?" Eden asked.

Hedger fumbled among the radishes. "I don't know if it's the proper kind of story to tell a girl."

She smiled; "Oh, forget about that! I've been balloon riding today. I like to hear you talk."

Her low voice was flattering. She had seemed like clay in his hands ever since they got on the boat to come home. He leaned back in his chair, forgot his food, and, looking at her intently, began to tell his story, the theme of which he somehow felt was dangerous tonight.

The tale began, he said, somewhere in Ancient Mexico, and concerned the daughter of a king. The birth of this Princess was preceded by unusual portents. Three times her mother dreamed that she was delivered of serpents, which betokened that the child she carried would have power with the rain gods. The serpent was the symbol of water. The Princess grew up dedicated to the gods, and wise men taught her the rain-making mysteries. She was with difficulty restrained from men and was guarded at all times, for it was the law of the Thunder that she be maiden until her marriage. In the years of her adolescence, rain was abundant with her people. The oldest man could not remember such fertility. When the Princess had counted eighteen summers, her father went to drive out a war party that harried his borders on the north and troubled his prosperity. The King destroyed the invaders and brought home many prisoners. Among the prisoners was a young chief, taller than any of his captors, of such strength and ferocity that the King's people came a day's journey to look at him. When the Princess beheld his great stature, and saw that his arms and breast were covered with the figures of wild animals, bitten into the skin and coloured, she begged his life from her father. She

desired that he should practise his art upon her, and prick upon her skin the signs of Rain and Lightning and Thunder, and stain the wounds with herb-juices, as they were upon his own body. For many days, upon the roof of the King's house, the Princess submitted herself to the bone needle, and the women with her marvelled at her fortitude. But the Princess was without shame before the Captive, and it came about that he threw from him his needles and his stains, and fell upon the Princess to violate her honour; and her women ran down from the roof screaming, to call the guard which stood at the gateway of the King's house, and none stayed to protect their mistress. When the guard came, the Captive was thrown into bonds, and he was gelded, and his tongue was torn out, and he was given for a slave to the Rain Princess.

The country of the Aztecs to the east was tormented by thirst, and their King, hearing much of the rain-making arts of the Princess, sent an embassy to her father, with presents and an offer of marriage. So the Princess went from her father to be the Queen of the Aztecs, and she took with her the Captive, who served her in everything with entire fidelity and slept upon a mat before her door.

The King gave his bride a fortress on the outskirts of the city, whither she retired to entreat the rain gods. This fortress was called the Queen's House, and on the night of the new moon the Queen came to it from the palace. But when the moon waxed and grew toward the round, because the god of Thunder had had his will of her, then the Queen returned to the King. Drought abated in the country and rain fell abundantly by reason of the Queen's power with the stars.

When the Queen went to her own house she took with her no servant but the Captive, and he slept outside her door and brought her food after she had fasted. The Queen had a jewel of great value, a turquoise that had fallen from the sun, and had the image of the sun upon it. And when she desired a young man whom she had seen in the army or among the slaves, she sent the Captive to him with the jewel, for a sign that he should come to her secretly at the Queen's House upon business concerning the welfare of all. And some, after she had talked with them, she sent away with rewards; and some she took into her chamber and kept them by her for one night or two. Afterward she called the Captive and bade him conduct the youth by the secret way he had come, underneath the chambers of the fortress. But for the going away of the Queen's lovers the Captive took out the bar that was beneath a stone in the floor of the passage, and put in its stead a rush-reed, and the youth stepped upon it and fell through into a cavern that was the bed of an underground river, and whatever was thrown into it was not seen again. In this service nor in any other did the Captive fail the Queen.

But when the Queen sent for the Captain of the Archers, she detained him four days in her chamber, calling often for food and wine, and was greatly content with him. On the fourth day she went to the Captive outside her door and said: "Tomorrow take this man up by the sure way, by which the King comes, and let him live."

In the Queen's door were arrows, purple and white.

When she desired the King to come to her publicly, with his guard, she sent him a white arrow; but when she sent the purple, he came secretly, and covered himself with his mantle to be hidden from the stone gods at the gate. On the fifth night that the Queen was with her lover, the Captive took a purple arrow to the King, and the King came secretly and found them together. He killed the Captain with his own hand, but the Queen he brought to public trial. The Captive, when he was put to the question, told on his fingers forty men that he had let through the underground passage into the river. The Captive and the Queen were put to death by fire, both on the same day, and afterward there was scarcity of rain.

Eden Bower sat shivering a little as she listened. Hedger was not trying to please her, she thought, but to antagonize and frighten her by his brutal story. She had often told herself that his lean, big-boned lower jaw was like his bull-dog's, but tonight his face made Caesar's most savage and determined expression seem an affectation. Now she was looking at the man he really was. Nobody's eyes had ever defied her like this. They were searching her and seeing everything; all she had concealed from Livingston, and from the millionaire and his friends, and from the newspaper men. He was testing her, trying her out, and she was more ill at ease than she wished to show.

"That's quite a thrilling story," she said at last, rising and winding her scarf about her throat. "It must be getting late. Almost every one has gone."

They walked down the Avenue like people who have quarrelled, or who wish to get rid of each other. Hedger did not take her arm at the street crossings, and they did not linger in the Square. At her door he tried none of the old devices of the Livingston boys. He stood like a post, having forgotten to take off his hat, gave her a harsh, threatening glance, muttered "good-night," and shut his own door noisily.

There was no question of sleep for Eden Bower. Her brain was working like a machine that would never stop. After she undressed, she tried to calm her nerves by smoking a cigarette, lying on the divan by the open window. But she grew wider and wider awake, combating the challenge that had flamed all evening in Hedger's eyes. The balloon had been one kind of excitement, the wine another; but the thing that had roused her, as a blow rouses a proud man, was the doubt, the contempt, the sneering hostility with which the painter had looked at her when he told his savage story. Crowds and balloons were all very well, she reflected, but woman's chief adventure is man. With a mind over active and a sense of life over strong, she wanted to walk across the roofs in the starlight, to sail over the sea and face at once a world of which she had never been afraid.

Hedger must be asleep; his dog had stopped sniffing under the double doors. Eden put on her wrapper and slippers and stole softly down the hall over the old carpet; one loose board creaked just as she reached the ladder. The trapdoor was open, as always on hot nights. When she stepped out on the roof she drew a long breath and walked across it, looking up at the sky. Her foot touched something soft; she heard a low growl, and on the instant Caesar's sharp little teeth

Street Scene
by John Sloan
1859

caught her ankle and waited. His breath was like steam on her leg. Nobody had ever intruded upon his roof before, and he panted for the movement or the word that would let him spring his jaw. Instead, Hedger's hand seized his throat.

"Wait a minute. I'll settle with him," he said grimly. He dragged the dog toward the manhole and disappeared. When he came back, he found Eden standing over by the dark chimney, looking away in an offended attitude.

"I caned him unmercifully," he panted. "Of course you didn't hear anything; he never whines when I beat him. He didn't nip you, did he?"

"I don't know whether he broke the skin or not," she answered aggrievedly, still looking off into the west.

"If I were one of your friends in white pants, I'd strike a match to find whether you were hurt, though I know you are not, and then I'd see your ankle, wouldn't I?"

"I suppose so."

He shook his head and stood with his hands in the pockets of his old painting jacket. "I'm not up to such boy-tricks. If you want the place to yourself, I'll clear out. There are plenty of places where I can spend the night, what's left of it. But if you stay here and I stay here—" He shrugged his shoulders.

Eden did not stir, and she made no reply. Her head drooped slightly, as if she were considering. But the moment he put his arms about her they began to talk, both at once, as people do in an opera. The instant avowal brought out a flood of trivial admissions. Hedger confessed his crime, was reproached and forgiven, and now Eden knew what it was in his look that she had found so disturbing of late.

Standing against the black chimney, with the sky behind and blue shadows before, they looked like one of Hedger's own paintings of that period; two figures, one white and one dark, and nothing whatever distinguishable about them but that they were male and female. The faces were lost, the contours blurred in shadow, but the figures were a man and a woman, and that was their whole concern and their mysterious beauty,—it was the rhythm in which they moved, at last, along the roof and down into the dark hole; he first, drawing her gently after him. She came down very slowly. The excitement and bravado and uncertainty of that long day and night seemed all at once to tell upon her. When his feet were on the carpet and he reached up to lift her down, she twined her arms about his neck as after a long separation, and turned her face to him, and her lips, with their perfume of youth and passion.

One Saturday afternoon Hedger was sitting in the window of Eden's music room. They had been watching the pigeons come wheeling over the roofs from their unknown feeding grounds.

"Why," said Eden suddenly, "don't we fix those big doors into your studio so they will open? Then, if I want you, I won't have to go through the hall. That illustrator is loafing about a good deal of late."

"I'll open them, if you wish. The bolt is on your side."

"Isn't there one on yours, too?"

"No. I believe a man lived there for years before I came in, and the nurse used to have these rooms herself. Naturally, the lock was on the lady's side."

Eden laughed and began to examine the bolt. "It's all stuck up with paint." Looking about, her eye lighted upon a bronze Buddha which was one of the nurse's treasures. Taking him by his head, she struck the bolt a blow with his squatting posteriors. The two doors creaked, sagged, and swung weakly inward a little way, as if they were too old for such escapades. Eden tossed the heavy idol into a stuffed chair. "That's better," she exclaimed exultantly. "So the bolts are always on the lady's side? What a lot society takes for granted!"

Hedger laughed, sprang up and caught her arms roughly. "Whoever takes you for granted—Did anybody, ever?"

"Everybody does. That's why I'm here. You are the only one who knows anything about me. Now I'll have to dress if we're going out for dinner."

He lingered, keeping his hold on her. "But I won't always be the only one, Eden Bower. I won't be the last."

"No, I suppose not," she said carelessly. "But what does that matter? You are the first."

As a long, despairing whine broke in the warm stillness, they drew apart. Caesar, lying on his bed in the dark corner, had lifted his head at this invasion of sunlight, and realized that the side of his room was broken open, and his whole world shattered by change. There stood his master and this woman, laughing at him! The woman was pulling the long black hair of this mightiest of men, who bowed his head and permitted it.

VI

In time they quarrelled, of course, and about an abstraction,—as young people often do, as mature people almost never do. Eden came in late one afternoon. She had been with some of her musical friends to lunch at Burton Ives' studio, and she began telling Hedger about its splendours. He listened a moment and then threw down his brushes. "I know exactly what it's like," he said impatiently. "A very good department-store conception of a studio. It's one of the show places."

"Well, it's gorgeous, and he said I could bring you to see him. The boys tell me he's awfully kind about giving people a lift, and you might get something out of it."

Hedger started up and pushed his canvas out of the way. "What could I possibly get from Burton Ives? He's almost the worst painter in the world; the stupidest, I mean."

Eden was annoyed. Burton Ives had been very nice to her and had begged her to sit for him. "You must admit that he's a very successful one," she said coldly.

"Of course he is! Anybody can be successful who will do that sort of thing. I wouldn't paint his pictures for all the money in New York."

"Well, I saw a lot of them, and I think they are

beautiful."

Hedger bowed stiffly.

"What's the use of being a great painter if nobody knows about you?" Eden went on persuasively. "Why don't you paint the kind of pictures people can understand, and then, after you're successful, do whatever you like?"

"As I look at it," said Hedger brusquely, "I am successful."

Eden glanced about. "Well, I don't see any evidences of it," she said, biting her lip. "He has a Japanese servant and a wine cellar, and keeps a riding horse."

Hedger melted a little. "My dear, I have the most expensive luxury in the world, and I am much more extravagant than Burton Ives, for I work to please nobody but myself."

"You mean you could make money and don't? That you don't try to get a public?"

"Exactly. A public only wants what has been done over and over. I'm painting for painters,—who haven't been born."

"What would you do if I brought Mr. Ives down here to see your things?"

"Well, for God's sake, don't! Before he left I'd probably tell him what I thought of him."

Eden rose. "I give up. You know very well there's only one kind of success that's real."

"Yes, but it's not the kind you mean. So you've been thinking me a scrub painter, who needs a helping hand from some fashionable studio man? What the devil have you had anything to do with me for, then?"

"There's no use talking to you," said Eden walking slowly toward the door. "I've been trying to pull wires for you all afternoon, and this is what it comes to." She had expected that the tidings of a prospective call from the great man would be received very differently, and had been thinking as she came home in the stage how, as with a magic wand, she might gild Hedger's future, float him out of his dark hole on a tide of prosperity, see his name in the papers and his pictures in the windows on Fifth Avenue.

Hedger mechanically snapped the midsummer leash on Caesar's collar and they ran downstairs and hurried through Sullivan Street off toward the river. He wanted to be among rough, honest people, to get down where the big drays bumped over stone paving blocks and the men wore corduroy trowsers and kept their shirts open at the neck. He stopped for a drink in one of the sagging bar-rooms on the water front. He had never in his life been so deeply wounded; he did not know he could be so hurt. He had told this girl all his secrets. On the roof, in these warm, heavy summer nights, with her hands locked in his, he had been able to explain all his misty ideas about an unborn art the world was waiting for; had been able to explain them better than he had ever done to himself. And she had looked away to the chattels of this uptown studio and coveted them for him! To her he was only an unsuccessful Burton Ives.

Then why, as he had put it to her, did she take up with him? Young, beautiful, talented as she was, why had she wasted herself on a scrub? Pity? Hardly; she wasn't sentimental. There was no explaining her. But in this passion that had seemed so fearless and so fated to be, his own position now looked to him ridiculous; a poor dauber without money or fame,—it was her caprice to load him with favours. Hedger ground his teeth so loud that his dog, trotting beside him, heard him and looked up.

While they were having supper at the oysterman's, he planned his escape. Whenever he saw her again, everything he had told her, that he should never have told any one, would come back to him; ideas he had never whispered even to the painter whom he worshipped and had gone all the way to France to see. To her they must seem his apology for not having horses and a valet, or merely the puerile boastfulness of a weak man. Yet if she slipped the bolt tonight and came through the doors and said, "Oh, weak man, I belong to you!" what could he do? That was the danger. He would catch the train out to Long Beach tonight, and tomorrow he would go on to the north end of Long Island, where an old friend of his had a summer studio among the sand dunes. He would stay until things came right in his mind. And she could find a smart painter, or take her punishment.

When he went home, Eden's room was dark; she was dining out somewhere. He threw his things into a hold-all he had carried about the world with him, strapped up some colours and canvases, and ran downstairs.

VII

Five days later Hedger was a restless passenger on a dirty, crowded Sunday train, coming back to town. Of course he saw now how unreasonable he had been in expecting a Huntington girl to know anything about pictures; here was a whole continent full of people who knew nothing about pictures and he didn't hold it against them. What had such things to do with him and Eden Bower? When he lay out on the dunes, watching the moon come up out of the sea, it had seemed to him that there was no wonder in the world like the wonder of Eden Bower. He was going back to her because she was older than art, because she was the most overwhelming thing that had ever come into his life.

He had written her yesterday, begging her to be at home this evening, telling her that he was contrite, and wretched enough.

Now that he was on his way to her, his stronger feeling unaccountably changed to a mood that was playful and tender. He wanted to share everything with her, even the most trivial things. He wanted to tell her about the people on the train, coming back tired from their holiday with bunches of wilted flowers and dirty daisies; to tell her that the fish-man, to whom she had often sent him for lobsters, was among the passengers, disguised in a silk shirt and a spotted tie, and how his wife looked exactly like a fish, even to her eyes, on which cataracts were forming. He could tell her, too, that he hadn't as much as unstrapped his canvases, —that ought to convince her.

In those days passengers from Long Island came into New York by ferry. Hedger had to be quick about getting his dog out of the express car in order to catch the first boat. The East River, and the bridges, and the city to the west, were burning in the conflagration of the sunset; there was that great home-coming reach of evening in the air.

The car changes from Thirty-fourth Street were too many and too perplexing; for the first time in his life Hedger took a hansom cab for Washington Square. Caesar sat bolt upright on the worn leather cushion beside him, and they jogged off, looking down on the rest of the world.

It was twilight when they drove down lower Fifth Avenue into the Square, and through the Arch behind them were the two long rows of pale violet lights that used to bloom so beautifully against the grey stone and asphalt. Here and yonder about the Square hung globes that shed a radiance not unlike the blue mists of evening, emerging softly when daylight died, as the stars emerged in the thin blue sky. Under them the sharp shadows of the trees fell on the cracked pavement and the sleeping grass. The first stars and the first lights were growing silver against the gradual darkening, when Hedger paid his driver and went into the house,—which, thank God, was still there! On the hall table lay his letter of yesterday, unopened.

He went upstairs with every sort of fear and every sort of hope clutching at his heart; it was as if tigers were tearing him. Why was there no gas burning in the top hall? He found matches and the gas bracket. He knocked, but got no answer; nobody was there. Before his own door were exactly five bottles of milk, standing in a row. The milk-boy had taken spiteful pleasure in thus reminding him that he forgot to stop his order.

Hedger went down to the basement; it, too, was dark. The janitress was taking her evening airing on the basement steps. She sat waving a palm-leaf fan majestically, her dirty calico dress open at the neck. She told him at once that there had been "changes." Miss Bower's room was to let again, and the piano would go tomorrow. Yes, she left yesterday, she sailed for Europe with friends from Chicago. They arrived on Friday, heralded by many telegrams. Very rich people they were said to be, though the man had refused to pay the nurse a month's rent in lieu of notice,—which would have been only right, as the young lady had agreed to take the rooms until October. Mrs. Foley had observed, too, that he didn't overpay her or Willy for their trouble, and a great deal of trouble they had been put to, certainly. Yes, the young lady was very pleasant, but the nurse said there were rings on the mahogany table where she had put tumblers and wine glasses. It was just as well she was gone. The Chicago man was uppish in his ways, but not much to look at. She supposed he had poor health, for there was nothing to him inside his clothes.

Hedger went slowly up the stairs—never had they seemed so long, or his legs so heavy. The upper floor was emptiness and silence. He unlocked his room, lit the gas, and opened the windows. When he went to put his coat in the closet, he found, hanging among his clothes, a pale, flesh-tinted dressing gown he had liked to see her wear, with a perfume—oh, a perfume that was still Eden Bower! He shut the door behind him and there, in the dark, for a moment he lost his

manliness. It was when he held this garment to him that he found a letter in the pocket.

The note was written with a lead pencil, in haste: She was sorry that he was angry, but she still didn't know just what she had done. She had thought Mr. Ives would be useful to him; she guessed he was too proud. She wanted awfully to see him again, but Fate came knocking at her door after he had left her. She believed in Fate. She would never forget him and she knew he would become the greatest painter in the world. Now she must pack. She hoped he wouldn't mind her leaving the dressing gown; somehow, she could never wear it again.

After Hedger read this, standing under the gas, he went back into the closet and knelt down before the wall; the knot hole had been plugged up with a ball of wet paper,—the same blue note-paper on which her letter was written.

He was hard hit. Tonight he had to bear the loneliness of a whole lifetime. Knowing himself so well, he could hardly believe that such a thing had ever happened to him, that such a woman had lain happy and contented in his arms. And now it was over. He turned out the light and sat down on his painter's stool before the big window. Caesar, on the floor beside him, rested his head on his master's knee. We must leave Hedger thus, sitting in his tank with his dog, looking up at the stars.

COMING, APHRODITE! This legend, in electric lights over the Lexington Opera House, had long announced the return of Eden Bower to New York after years of spectacular success in Paris. She came at last, under the management of an American Opera Company, but bringing her own *chef d' orchestre*.

One bright December afternoon Eden Bower was going down Fifth Avenue in her car, on the way to her broker, in Williams Street. Her thoughts were entirely upon stocks,—Cerro de Pasco, and how much she should buy of it,—when she suddenly looked up and realized that she was skirting Washington Square. She had not seen the place since she rolled out of it in an old-fashioned four-wheeler to seek her fortune, eighteen years ago.

"Arrêtez, Alphonse. Attendez moi," she called, and opened the door before he could reach it. The children who were streaking over the asphalt on roller skates saw a lady in a long fur coat, and short, high-heeled shoes, alight from a French car and pace slowly about the Square, holding her muff to her chin. This spot, at least, had changed very little, she reflected; the same trees, the same fountain, the white arch, and over yonder, Garibaldi, drawing the sword of freedom. There, just opposite her, was the old red brick house.

"Yes, that is the place," she was thinking. "I can smell the carpets now, and the dog,—what was his name? That grubby bathroom at the end of the hall, and that dreadful Hedger—still, there was something about him, you know—" She glanced up and blinked against the sun. From somewhere in the crowded quarter south of the Square a flock of pigeons rose, wheeling quickly upward into the brilliant blue sky. She threw back her head, pressed her muff closer to her chin, and watched them with a smile of amazement and delight. So they still rose, out of all that dirt and noise and squalor, fleet and silvery, just as they used to rise that summer when she was twenty and went up in a balloon on Coney Island!

Alphonse opened the door and tucked her robes about her. All the way down town her mind wandered from Cerro de Pasco, and she kept smiling and looking up at the sky.

When she had finished her business with the broker, she asked him to look in the telephone book for the address of M. Gaston Jules, the picture dealer, and slipped the paper on which he wrote it into her glove. It was five o'clock when she reached the French Galleries, as they were called. On entering she gave the attendant her card, asking him to take it to M. Jules. The dealer appeared very promptly and begged her to come into his private office, where he pushed a great chair toward his desk for her and signalled his secretary to leave the room.

"How good your lighting is in here," she observed, glancing about. "I met you at Simon's studio, didn't I? Oh, no! I never forget anybody who interests me." She threw her muff on his writing table and sank into the deep chair. "I have come to you for some information that's not in my line. Do you know anything about an American painter named Hedger?"

He took the seat opposite her. "Don Hedger? But, certainly! There are some very interesting things of his in an exhibition at V——'s. If you would care to—"

She held up her hand. "No, no. I've no time to go to exhibitions. Is he a man of any importance?"

"Certainly. He is one of the first men among the moderns. That is to say, among the very moderns. He is always coming up with something different. He often exhibits in Paris, you must have seen—"

"No, I tell you I don't go to exhibitions. Has he had great success? That is what I want to know."

M. Jules pulled at his short grey moustache. "But, Madame, there are many kinds of success," he began cautiously.

Madame gave a dry laugh. "Yes, so he used to say. We once quarrelled on that issue. And how would you define his particular kind?"

M. Jules grew thoughtful. "He is a great name with all the young men, and he is decidedly an influence in art. But one can't definitely place a man who is original, erratic, and who is changing all the time."

She cut him short. "Is he much talked about at home? In Paris, I mean? Thanks. That's all I want to know." She rose and began buttoning her coat. "One doesn't like to have been an utter fool, even at twenty."

"*Mais, non!*" M. Jules handed her her muff with a quick, sympathetic glance. He followed her out through the carpeted show-room, now closed to the public and draped in cheesecloth, and put her into her car with words appreciative of the honour she had done him in calling.

Leaning back in the cushions, Eden Bower closed her eyes, and her face, as the street lamps flashed their ugly orange light upon it, became hard and settled, like a plaster cast; so a sail, that has been filled by a strong breeze, behaves when the wind suddenly dies. Tomorrow night the wind would blow again, and this mask would be the golden face of Aphrodite. But a "big" career takes its toll, even with the best of luck.

To His Coy Mistress
by Andrew Marvell

Had we but world enough, and time,
This coyness, lady, were no crime.
We would sit down, and think which way
To walk, and pass our long love's day.
Thou by the Indian Ganges' side
Shouldst rubies find: I by the tide
Of Humber would complain. I would
Love you ten years before the flood,
And you should, if you please, refuse
Till the conversion of the Jews;
My vegetable love should grow
Vaster than empires and more slow;
An hundred years should go to praise
Thine eyes, and on thy forehead gaze;
Two hundred to adore each breast,
But thirty thousand to the rest;
An age at least to every part,
And the last age should show your heart.
For, lady, you deserve this state;
Nor would I love at lower rate.

But at my back I always hear
Time's wingéd chariot hurrying near;
And yonder all before us lie
Deserts of vast eternity.
Thy beauty shall no more be found,
Nor in thy marble vault shall sound
My echoing song; then worms shall try
That long preserved virginity;
And your quaint honor turn to dust,
And into ashes all my lust:
The grave's a fine and private place,
But none, I think, do there embrace.

Now therefore, while the youthful hue
Sits on thy skin like morning dew,
And while thy willing soul transpires
At every pore with instant fires,
Now let us sport us while we may,
And now, like amorous birds of prey,
Rather at once our time devour
Than languish in his slow-chapped power,
Let us roll all our strength and all
Our sweetness up into one ball,
And tear our pleasures with rough strife
Through the iron gates of life:
Thus, though we cannot make our sun
Stand still, yet we will make him run.

detail from

The Garden of Love
by Peter Paul Rubens
1638

"Tonight, same time, same place."

Anonymous

Illustration
by Weber
1978

CELEBRATIONS

Birthday
by Marc Chagall
1915

You're the Top
Lyrics by Cole Porter

At words poetic, I'm so pathetic
That I always have found it best,
Instead of getting 'em off my chest,
To let 'em rest unexpressed.
I hate parading
My serenading
As I'll probably miss a bar,
But if this ditty
Is not so pretty,
At least it'll tell you
How great you are

You're the top!
You're the Colosseum.
You're the top!
You're the Louvre Museum.
You're a melody from a symphony
    by Strauss,
You're a Bendel bonnet,
A Shakespeare sonnet,
You're Mickey Mouse.
You're the Nile,
You're the Tow'r of Pisa,
You're the smile
On the Mona Lisa.
I'm a worthless check, a total wreck,
    a flop,
But if, Baby, I'm the bottom,
You're the top!

Your words poetic are not pathetic
On the other hand, boy, you shine
And I can feel after every line
A thrill divine
Down my spine.
Now gifted humans like Vincent
    Youmans
Might think that your song is bad,
But for a person who's just rehearsin'
Well I gotta say this my lad:

You're the top!
You're Mahatma Gandhi.
You're the top!
You're Napoleon brandy.
You're the purple light of a summer
    night in Spain,
You're the National Gall'ry,
You're Garbo's sal'ry,
You're cellophane.

You're sublime,
You're a turkey dinner,
You're the time
Of the Derby winner.
I'm a toy balloon that is fated soon
    to pop,
But if, Baby, I'm the bottom
You're the top!

You're the top!
You're a Ritz hot toddy.
You're the top!
You're a Brewster body.
You're the boats that glide on the
    sleepy Zuider Zee,
You're a Nathan panning,
You're Bishop Manning,
You're broccoli.
You're a prize,
You're a night at Coney,
You're the eyes
Of Irene Bordoni.
I'm a broken doll, a fol-de-rol,
    a blop,
But if, Baby, I'm the bottom
You're the top!

You're the top!
You're an Arrow collar.
You're the top!
You're a Coolidge dollar.
You're the nimble tread of the feet
    of Fred Astaire,
You're an O'Neill drama,
You're Whistler's mama,
You're Camembert.
You're a rose,
You're Inferno's Dante,
You're the nose
On the great Durante.
I'm just in the way, as the French
    would say
"De trop,"
But if, Baby, I'm the bottom
You're the top.

You're the top!
You're a Waldorf salad.
You're the top!
You're a Berlin ballad.

You're a baby grand of a lady and
    a gent,
You're an old Dutch master,
You're Mrs. Astor,
You're Pepsodent.
You're romance,
You're the steppes of Russia,
You're the pants on a Roxy usher.
I'm a lazy lout that's just about
    to stop,
But if, Baby, I'm the bottom
You're the top.

You're the top!
You're a dance in Bali.
You're the top!
You're a hot tamale.
You're an angel, you, simply too, too,
    too diveen,
You're a Botticelli,
You're Keats,
You're Shelley,
You're Ovaltine.
You're a boon,
You're the dam at Boulder,
You're the moon over Mae West's
    shoulder.
I'm a nominee of the G.O.P.
or GOP,
But if, Baby, I'm the bottom,
You're the top.

You're the top!
You're the Tower of Babel.
You're the top!
You're the Whitney Stable.
By the River Rhine,
You're a sturdy stein of beer,
You're a dress from Saks's,
You're next year's taxes,
You're stratosphere.
You're my thoist,
You're a Drumstick Lipstick,
You're da foist
In da Irish svipstick.
I'm a frightened frog
That can find no log
To hop,
But if, Baby, I'm the bottom,
You're the top!

---

from Quatre Proverbes, a de luxe album
"Qui Trop Embrasse"
by Tito
circa 1920

Taking the Hands
by Robert Bly

Taking the hands of someone you love,
You see they are delicate cages...
Tiny birds are singing
In the secluded prairies
And in the deep valleys of the hand.

opposite

Sethos I with Queen Hathor

XIX Dynasty

above, detail from

The Tomb of Ramses I

Valley of Kings, Thebes

April, Late April
by Thomas Wolfe

Autumn was kind to them, winter was long to them—but in April, late April, all the gold sang.

Spring came that year like magic and like music and like song. One day its breath was in the air, a haunting premonition of its spirit filled the hearts of men with its transforming loveliness, working its sudden and incredible sorcery upon grey streets, grey pavements, and on grey faceless tides of manswarm ciphers. It came like music faint and far, it came with triumph and a sound of singing in the air, with lutings of sweet bird cries at the break of day and the high, swift passing of a wing, and one day it was there upon the city streets with a strange, sudden cry of green, its sharp knife of wordless joy and pain.

Not the whole glory of the great plantation of the earth could have outdone the glory of the city streets that Spring. Neither the cry of great, green fields, nor the song of the hills, nor the glory of young birch trees bursting into life again along the banks of rivers, nor the oceans of bloom in the flowering orchards, the peach trees, the apple trees, the plum and cherry trees—not all of the singing and the gold of Spring, with April bursting from the earth in a million shouts of triumph, and the visible stride, the flowered feet of the Springtime as it came on across the earth, could have surpassed the wordless and poignant glory of a single tree in a city street that Spring.

Monk had given up his tiny room in the dingy little hotel and had taken possession of the spacious floor in the old house on Waverly Place. There had been a moment's quarrel when he had said that from that time on he would pay the rent. She had objected that the place was hers, that she had found it—she wanted him to come, she would like to think of him as being there, it would make it seem more "theirs"—but she had been paying for it, and would continue, and it

Man and Woman
by Pierre Bonnard
Circa 1906

---

didn't matter. But he was adamant and said he wouldn't come at all unless he paid his way, and in the end she yielded.

And now each day he heard her step upon the stairs at noon. At noon, at high, sane, glorious noon, she came, the mistress of that big, disordered room, the one whose brisk, small step on the stairs outside his door woke a leaping jubilation in his heart. Her face was like a light and like a music in the light of noon: it was jolly, small, and tender, as delicate as a plum, and as rosy as a flower. It was young and good and full of health and delight; its sweetness, strength, and noble beauty could not be equaled anywhere on earth. He kissed it a thousand times because it was so good, so wholesome, and so radiant in its loveliness.

Everything about her sang out with hope and morning. Her face was full of a thousand shifting plays of life and jolly humor, as swift and merry as a child's, and yet had in it always, like shadows in the sun, all of the profound, brooding, and sorrowful depths of beauty.

Thus, when he heard her step upon the stairs at noon, her light knuckles briskly rapping at the door, her key turning in the lock, she brought the greatest health and joy to him that he had ever known. She came in like a cry of triumph, like a shout of music in the blood, like the deathless birdsong in the first light of the morning. She was the bringer of hope, the teller of good news. A hundred sights and magical colors which she had seen in the streets that morning, a dozen tales of life and work and business, sprang from her merry lips with the eager insistence of a child.

She got into the conduits of his blood, she began to sing and pulse through the vast inertia of his flesh, still heavied with great clots of sleep, until he sprang up with the goat cry in his throat, seized, engulfed, and devoured her, and felt there was nothing on earth he could not do, nothing on earth he could not conquer. She gave a tongue to all the exultant music of the Spring whose great pulsations trembled in the gold and sapphire singing of the air. Everything—the stick-candy whippings of a flag, the shout of a child, the smell of old, worn plankings in the sun, the heavy, oily, tarry exhalations of the Spring-warm streets, the thousand bobbing and weaving colors and the points of light upon the pavements, the smell of the markets, of fruits, flowers, vegetables, and loamy earth, and the heavy shattering *baugh* of a great ship as it left its wharf at noon on Saturday—was given intensity, structure, and a form of joy because of her.

She had never been as beautiful as she was that Spring, and sometimes it drove him almost mad to see her look so fresh and fair. Even before he heard her step upon the stair at noon he always knew that she was there. Sunken in sleep at twelve o'clock, drowned fathoms deep at noon in a strange, wakeful sleep, his consciousness of her was so great that he knew instantly the moment when she had entered the house, whether he heard a sound or not.

She seemed to be charged with all the good and joyful living of the earth as she stood there in the high light of noon. In all that was delicate in her little bones, her trim figure, slim ankles, full, swelling thighs, deep breast and straight, small shoulders, rose lips and flower face, and all the winking lights of her fine hair, jolliness, youth, and noble beauty—she seemed as rare, as rich, as high and grand a woman as any on earth could be. The first sight of her at noon always brought hope, confidence, belief, and sent through the huge inertia of his flesh, still drugged with the great anodyne of sleep, a tidal surge of invincible strength.

She would fling her arms around him and kiss him furiously, she would fling herself down beside him on his cot and cunningly insinuate herself into his side, presenting her happy, glowing little face insatiably to be kissed, covered, plastered with a thousand kisses. She was as fresh as morning, as tender as a plum, and so irresistible he felt he could devour her in an instant and entomb her in his flesh forever. And then, after an interval, she would rise and set briskly about the preparation of a meal for him.

There is no spectacle on earth more appealing than that of a beautiful woman in the act of cooking dinner for someone she loves. Thus the sight of Esther as, delicately flushed, she bent with the earnest devotion of religious ceremony above the food she was cooking for him, was enough to drive him mad with love and hunger.

In such a moment he could not restrain himself. He would get up and begin to pace the room in a madness of wordless ecstasy. He would lather his face for shaving, shave one side of it, and then begin to walk up and down the room again, singing, making strange noises in his throat, staring vacantly out of the window at a cat that crept along the ridges of the fence; he would pull books from the shelves, reading a line or page, sometimes reading her a passage from a poem as she cooked, and then forgetting the book, letting it fall upon the cot or on the floor, until the floor was covered with them. Then he would sit on the edge of the cot for minutes, staring stupidly and vacantly ahead, holding one sock in his hand. Then he would spring up again and begin to pace the room, shouting and singing, with a convulsion of energy surging through his body that could find no utterance and that ended only in a wild, goatlike cry of joy.

From time to time he would go to the door of the kitchen where she stood above the stove, and for a moment he would draw into his lungs the maddening fragrance of the food. Then he would fling about the room again, until he could control himself no longer. The sight of her face, earnestly bent and focused in its work of love, her sure and subtle movements, and her full, lovely figure—all that was at once both delicate and abundant in her, together with the maddening fragrance of glorious food, evoked an emotion of wild tenderness and hunger in him which was unutterable.

your little voice
by e. e. cummings

your little voice
                    Over the wires came leaping
and i felt suddenly
dizzy
        With the jostling and shouting of merry flowers
wee skipping high-heeled flames
courtesied before my eyes
                                or twinkling over to my side
Looked up
with impertinently exquisite faces
floating hands were laid upon me
I was whirled and tossed into delicious dancing
up
Up
with the pale important
                          stars and the Humorous
                                                    moon
dear girl
How i was crazy how i cried when i heard
                                        over time
and tide and death
leaping
Sweetly
            your voice

Le Bal à Bougival
by Pierre Auguste Renoir
1883

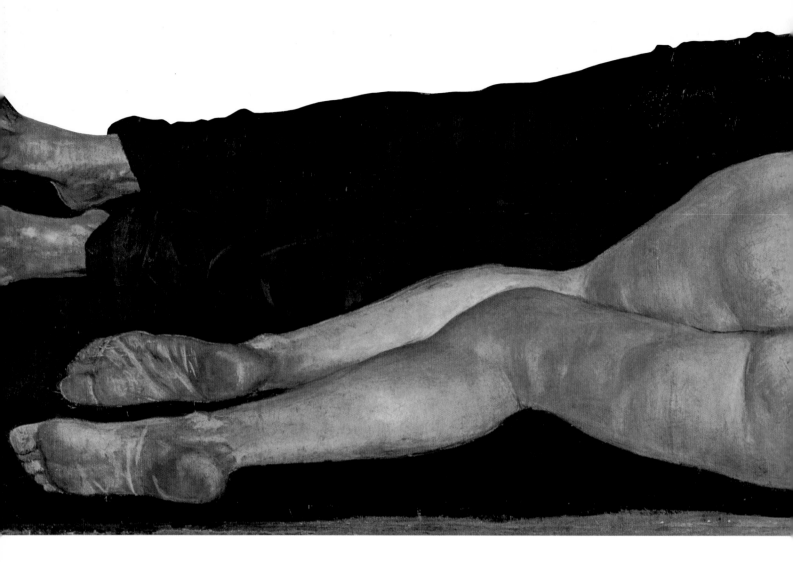

From Pent-up, Aching Rivers
by Walt Whitman

From pent-up, aching rivers;
From that of myself, without which I were nothing;
From what I am determined to make illustrious, even
  if I stand sole among men;
From my own voice resonant—singing the phallus,
Singing the song of procreation,
Singing the need of superb children, and therein superb
  grown people,
Singing the muscular urge and the blending,
Singing the bedfellow's song, (O resistless yearning!
O for any and each, the body correlative attracting!
O for you, whoever you are, your correlative body! O it,
  more than all else, you delighting!)
—From the hungry gnaw that eats me night and day;
From native moments—from bashful pains—singing
  them;
Singing something yet unfound, though I have diligently
  sought it, many a long year,

Singing the true song of the Soul, fitful, at random;
Singing what, to the Soul, entirely redeemed her, the
  faithful one, even the prostitute, who detained me
  when I went to the city;
Singing the song of prostitutes;
Renascent with grossest Nature, or among animals;
Of that—of them, and what goes with them, my poems
  informing;
Of the smell of apples and lemons—of the pairing of
  birds,
Of the wet of woods—of the lapping of waves,
Of the mad pushes of waves upon the land—I them
  chanting;
The overture lightly sounding—the strain anticipating;
The welcome nearness—the sight of the perfect body;
The swimmer swimming naked in the bath, or motion-
  less on his back lying and floating;
The female form approaching—I, pensive, love-flesh
  tremulous, aching;
The divine list, for myself or you, or for any one, making;
The face—the limbs—the index from head to foot, and
  what it arouses;
The mystic deliria—the madness amorous—the utter
abandonment;
(Hark close, and still, what I now whisper to you,
I love you—O you entirely possess me,
O I wish that you and I escape from the rest, and go
  utterly off—O free and lawless,

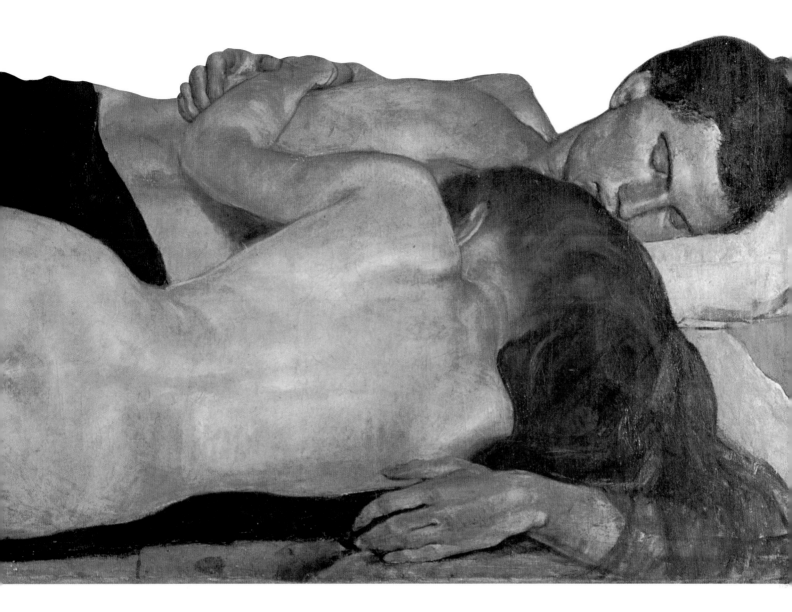

Two hawks in the air—two fishes swimming in the sea
 not more lawless than we;)
—The furious storm through me careering—I passion-
 ately trembling;
The oath of the inseparableness of two together—of the
 woman that loves me, and whom I love more than
 my life—that oath swearing;
(O I willingly stake all, for you!
O let me be lost, if it must be so!
O you and I—what is it to us what the rest do or think?
What is all else to us? only that we enjoy each other,
 and exhaust each other, if it must be so;)
—From the master—the pilot I yield the vessel to;
The general commanding me, commanding all—from
 him permission taking;
From time the programme hastening, (I have loitered
 too long, as it is;)
From sex—From the warp and from the woof;
(To talk to the perfect girl who understands me,
To waft to her these from my own lips—to effuse them
 from my own body;)
From privacy—from frequent repinings alone;
From plenty of persons near, and yet the right person
 not near;
From the soft sliding of hands over me, and thrusting
 of fingers through my hair and beard;
From the long sustained kiss upon the mouth or
 bosom;

From the close pressure that makes me or any man
 drunk, fainting with excess;
From what the divine husband knows—from the work
 of fatherhood;
From exultation, victory, and relief—from the bedfellow's
 embrace in the night;
From the act-poems of eyes, hands, hips, and bosoms,
From the cling of the trembling arm,
From the bending curve and the clinch,
From side by side, the pliant coverlid off-throwing,
From the one so unwilling to have me leave—and me
 just as unwilling to leave,
(Yet a moment, O tender waiter, and I return;)
—From the hour of shining stars and dropping dews,
From the night, a moment, I, emerging, flitting out,
Celebrate you, act divine—and you, children prepared
 for,
And you, stalwart loins.

---

detail from

Night

by Ferdinand Hodler

1890

How Do I Love Thee?
by Elizabeth Barrett Browning

How do I love thee? Let me count the ways.
I love thee to the depth and breadth and height
My soul can reach, when feeling out of sight
For the ends of Being and ideal Grace.
I love thee to the level of everyday's
Most quiet need, by sun and candlelight.
I love thee freely, as men strive for Right;
I love thee purely, as they turn from praise.
I love thee with the passion put to use
In my old griefs, and with my childhood's faith.
I love thee with a love I seemed to lose–
With my lost saints,–I love thee with the breath,
Smiles, tears, of all my life!–and, if God choose,
I shall but love thee better after death.

Krishna and Radha in the Groves of Brindaban
Indian Painting
Nineteenth to Twentieth Century

And One Shall Live in Two
by Jonathan Henderson Brooks

Though he hung dumb upon her wall
And was so very still and small—
A miniature, a counterpart,
Yet did she press him to her heart
On countless, little loving trips,
And six times pressed him to her lips!
As surely as she kissed him six,
As sure as sand and water mix,
Sure as canaries sweetly sing,
And lilies come when comes the spring,
The two have hopes for days of bliss
When four warm lips shall meet in kiss;
Four eyes shall blend to see as one,
Four hands shall do what two have done,
Two sorrow-drops will be one tear—
And one shall live in two each year.

Romance
by Thomas Hart Benton
1931–1932

Heart Exchange
by Sir Philip Sidney

My true love hath my heart, and I have his,
By just exchange, one for the other giv'n:
I hold his dear, and mine he cannot misse:
There never was a bargain better driv'n.

His heart in me keeps me and him in one,
My heart in him his thoughts and senses guides:
He loves my heart, for once it was his own:
I cherish his, because in me it bides.

His heart his wound received from my sight:
My heart was wounded with his wounded heart.
For as from me on him his hurt did light:
So still me thought in me his heart did smart:
   Both equal hurt, in his change sought our bliss:
   My true Love hath my heart, and I have his.

Self-Portrait with Isabella Brandt in the Honeysuckle Bower
by Peter Paul Rubens
1609

from
Thirty-five Tanka
by Ki no Tsurayuki

Along the Yodo
where they cut wild rice,
when it rains the marsh waters overflow,
like my love,
growing deeper than ever

Azuma and Yogoro
by Hokusai
Circa 1798

somewhere i have never travelled, gladly beyond

by e. e. cummings

somewhere i have never travelled, gladly beyond
any experience, your eyes have their silence:
in your most frail gesture are things which enclose me,
or which i cannot touch because they are too near

your slightest look easily will unclose me
though i have closed myself as fingers,
you open always petal by petal myself as Spring opens
(touching skilfully, mysteriously) her first rose

or if your wish be to close me, i and
my life will shut very beautifully, suddenly,
as when the heart of this flower imagines
the snow carefully everywhere descending;
nothing which we are to perceive in this world equals
the power of your intense fragility: whose texture
compels me with the color of its countries,
rendering death and forever with each breathing

(i do not know what it is about you that closes
and opens; only something in me understands
the voice of your eyes is deeper than all roses)
nobody, not even the rain, has such small hands

Symphony in White, No. 2

James Abbott McNeill Whistler

1864

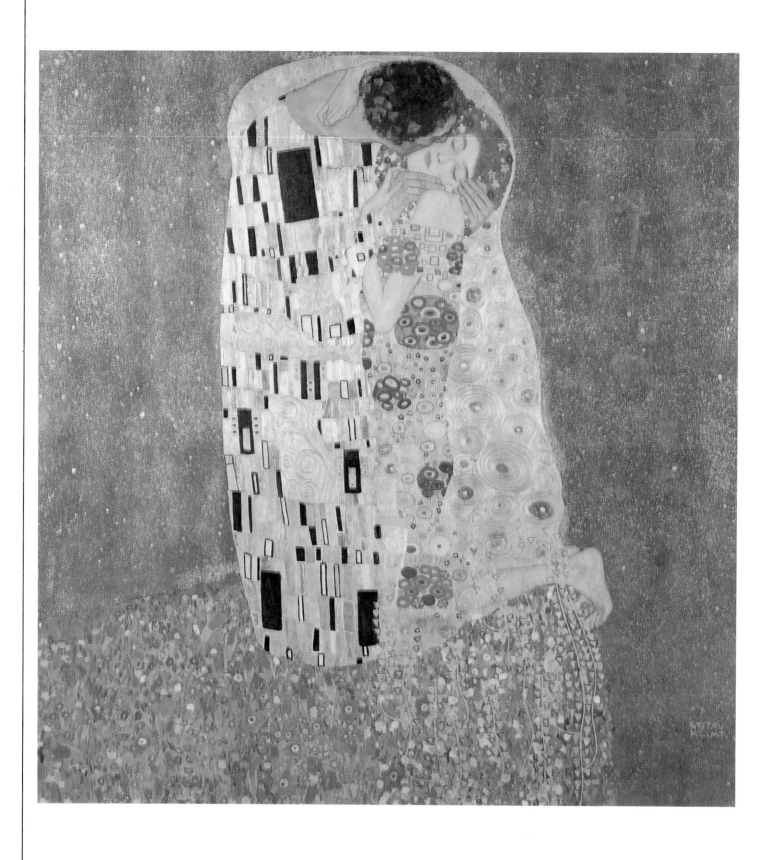

PASSION

The Kiss
by Gustav Klimt
1907–1908

"Let thy love in kisses rain..."

Percy Bysshe Shelley

above

The
Stolen Kiss
by Jean Honoré Fragonard
Circa 1761–1765

opposite, detail from

Francesca da Rimini and
Paolo Malatesta
by Ingres
1819

below
Hindu Temple Sculpture
Khajurāho, India
Tenth to Eleventh Century

opposite
The Kiss
by Francesco Hayez
Circa 1859

from
Ulysses
by James Joyce

...and then I asked him with my eyes to ask again yes
and then he asked me would I yes...
and first I put my arms around him yes
and drew him down to me so he could feel my breasts all perfume yes
and his heart was going like mad
and yes I said yes I will Yes.

Hindu Temple Sculpture
Khajurāho, India
Tenth to Eleventh Century

from
Earthly Paradise
by Colette

Equestrian
by Marc Chagall
1931

One night M. Willy was awakened by the violent ringing of the telephone. He lifted the receiver and heard a confused noise of sobs and muffled cries: "Vili! Oh Vili!... Come quick! I'm dying."

A short outburst of curses, and M. Willy leapt from his bed, flung a topcoat over his Russian-embroidered nightgown and hurried off, calling a few brief orders to me over his shoulder:

"Dress. Get there as soon as you can. I don't know what's up at Polaire's, but it looks as if tonight's takings were bitched."

He found, we found, Polaire on the floor of her bedroom, half under the bed. Sitting on the bed, and most admirably lit by a pink-frilled table lamp, was a young man in pajamas, Pierre L——. His eyes glowered, and with arms folded on his chest, he was breathing quickly through his nostrils like a boxer at the end of a round.

Down for the count, Polaire lay prostrate, if indeed the word "prostrate" can be applied to the stricken serpent, the frantic panther, to every live creature that can writhe and toss and buckle madly, tear the ground with its claws, sob, roar. The young man looked down at her in silence, motionless, making no attempt to help or soothe.

"Good God!" gasped M. Willy. "Whatever is the matter with her?"

Pierre L——'s handsome mouth remained grimly closed, but an answer issued, panting and incoherent, from underneath the bed:

"Vili! He hit me!... The brute! The brute!... Here... and here... and here!... Vili! I want to die!... Oh! Oh! Oh! Oh! I'm *so* unhappy!... Get a policeman! Get a policeman! I'll have him sent to prison! I'll have him put in irons!"

M. Willy wiped his forehead and inquired anxiously (first things first):

"Is she badly hurt?"

Pierre L——shrugged his shoulders.

"Hurt? Don't be funny! A couple of wallops..."

The prostrate victim sprang to her feet. Crowned with curl papers large as the largest Roman snails, puffed with tears, swollen with sighs and cries, she still glowed, in her long nightdress, like some fiery Eastern sorceress; nothing that was excessive or frenzied could ever make her ugly.

"A couple of wallops?" she repeated. "And what about this?... And this?"

She pointed to her arms, her neck, her shoulder, her thighs that were made to grip the bare flanks of a horse.

"The police!" she whispered childishly. "Call the police."

Tears of exhaustion and defeat overcame her, and she sank to the ground again. M. Willy, much relieved, sat down on the bed beside Pierre L——.

"My dear old fellow! This sort of thing isn't decent. You must forgive me if I tell you, as a friend, that a decent-hearted man, a man of feeling..."

The dear fellow laid a large, white, well-kept hand upon his unfeeling heart:

"In the first place I don't care a damn," he declared, "whether I'm decent or not. As for tonight——she said something I couldn't stand. No!" he suddenly shouted. "No! I can't and I won't stand it!"

He got up, scrabbling with his fingers in his thick, ash-gold hair.

"Can't you tell me what happened?" suggested M. Willy in a conciliatory tone. "You know you can trust me."

"She said—" began Pierre L——at the top of his voice. "She said—that I wasn't gentle!"

Below him, on the carpet, Polaire stirred feebly, shook her cluster of monster snails, moaned.

"That—I—was—not—gentle!" Pierre L——barked out. "When I heard that, I saw red.... Not gentle! I! I!"

He struck his fine chest with his fists.

"I—! Everybody knows it! I'm the mildest of men! *I*, not gentle!..."

Groans came from the carpet, broken and despairing....

"No, you're not, You're not gentle.... You don't understand anything.... You don't know what gentleness and understanding are.... What a woman really wants from love isn't what you think it is.... It's..."

"Do you hear her?" Pierre L——thundered. "She's at it again! My God!"

He threw off his pajama jacket, bent over the floor. M. Willy was about to intervene when two amber arms rose and closed about the smooth neck of the mildest of men.

"Pierre... I'm so unhappy.... Nobody loves me.... Pierre..."

"My little duck.... My lovey girl.... Popo, darling.... Who said nobody loved you?"

He picked her up, held her slung across his breast like a dark gazelle, carried her, humming softly, back and forth about the great Louis XV bed. M. Willy turned to me:

"I feel that our presence is no longer essential. But they did give me a turn! They're killing, don't you think?"

He wiped his forehead and laughed, but I could not do the same. Standing there, unwanted, almost in silence, I had had ample time to watch a strange, unknown sight—love in its youth and its violence, an outraged lover, naked to the waist, the silky woman's skin above the perfect muscles, the rippling play of light upon the proud, careless body, his easy assurance as he stepped over and then picked up the fallen body of Polaire.

I saw the back of his trim, well-shaped neck and the ash-gold hair falling like rain over Polaire's hidden face. Her arms about him, he rocked his victim gently, and she had forgotten we were there.

"Hey! Young Pierrot! Can you promise not to try our star's nerves too hard? Not to give her advice so—er—convincingly?"

The young head lifted and we saw the flushed, ferocious face, the mouth still moist from the interrupted kiss.

"Only when it's absolutely necessary, old man. I promise..."

I joined M. Willy, who, by the way of being funny, was tripping to the door on tiptoe, and we went out.

M. Willy, his mind now entirely at rest, seemed greatly amused by our night's adventure. I was not so entertained.

"Are you cold? You don't want to go home on foot, do you?"

No, I was not cold. Yes, I was cold. All the same, I would have liked to go home on foot. Or not to go home at all. Walking beside him, I looked back in my mind at the room we had just left. I can see something of it still—highlights of pale blue against a dim background, lamps that shone pink in their little embroidered shades, the tumbled, white expanse of a lovers' bed. I have kept the memory of a prolonged, uneasy sadness that I ought, perhaps, to call jealousy.

detail from a study for

Country Dance
by Pierre Auguste Renoir

from a play
The Greeks
by John Barton and Kenneth Cavander

Once long ago
in the mountains of the northland
lived a man named Peleus.
He was a master wrestler.
He fell in love with a sea-nymph,
Thetis, who was so fair
that the gods themselves
wanted her in their bed.
Peleus decided to try and capture her,
so he waited by the sea.
And one full-moon night, he saw her,
swimming shorewards, her body touched
with silver.
So when she was high and dry,
shaking out her hair, a free thing,
Peleus leapt out and seized her.
He tried every trick he knew as a wrestler.
She used every trick a sea-nymph knows.
She changed shape.
She became water—and soaked him.
She became fire—and singed him.
She became a lioness—and bit him.
She became a serpent—and stung him.
She became a cuttlefish—and squirted him
with purple ink all over.
She became a bird—and she tried to fly.
And she slipped and slid through his fingers.
Then just as he was tiring
he saw in his hands
A little silver fish,
wet, delicate, and tender.
It gasped, and arched its back
like a loving woman.
And he knew, that it was
the girl he so wanted.
So he stroked her,
and took her,
and loved her,
and they wrestled, as the dawn broke in sky.

detail from
Greek Red-figure Vase
by the Brygos Painter
500–480 B.C.

from the Sanskrit
When We Have Loved...

When we have loved, my love,
Panting and pale from love,
Then from your cheeks, my love,
Scent of the sweat I love:
And when our bodies love
Now to relax in love
After the stress of love,
Ever still more I love
Our mingled breath of love.

Two Lovers
by Reza-ye Abbasi
Safavid Period, 1630

That Act

by Tanikawa Shuntarō

I don't think I'm being manipulated.
But to do something one can't do anything about
as if by one's own will
is comical, sad, and yet peaceful.
While lying by you like this,
waiting for our breathing to calm down,
there's no way of thinking about things like love.
What were they—
those smooth, hot, and endless things?
Just because those odd things touched each other,
even my heart relaxed and breathed deeply,
my eyes looked at the starless darkness,
my ears heard moans that could not form words,
and I was about to melt and cease to be,
when you became unfathomably gentle and rich,
and in the void where any relation between persons doesn't
    catch up,
the very first thing of this world,
trying to be born, spurted out of me.
Out of this total silence now
what can I begin to say?
I simply rise to my feet in the darkness, for a glass of water.

Lovers

by Kitagawa Utamaro
1788

102/250   Picasso

from

Lady Chatterley's Lover
by D. H. Lawrence

Connie went to the wood directly after lunch. It was really a lovely day, the first dandelions making suns, the first daisies so white. The hazel thicket was a lacework of half-open leaves, and the last dusty perpendicular of the catkins. Yellow celandines now were in crowds, flat open, pressed back in urgency, and the yellow glitter of themselves. It was the yellow, the powerful yellow of early summer. And primroses were broad, and full of pale abandon, thick-clustered primroses no longer shy. The lush, dark green of hyacinths was a sea, with buds rising like pale corn, while in the riding the forget-me-nots were fluffing up, and columbines were unfolding their ink-purple riches, and there were bits of bluebird's eggshell under a bush. Everywhere the bud-knots and the leap of life!

The keeper was not at the hut. Everything was serene, brown chickens running lustily. Connie walked on towards the cottage, because she wanted to find him.

The cottage stood in the sun, off the wood's edge. In the little garden the double daffodils rose in tufts, near the wide open door, and red double daisies made a border to the path. There was the bark of a dog, and Flossie came running.

The wide-open door! so he was at home. And the sunlight falling on the red-brick floor! As she went up the path, she saw him through the window, sitting at the table in his shirtsleeves, eating. The dog wuffed softly, slowly wagging her tail.

He rose, and came to the door, wiping his mouth with a red handkerchief, still chewing.

"May I come in?" she said.

"Come in!"

The sun shone into the bar room, which still smelled of a mutton chop, done in a dutch oven before the fire, because the dutch oven still stood on the fender, with the black potato-saucepan on a piece of paper beside it on the white hearth. The fire was red, rather low, the bar dropped, the kettle singing.

On the table was his plate, with potatoes and the remains of the chop; also bread in a basket, salt, and a blue mug with beer. The tablecloth was white oil-cloth. He stood in the shade.

"You are very late," she said. "Do go on eating!"

She sat down on a wooden chair, in the sunlight by the door.

"I had to go to Uthwaite," he said, sitting down at table but not eating.

"Do eat," she said.

But he did not touch the food.

"Shall y'ave something?" he asked her. "Shall y'ave a cup of tea? t' kettle's on t' boil." He half rose again from his chair.

"If you'll let me make it myself," she said rising. He seemed sad, and she felt she was bothering him.

"Well, teapot's in there,"—he pointed to a little, drab corner cupboard; "an' cups. An' tea's on t' mantel ower yer 'ead."

She got the black teapot, and the tin of tea from the mantleshelf. She rinsed the teapot with hot water, and stood a moment wondering where to empty it.

"Thrown it out," he said, aware of her. "It's clean."

She went to the door and threw the drop of water down the path. How lovely it was here, so still, so really woodland. The oaks were putting out ochre yellow leaves; in the garden the red daisies were like red plush buttons. She glanced at the big, hollow sandstone slab of the threshold, now crossed by so few feet.

"But it's lovely here," she said. "Such a beautiful stillness, everything alive and still."

He was eating again, rather slowly and unwillingly, and she could feel he was discouraged. She made the tea in silence, and set the teapot on the hob, as she knew the people did. He pushed his plate aside and went to the back place; she heard a latch click, then he came back with cheese on a plate, and butter.

She set the two cups on the table, there were only two.

"Will you have a cup of tea?" she said.

"If you like. Sugar's in the' cupboard, an' there's a little cream-jug. Milk's in a jug in th' pantry."

Man and Woman
by Pablo Picasso
1927

"Shall I take your plate away?" she asked him. He looked up at her with a faint ironical smile.

"Why . . . if you like," he said, slowly eating bread and cheese. She went to the back, into the penthouse scullery, where the pump was. On the left was a door, no doubt the pantry door. She unlatched it, and almost smiled at the place he called a pantry; a long narrow whitewashed slip of a cupboard. But it managed to contain a little barrel of beer, as well as a few dishes and bits of food. She took a little milk from the yellow jug.

"How do you get your milk?" she asked him, when she came back to the table.

"Flints! They leave me a bottle at the warren end. You know, where I met you!"

But he was discouraged.

She poured out the tea, poising the cream-jug.

"No milk," he said; then he seemed to hear a noise, and looked keenly through the doorway.

"'Appen we'd better shut," he said.

"It seems a pity," she replied. "Nobody will come, will they?"

"No unless it's one in a thousand, but you never know."

"And even then it's no matter," she said. "It's only a cup of tea. Where are the spoons?"

He reached over, and pulled open the table drawer. Connie sat at table in the sunshine of the doorway.

"Flossie!" he said to the dog, who was lying on a little mat at the stair foot. "Go an' hark, hark!"

He lifted his finger, and his "hark!" was very vivid. The dog trotted out to reconnoitre.

"Are you sad today?" she asked him.

He turned his blue eyes quickly, and gazed direct on her.

"Sad! no, bored! I had to go getting summonses for two poachers I caught, and oh well, I don't like people."

He spoke cold, good English, and there was anger in his voice.

"Do you hate being a gamekeeper?" she asked.

"Being a gamekeeper, no! So long as I'm left alone. But when I have to go messing around at the police station, and various other places, and waiting for a lot of fools to attend to me . . . oh well, I get mad . . ." and he smiled, with a certain faint humour.

"Couldn't you be really independent?" she asked.

"Me? I suppose I could, if you mean manage to exist on my pension. I could! But I've got to work, or I should die. That is, I've got to have something that keeps me occupied. And I'm not in a good enough temper to work for myself. It's got to be a sort of job for somebody else, or I should throw it up in a month, out of bad temper. So altogether I'm very well off here, especially lately. . . ."

He laughed at her again, with mocking humour.

"But why are you in a bad temper?" she asked. "Do you mean you are *always* in a bad temper?"

"Pretty well," he said, laughing. "I don't quite digest my bile."

"But what bile?" she said.

"Bile!" he said. "Don't you know what that is?" She was silent, and disappointed. He was taking no notice of her.

"I'm going away for a while next month," she said.

"You are! Where to?"

"Venice."

"Venice! With Sir Clifford? For how long?"

"For a month or so," she replied. "Clifford won't go."

"He'll stay here?" he asked.

"Yes! He hates to travel as he is."

"Ay, poor devil!" he said, with sympathy.

There was a pause.

"You won't forget me when I'm gone, will you?" she asked. Again he lifted his eyes and looked full at her.

"Forget?" he said. "You know nobody forgets. It's not a question of memory."

She wanted to say: "What then?" but she didn't. Instead, she said in a mute kind of voice: "I told Clifford I might have a child."

Now he really looked at her, intense and searching.

"You did?" he said at last. "And what did he say?"

"Oh, he wouldn't mind. He'd be glad, really, so long as it seemed to be his." She dared not look up at him.

He was silent a long time, then he gazed again on her face.

"No mention of *me*, of course?" he said.

"No. No mention of you," she said.

"No, he'd hardly swallow me as a substitute breeder. —Then where are you supposed to be getting the child?"

"I might have a love affair in Venice," she said.

"You might," he replied slowly. "So that's why you're going?"

"Not to have the love affair," she said, looking up at him, pleading.

"Just the appearance of one," he said.

There was silence. He sat staring out of the window, with a faint grin, half mockery, half bitterness, on his face. She hated his grin.

"You've not taken any precautions against having a child then?" he asked her suddenly, "Because I haven't."

"No," she said faintly. "I should hate that."

He looked at her, then again with the peculiar subtle grin out of the window. There was a tense silence.

At last he turned to her and said satirically:

"That was why you wanted me then, to get a child?"

She hung her head.

"No. Not really," she said.

"What then, *really*?" he asked rather bitingly.

She looked up at him reproachfully, saying: "I don't know." He broke into a laugh.

"Then I'm damned if I do," he said.

There was a long pause of silence, a cold silence.

"Well," he said at last. "It's as your Ladyship likes. If you get the baby, Sir Clifford's welcome to it. I shan't have lost anything. On the contrary. I've had a very nice experience, very nice indeed!" and he stretched in a half suppressed sort of yawn. "If you've made use of me," he said, "it's not the first time I've been made use of; and I don't suppose it's ever been as pleasant as this time; though of course one can't feel tremendously dignified about it." He stretched again, curiously, his muscles quivering, and his jaw oddly set.

"But I didn't make use of you," she said, pleading.

"At your Ladyship's service," he replied.

"No," she said. "I liked your body."

"Did you?" he replied, and he laughed. "Well then, we're quits, because I liked yours."

He looked at her with queer darkened eyes.

"Would you like to go upstairs now?" he asked her, in a strangled sort of voice.

"No, not here. Not now!" she said heavily, though if he had used any power over her, she would have gone, for she had no strength against him.

He turned his face away again, and seemed to forget her.

"I want to touch you like you touch me," she said. "I've never really touched your body."

He looked at her, and smiled again. "Now?" he said.

"No! No! Not here! At the hut. Would you mind?"

"How do I touch you?" he asked.

"When you feel me."

He looked at her, and met her heavy, anxious eyes.

"And do you like it when I feel you?" he asked, laughing at her still.

"Yes, do you?" she said.

"Oh, me!" Then he changed his tone. "Yes," he said. "You know without asking." Which was true.

She rose and picked up her hat. "I must go," she said.

"Will you go?" he replied politely.

She wanted him to touch her, to say something to her, but he said nothing, only waited politely.

"Thank you for the tea," she said.

"I haven't thanked your Ladyship for doing me the honours of my teapot," he said.

She went down the path, and he stood in the doorway, faintly grinning. Flossie came running with her tail lifted. And Connie had to plod dumbly across into the wood, knowing he was standing there watching her, with that incomprehensible grin on his face.

She walked home very much downcast and annoyed. She didn't at all like his saying he had been made use of; because in a sense it was true. But he oughtn't to have said it. Therefore, again, she was divided between two feelings; resentment against him, and a desire to make it up with him.

She passed a very uneasy and irritated teatime, and at once went up to her room. But when she was there it was no good; she could neither sit nor stand. She would have to do something about it. She would have to go back to the hut; if he was not there, well and good.

She slipped out of the side door, and took her way direct and a little sullen. When she came to the clearing she was terribly uneasy. But there he was again, in his shirtsleeves, stooping, letting the hens out of the coops, among the chicks that were now growing a little gawky, but were much more trim than hen-chickens.

She went straight across to him.

"You see I've come!" she said.

"Ay, I see it!" he said, straightening his back, and looking at her with a faint amusement.

"Do you let the hens out now?" she asked.

"Yes, they've sat themselves to skin and bone," he said. "An' now they're not all that anxious to come out an' feed. There's no self in a sitting hen; she's all in the eggs or the chicks."

The poor mother hens; such blind devotion! Even to eggs not their own! Connie looked at them in compassion. A helpless silence fell between the man and the woman.

Danaë
by Gustav Klimt
1907–1908

"Shall us go i' th' 'ut?" he asked.

"Do you want me?" she asked, in a sort of mistrust.

"Ay, if you want to come."

She was silent.

"Come then!" he said.

And she went with him to the hut. It was quite dark when he had shut the door, so he made a small light in the lantern, as before.

"Have you left your underthings off?" he asked her.

"Yes!"

"Ay, well, then I'll take my things off too."

He spread the blankets, putting one at the side for a coverlet. She took off her hat, and shook her hair. He sat down, taking off his shoes and gaiters, and undoing his cord breeches.

"Lie down then!" he said, when he stood in his shirt. She obeyed in silence, and he lay beside her, and pulled the blanket over them both.

"There!" he said.

And he lifted her dress right back, till he came even to her breasts. He kissed them softly, taking the nipples in his lips in tiny caresses.

"Eh, but tha'rt nice, tha'rt nice!" he said, suddenly rubbing his face with a snuggling movement against her warm belly.

And she put her arms round him under his shirt, but she was afraid, afraid of his thin, smooth, naked body, that seemed so powerful, afraid of the violent muscles. She shrank afraid.

And when he said, with a sort of sigh: "Eh, tha'rt nice!" something in her quivered, and something in her spirit stiffened in resistance: stiffened from the terribly physical intimacy, and from the peculiar haste of his possession. And this time the sharp ecstasy of her own passion did not overcome her; she lay with her hands inert on his striving body, and do what she might, her spirit seemed to look on from the top of her head, and the butting of his haunches seemed ridiculous to her, and the sort of anxiety of his penis to come to its little evacuating crisis seemed farcical. Yes, this was love, this ridiculous bouncing of the buttocks, and the wilting of the poor insignificant, moist little penis. This was the divine love! After all, the moderns were right when they felt contempt for the performance; for it was a performance. It was quite true, as some poets said, that the God who created man must have had a sinister sense of humour, creating him a reasonable being, yet forcing him to take this ridiculous posture, and driving him with blind craving for this ridiculous performance. Even a Maupassant found it a humiliating anticlimax. Men despised the intercourse act, and yet did it.

Cold and derisive her queer female mind stood apart, and though she lay perfectly still, her impulse was to heave her loins, and throw the man out, escape his ugly grip, and the butting over-riding of his absurd haunches. His body was a foolish, impudent, imperfect thing, a little disgusting in its unfinished clumsiness. For surely a complete evolution would eliminate this performance, this "function."

And yet when he had finished, soon over, and lay very very still, receding into silence, and a strange, motionless distance, far, farther than the horizon of her awareness, her heart began to weep. She could feel him ebbing away, ebbing away, leaving her there like a stone on a shore. He was withdrawing, his spirit was leaving her. He knew.

And in real grief, tormented by her own double consciousness and reaction, she began to weep. He took no notice, or did not even know. The storm of weeping swelled and shook her, and shook him.

"Ay!" he said. "It was no good that time. You wasn't there." So he knew! Her sobs became violent.

"But what's amiss?" he said. "It's once in a while that way."

"I . . . I can't love you," she sobbed, suddenly feeling her heart breaking.

"Canna ter? Well, dunna fret! There's no law says as tha's got to. Ta'e it for what it is."

He still lay with his hand on her breast. But she had drawn both her hands from him.

His words were small comfort. She sobbed aloud.

"Nay, nay," he said. "Ta'e the thick wi' th' thin. This wor' a bit o' thin for once."

She wept bitterly, sobbing: "But I want to love you, and I can't. It only seems horrid."

He laughed a little, half bitter, half amused.

"It isna horrid," he said, "even if tha thinks it is. An' tha canna ma'e it horrid. Dunna fret thysen about lovin' me. Tha'lt niver force thysen to 't. There's sure to be a bad nut in a basketful. Tha mun ta'e th' rough wi' th' smooth."

He took his hand away from her breast, not touching her. And now she was untouched she took an almost perverse satisfaction in it. She hated the dialect: the *thee* and the *tha* and the *thysen*. He could get up if he liked, and stand there above her buttoning down those absurd corduroy breeches, straight in front of her. After all, Michaelis had had the decency to turn away. This man was so assured in himself, he didn't know what a clown other people found him, a half-bred fellow.

"Don't! Don't go! Don't leave me! Don't be cross with me! Hold me! Hold me fast!" she whispered in blind frenzy, not even knowing what she said, and clinging to him with uncanny force. It was from herself she wanted to be saved, from her own inward anger and resistance. Yet how powerful was that inward resistance that possessed her!

He took her in his arms again and drew her to him, and suddenly she became small in his arms, small and nestling. It was gone, the resistance was gone, and she began to melt in a marvellous peace. And as she melted small and wonderful in his arms, she became infinitely desirable to him, all his blood-vessels seemed to scald with intense yet tender desire, for her, for her softness, for the penetrating beauty of her in his arms, passing into his blood. And softly, with that marvellous swoon-like caress of his hand in pure soft desire, softly he stroked the silky slope of her loins, down, down between her soft warm buttocks, coming nearer and nearer to the very quick of her. And she felt him like a flame of desire, yet tender, and she felt herself melting in the flame. She let herself go. She felt his penis risen against her with silent amazing force and assertion, and she let herself go to him. She yielded with a quiver that was like death, she went all open to him. And oh, if he were not tender to her now, how cruel, for she was all open to him and helpless!

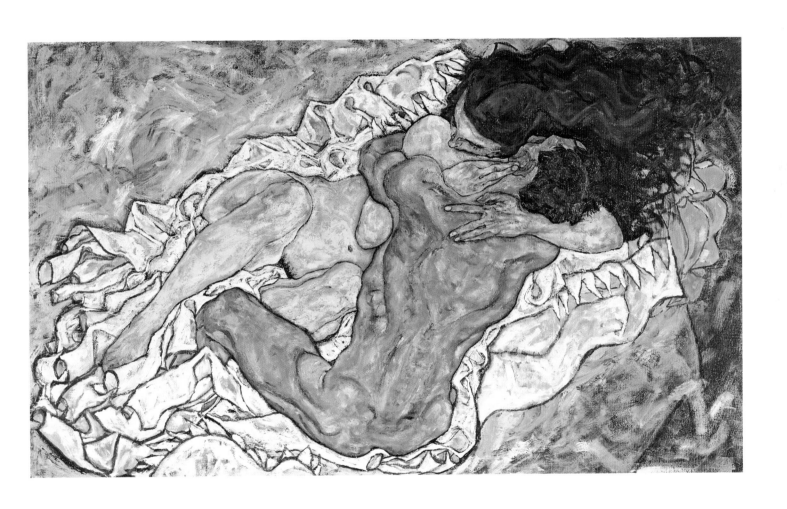

The Embrace
by Egon Schiele
1917

She quivered again at the potent inexorable entry inside her, so strange and terrible. It might come with the thrust of a sword in her softly-opened body, and that would be death. She clung in a sudden anguish of terror. But it came with a strange slow thrust of peace, the dark thrust of peace and a ponderous, primordial tenderness, such as made the world in the beginning. And her terror subsided in her breast, her breast dared to be gone in peace, she held nothing. She dared to let go everything, all herself, and be gone in the flood.

And it seemed she was like the sea, nothing but dark waves rising and heaving, heaving with a great swell, so that slowly her whole darkness was in motion, and she was ocean rolling its dark, dumb mass. Oh, and far down inside her the deeps parted and rolled asunder, in long, far-travelling billows, and ever, at the quick of her, the depths parted and rolled asunder, from the centre of soft plunging, as the plunger went deeper and deeper, touching lower, and she was deeper and deeper and deeper disclosed, and heavier the billows of her rolled away to some shore, uncovering her, and closer and closer plunged the palpable unknown, and further and further rolled the waves of herself away from herself, leaving her, till suddenly, in a soft, shuddering convulsion, the quick of all her plasm was touched, she knew herself touched, the consummation was upon her, and she was gone. She was gone, she was not, and she was born: a woman.

Ah, too lovely, too lovely! In the ebbing she realised all the loveliness. Now all her body clung with tender love to the unknown man, and blinding to the wilting penis, as it so tenderly, frailly, unknowingly withdrew, after the fierce thrust of its potency. As it drew out and left her body, the secret, sensitive thing, she gave an unconscious cry of pure loss, and she tried to put it back. It had been so perfect! And she loved it so!

And only now she became aware of the small, bud-like reticence and tenderness of the penis, and a little cry of wonder and poignancy escaped her again, her woman's heart crying out over the tender frailty of that which had been the power.

"It was so lovely!" she moaned. "It was so lovely!" But he said nothing, only softly kissed her, lying still above her. And she moaned with a sort of bliss, as a sacrifice, and a new-born thing.

And now in her heart the queer wonder of him was awakened. A man! the strange potency of manhood upon her! Her hands strayed over him, still a little afraid. Afraid of that strange, hostile, slightly repulsive thing that he had been to her, a man. And now she touched him, and it was the sons of god with the daughters of men. How beautiful he felt, how pure in tissue! How lovely, how lovely, strong, and yet pure and delicate, such stillness of the sensitive body! Such utter stillness of potency and delicate flesh! How beautiful! How beautiful! Her hands came timorously down his back, to the soft, smallish globes of the buttocks. Beauty! What beauty! a sudden little flame of new awareness went through her. How was it possible, this beauty here, where she had previously only been repelled? The unspeakable beauty to the touch, of the warm, living buttocks! The life within life, the sheer warm, potent loveliness. And the strange weight of the balls between his legs! What a mystery! What a strange heavy weight of mystery, that could lie soft and heavy in one's hand! The roots, root of all that is lovely, the primeval root of all full beauty.

She clung to him, with a hiss of wonder that was almost awe, terror. He held her close, but he said nothing. He would never say anything. She crept nearer to him, nearer, only to be near to the sensual wonder of him. And out of his utter, incomprehensible stillness, she felt again the slow, momentous, surging rise of the phallus again, the other power. And her heart melted out with a kind of awe.

And this time his being within her was all soft and iridescent, purely soft and iridescent, such as no consciousness could seize. Her whole self quivered unconscious and alive, like plasm. She could not know what it was. She could not remember what it had been. Only that it had been more lovely than anything ever could be. Only that. And afterwards she was utterly still, utterly unknowing, she was not aware for how long. And he was still with her, in an unfathomable silence along with her. And of this, they would never speak.

When awareness of the outside began to come back, she clung to his breast, murmuring: "My love! my love!" And he held her silently. And she curled on his breast, perfect.

But his silence was fathomless. His hands held her like flowers, so still and strange. "Where are you?" she whispered to him. "Where are you? Speak to me!"

He kissed her softly, murmuring: "Ay, my lass!"

But she did not know what he meant, she did not know where he was. In his silence he seemd lost to her.

"You love me, don't you?" she murmured.

"Ay, tha knows!" he said.

"But tell me!" she pleaded.

"Ay! Ay! 'asn't ter felt it?" he said dimly, but softly and surely. And she clung close to him, closer. He was so much more peaceful in love than she was, and she wanted him to reassure her.

"You do love me!" she whispered, assertive. And his hands stroked her softly, as if she were a flower, without the quiver of desire, but with delicate nearness. And still there haunted her a restless necessity to get a grip on love.

"Say you'll always love me!" she pleaded.

"Ay!" he said, abstractedly. And she felt her questions driving him away from her.

"Mustn't we get up?" he said at last.

"No!" she said.

But she could feel his consciousness straying, listening to the noises outside.

"It'll be nearly dark," he said. And she heard the pressure of circumstance in his voice. She kissed him, with a woman's grief at yielding up her hour.

He rose, and turned up the lantern, then began to pull on his clothes, quickly disappearing inside them. Then he stood there, above her, fastening his breeches and looking down at her with dark, wide eyes, his face a little flushed and his hair ruffled, curiously warm and still and beautiful in the dim light of the lantern, so beautiful, she would never tell him how beautiful. It made her want to cling fast to him, to hold him, for there was a warm, half-sleepy remoteness in his beauty that made her want to cry out and clutch him, to have him. She would never have him. So she lay on the blanket with curved, soft naked haunches, and he had no idea what she was thinking, but to him too she was beautiful, the soft, marvellous thing he could go into, beyond everything.

"I love thee that I can go into thee," he said.

"Do you like me?" she said, her heart beating.

"It heals it all up, that I can go into thee. I love thee that tha opened to me. I love thee that I came into thee like that."

He bent down and kissed her soft flank, rubbed his cheek against it, then covered it up.

"And will you never leave me?" she said.

"Dunna ask them things," he said.

"But you do believe I love you?" she said.

"Tha loved me just now, wider than iver tha thout tha would. But who knows what'll 'appen, once tha starts thinkin' about it!"

"No, don't say those things!—And you don't really think I wanted to make use of you, do you?"

"How?"

"To have a child—?"

"Now anybody can 'ave any child i' th'world," he said, as he sat down fastening on his leggings.

"Ah no!" she cried. "You don't mean it?"

"Eh well!" he said, looking at her under his brows. "This wor t' best."

She lay still. He softly opened the door. The sky was dark blue, with crystalline, turquoise rim. He went out, to shut up the hens, speaking softly to his dog. And she lay and wondered at the wonder of life, and of being.

When he came back she was still lying there, glowing like a gypsy. He sat on the stool by her.

"Tha mun come one naight ter th' cottage, afore tha goos; sholl ter?" he asked, lifting his eyebrows as he looked at her, his hands dangling between his knees.

"Sholl ter?" she echoed, teasing.

He smiled.

"Ay, sholl ter?" he repeated.

"Ay! she said, imitating the dialect sound.

"Yi!" he said.

"Yi!" she repeated.

"An' slaip wi' me," he said. "It needs that. When sholt come?"

"When sholl I?" she said.

"Nay," he said, "tha canna do't. When sholt come then?"

"'Appen Sunday," she said.

"'Appen a' Sunday! Ay!"

He laughed at her quickly.

"Nay, tha canna," he protested.

"Why canna I?" she said.

He laughed. Her attempts at the dialect were so ludicrous, somehow.

"Coom then, tha mun goo!" he said.

"Mun I?" she said.

"Maun Ah!" he corrected.

"Why should I say *maun* when you said *mun*," she protested. "You're not playing fair."

"Arena Ah!" he said, leaning forward and softly stroking her face.

"Th'art good cunt, though, aren't ter? Best bit o' cunt left on earth. When ter likes! When tha'rt willin'!"

"What is cunt?" she said.

"An' doesn't ter know? Cunt! It's thee down theer; an' what I get when I'm i'side thee, and what tha gets when I'm i'side thee; it's a' as it is, all on't."

"All on't," she teased. "Cunt! It's like fuck then."

"Nay nay! Fuck's only what you do. Animals fuck. But cunt's a lot more than that. It's thee, dost see: an' tha't a lot beside an animal, aren't ter? even ter fuck! Cunt! Eh, that's the beauty o' thee, lass!"

She got up and kissed him between the eyes, that looked at her so dark and soft and unspeakably warm, so unbearably beautiful.

"Is it?" she said. "And do you care for me?"

He kissed her without answering.

"Tha mun goo, let me dust thee," he said.

His hand passed over the curves of her body, firmly, without desire, but with soft, intimate knowledge.

As she ran home in the twilight the world seemed a dream; the trees in the park seemed bulging and surging at anchor on a tide, and the heave of the slope to the house was alive.

COMMITMENT

"William, do you have the courage to love?"

Illustration
by Koren
1977

from

Chapter Two
by Neil Simon

ACT TWO, SCENE 7

His apartment, about an hour later. GEORGE *comes out of the bedroom, wearing a sports jacket and carrying a raincoat and fully packed suitcase and attaché case. He puts a note on the desk and starts for the door.*

JENNIE *enters, looking a little glum, sees* GEORGE *and his luggage.*

GEORGE   Hi.

JENNIE   Hi.

GEORGE   You had some messages. (*Takes the piece of notepaper from the desk*) I was going to leave this for you. I don't know if you can read my writing... Jill James at CBS called and said you start shooting again on Monday. They'll send the pages over tonight. Also, Helen Franklyn called and said you have a reading for the new Tom Stoppard play Monday at ten. And Faye called a few minutes ago, said it was urgent she talk to you and can you have lunch with her on Tuesday, Wednesday, Thursday and Friday... And that was it.

JENNIE (*Stunned; doesn't respond immediately*)   I'm sorry, I wasn't listening... I couldn't take my eyes off your suitcase.

GEORGE   I tried to explain everything in a letter. I left it on the bed.

JENNIE   Good. I was worried that I wasn't getting any mail... Where are you going?

GEORGE   Los Angeles. Someone at Paramount is interested in *The Duchess of Limehouse* as a film.

JENNIE   When did all this come up?

GEORGE   Two weeks ago.

JENNIE   Why didn't you tell me?

GEORGE   I had no reason to go two weeks ago.

JENNIE   Leave it to you to make a point clear. How long will you be gone?

GEORGE   I don't know.

JENNIE   Where will you stay?

GEORGE   I don't know.

JENNIE   Just going to circle the airport for a few days?

GEORGE   You never lose your equilibrium, do you?

JENNIE   You think not? I'd hate to see an X-ray of my stomach right now.

GEORGE   I don't think being apart for a while is going to do us any damage.

JENNIE   Probably no worse than being together the past few days.

GEORGE   But if it's really important to get in touch with me, Leo will know where I am.

JENNIE   And I'll know where Leo is.

GEORGE (*Goes to the door, turns back uncomfortably*)   I don't think I have anything else to say. How about you?

JENNIE (*Shrugs*)   I have no statement to make at this time.

GEORGE   I'm glad a lot of work is coming your way. I know it's important to you. It's what you want.

JENNIE   I'm glad you know what I want, George... If you told me five years ago, I could have saved a lot of doctor money.

GEORGE   I was busy five years ago.

JENNIE   You don't have to remind me. Interesting how this all worked out. You pack up and go and leave *me* with all your memories.

GEORGE   I'm sorry, but you can't get a five-room apartment in the overhead rack.

JENNIE   Is there anything you want me to take care of while you're gone?

GEORGE   You seem to be taking care of it fine right now.

JENNIE   Oh, I tripped over the wire and set off the trap, didn't I?... Everything I say can be so cleverly twisted around by you that you always end up the victim and I'm the perpetrator. God forbid I'm not as fast with a thought or a phrase as you, and you pounce on it like a fat cat.

GEORGE   Fat cats are very slow on the pounce because they're fat, but I got your point.

JENNIE (*Very angry*)   Oh, go on, get the hell out of here, will you! If you're going to leave, leave! Go! Your Mystery Plane is waiting to take you shrouded in secrecy, to your Phantom Hotel on the intriguing West Coast. Even your life is turning into a goddamn spy novel—

GEORGE (*Puts down the valise*)   I've got a few minutes. I don't want to miss what promises to be our most stimulating conversation since I thought you were an eighty-five-year-old woman on the phone.

151

JENNIE   Isn't it amazing the minute I get angry and abusive, it's one of the few times I can really hold your attention... What can I say that will really hurt you, George? I want to send you off happy. *(She swarms over him, punching him. He throws her onto the sofa)*

GEORGE   Just going is reward enough.
(He starts out. She runs out. She runs ahead of him and grabs the suitcase to fling it out. He throws her to the floor)

JENNIE   You know what you want better than me, George... I don't know what you expect to find out there, except a larger audience for your two shows a day of suffering... I know I'm not as smart as you. Maybe I can't analyze and theorize and speculate on why we behave as we do and react as we do and suffer guilt and love and hate. You read all those books, not me... But there's one thing I *do* know. I know how I *feel*. I know I can stand here watching you try to destroy everything I've ever wanted in my life, wanting to smash your face with my fists because you won't even make the slightest effort to opt for happiness—and still know that I love you. That's always so clear to me. It's the one place I get all my strength from... You mean so much to me that I am willing to take all your abuse and insults and insensitivity—because that's what you need to do to prove I'm not going to leave you. I can't promise I'm not going to die, George, that's asking too much. But if you want to test me, go ahead and test me. You want to leave, leave! But *I'm* not the one who's going to walk away. I don't know if I can take it forever, but I can take it for tonight and I can take it next week. Next month I may be a little shaky... But I'll tell you something, George. No matter what you say about me, I feel so good about myself—better than I felt when I ran from Cleveland and was frightened to death of New York. Better than I felt when Gus was coming home at two o'clock in the morning just to change his clothes. Better than I felt when I thought there was no one in the world out there for me, and better than I felt the night before we got married and I thought that I wasn't good enough for you... Well, I am! I'm wonderful! I'm nuts about me! And if you're stupid enough to throw someone sensational like me aside, then you don't deserve as good as you've got! I am sick and tired of running from places and people and relationships... And don't tell me what I want because *I'll* tell you what I want. I want a home and I want a family—and I want a career, too. And I want a dog and I want a cat and I want three goldfish. I want *everything*! There's no harm in wanting it, George, because there's not a chance in hell we're going to get it all, anyway. But if you don't *want* it, you've got even less chance than that... Everyone's out there looking for easy answers. And if you don't find it at home, hop into another bed and maybe you'll come up lucky. *Maybe!* You'd be just as surprised as me at some of the "maybe's" I've seen out there lately. Well, none of that for me, George... You want me, then fight for me, because I'm fighting like hell for you. I think we're both worth it. I will admit, however that I *do* have one fault. One glaring, major, monumental fault... Sometimes I don't know when to stop talking. For that I'm sorry, George, and I apologize. I am now through!
(She sits back on the sofa, exhausted)

GEORGE *(Looks at her for a long time, then says warmly)* I'll tell you one thing—I'm glad you're on *my* side.

JENNIE *(Looks over at him)* Do you mean it, George?

GEORGE   I didn't hear half of what you said because I was so mesmerized by your conviction. I'm not a doctor, Jennie, but I can tell you right now, you're one of the healthiest people I ever met in my life.

JENNIE *(Smiles)* Funny, I don't look it.

GEORGE   I am crazy about you. I want you to know that.

JENNIE   I know that.

GEORGE   No. You don't know that I'm absolutely crazy nuts for you.

JENNIE   Oh. No, I didn't know that. You're right.

GEORGE   I want to walk over now and take you in my arms and say, "Okay, we're finished with the bad part. Now, what's for dinner?" But I'm stuck, Jennie... I'm just stuck someplace in my mind and it's driving me crazy. Something is keeping me here, glued to this spot like a big, dumb, overstuffed chair.

JENNIE   I could rearrange the furniture.

GEORGE   Don't make it so easy for me. I'm fighting to hold on to self-pity, and just my luck I run into the most understanding girl in the world.

JENNIE   I'm not so understanding.

GEORGE   Yes, you are. You just said so yourself. And I swear to God, Jennie, I can't find a thing I would want to change about you... So let me go to Los Angeles. Let me try to get unstuck... I'll be at the Chateau Marmont Hotel. I'll be in my room unsticking like crazy.

JENNIE   Couldn't I go with you. I wouldn't bother you. I would just watch.

GEORGE   Then the people next door would want to watch, and pretty soon we'd have a crowd. *(He picks up his suitcase)* Take care of yourself.

JENNIE   George! *(He stops, looks at her)* Would you mind very much if I slept in my apartment while you're gone? I feel funny about staying in this place alone.

GEORGE *(Nods)* I understand...

JENNIE   If you don't call me, can I call you?

GEORGE *(A pause)* You know, we may have one of the most beautiful marriages that was ever in trouble. *(He goes out. She goes to the door, watches him go, then comes in and closes the door. Dimout)*

ACT TWO, SCENE 9

His apartment. The door opens. GEORGE *enters and turns on the lights. He looks a little travel-weary.*

GEORGE *(Putting down his suitcase)* Jennie? Jennie? *(He looks around, then goes into the bedroom. It's apparent no one is home. He comes back into the living room. In her apartment,* JENNIE *goes to the refrigerator, takes out an apple, then goes to the sofa and sits.* GEORGE *picks up the phone, and starts to dial just as* JENNIE *picks up the receiver. She dials 213-555-1212. He finishes dialing and gets a busy signal. He hangs up, takes a manuscript from his attaché case)*

JENNIE *(Into the phone)* Los Angeles ... I'd like the number of the Chateau Marmont Hotel ... Yes, I think it *is* West Hollywood ... *(She waits. He paces)* 656-1010 Thank you. *(She disconnects with her finger, then starts to dial just as he goes back to the phone, picks it up and starts to dial. She gets halfway through the number when she suddenly hangs up)* Patience, Jennie! Don't pressure him. *(She sits back just as he completes his dial. Her phone rings. She jumps and clutches her bosom)* Oh God, I'm so smart! *(She reaches over and picks up the phone)* Hello?

GEORGE Serene?

JENNIE Who?

GEORGE Is this Serene Jurgens? ... It's George Schneider, Leo's brother ... I just arrived on the Coast, darling. At last, I'm free.

JENNIE *(Near tears)* Tell me you're joking, George. Right now I wouldn't know humor if it hit me with a truck.

GEORGE Oh. Well, then you'd better pull off the highway ... How are you? What have you been doing?

JENNIE Watching the telephone. Nothing good on until now ... How's the weather there?

GEORGE *(Looks around)* Oh, about eighty-four degrees. A little humid.

JENNIE Same here ... How are you, George?

GEORGE Dumb. Dummy Dumbo.

JENNIE Why?

GEORGE Well, when Barbara and I had a fight, I'd walk around the block and come back twenty minutes later feeling terrific ... At the airport I said to myself, "Of course. That's what I should do." And that's what I did.

JENNIE I can't believe it. You mean, you just walked around the block?

GEORGE Yes.

JENNIE What's so dumb about that?

GEORGE I was in the Los Angeles airport when I thought of it.

JENNIE Well, where are you? Here or there?

GEORGE Wait, I'll look. *(He looks around)* Looks like here.

JENNIE You're back! You're in New York!

GEORGE I never even checked into the Chateau Marmont ... I got unstuck in the TWA lounge.

JENNIE Oh, George ...

GEORGE I sat there drinking my complimentary Fresca, and I suddenly remembered a question Dr. Ornstein told me to ask myself whenever I felt trouble coming on. The question is "What is it you're most afraid would happen *if*?"

JENNIE I'm listening.

GEORGE So I said to myself, "George, what is it you're most afraid would happen—*if* you went back to New York ... to Jennie ... and started your life all over again?" And the answer was so simple ... I would be happy! I have stared happiness in the face, Jennie—and I embrace it.

JENNIE *(Tearfully)* Oh, George. You got any left to embrace me?

GEORGE From here? No. You need one of those long-armed fellas for that.

JENNIE Well, what are we waiting for? Your place or mine?

GEORGE Neither. I think we have to find a new one called "Ours."

JENNIE Thank you, George. I was hoping we would.

GEORGE Thus, feeling every bit as good about me as you do about you, I finished the last chapter of the new book on the plane. *(He takes up the manuscript. The last few pages are handwritten)* I've got it with me. You want to hear it?

JENNIE The last chapter?

GEORGE No. The whole book.

JENNIE Of course. I'll be right over.

GEORGE No, I'll read it to you. I don't want to lose my momentum. *(He opens the manuscript folder, settles back; so does she. He reads)* You ready? ... *Falling Into Place*, by George Schneider. Dedication: "To Jennie ... A nice girl to spend the rest of your life with ..." *(He turns the page)* Chapter One ... "Walter Maslanski looked in the mirror and saw what he feared most ... Walter Maslanski ..." *(The curtain begins to fall)* "Not that Walter's features were awesome by any means ... He had the sort of powder-puff eyes that could be stared down in an abbreviated battle by a one-eyed senior-citizen canary ..."

Curtain

from the Sanskrit
Although I Conquer
All the Earth

Although I conquer all the earth,
yet for me there is only one city.
In that city there is for me only one house;
And in that house, one room only;
And in that room, a bed.
And one woman sleeps there,
The shining joy and jewel of all my kingdom.

detail from
By the Seashore
by Pierre Auguste Renoir
1883

The Queen
by Anna Wahlenberg

Many hundreds of years ago there lived a young maiden who was famous in several kingdoms. Adelgunda was indeed a remarkable young girl. She was slight, delicate, and pale as a lily, but it was not so much her beauty that people spoke of. Nor was it her good sense, though one and all could see intelligence shining on her brow.

No, what Adelgunda was renowned for were her two wonderful eyes, which could speak much more plainly than her lips. Her eyes could also see better than anyone else's; they saw what people were thinking and things that lay hidden deep in their souls.

Yet no one was afraid of Adelgunda's eyes which saw and expressed so much; rather, anyone who looked at them was glad. Adelgunda's gaze rested long on good and beautiful things, and when her eyes saw something ugly and evil, they said so, not with hatred and contempt but with sorrow and compassion. Adelgunda's eyes spoke a language that everyone understood.

continued

Illustration
by John Bauer
1914

Anyone who met the young girl became fond of her and left hoping to see her again. Only the really wicked and those with uneasy consciences shunned her. They never dared show themselves in the neighborhood of the old castle where she lived with her father, Sir Hubert.

But one day a messenger announced the arrival at the knight's castle of a very special guest.

Prince Sigmund, who would one day inherit the realm from his father, the king, was wooing a handsome princess in a powerful nearby kingdom. This princess had already almost promised Sigmund her hand; now the two were to meet to see if they really suited each other. And since his road took him past Sir Hubert's castle, Sigmund decided to stay there a day and see young Adelgunda, of whom he had heard so many remarkable things.

Adelgunda was also curious about the prince, for she had heard how brave, handsome, and chivalrous he was, and how much his people loved him. But suppose she saw something in him, something that others did not see, something which was not beautiful, but which her eyes would nevertheless speak of, since she could not hide anything they saw? How terrible that would be! And how ashamed her father would be if such a thing happened to the young prince in his home.

At last Adelgunda decided what she would do. She would hide, and steal a glance at the prince before he entered her father's castle. Then if she saw anything that her eyes ought not to reveal, she would run into the forest and not return until Prince Sigmund had left.

Silently and alone, she slipped from the castle and walked towards the road on which the prince was expected to arrive. When she saw a cloud of dust at the top of the hill, she hid behind a wild rose bush, where she could watch without being seen.

The cloud of dust drew nearer and nearer, bringing with it a big wagon drawn by four horses and loaded with baggage. Two valets in gold-braided livery sat on top. The prince's servants were travelling ahead of their master.

After a while, however, another cloud of dust rose at the top of the hill. This time four riders approached at a fast gallop. One was taller and more distinguished than the others, and Adelgunda realized it must be the prince. Just as the riders reached the rose bush where she was hiding, the prince's horse stumbled on a stone and fell heavily.

His frightened companions reined in, dismounted, and gathered anxiously around Prince Sigmund to see if he had been hurt. But he was already on his feet examining his horse, which was trying to stand.

"It's nothing serious," he said, "but my horse has sprained a leg so I won't get back into the saddle."

"Will your Highness take my horse then?" asked the nearest knight, bringing up his mount.

But the prince slapped him warmly on the shoulder and refused. "Should one of you, my trusted and faithful comrades in peace and war, walk while I ride?" he asked. "No, indeed. That will never do. Let's ask at that farm cottage if they will lend us a horse."

The knight rode towards a nearby cottage, and soon he returned with a large, heavy drayhorse, shaggy,

unkempt, and ugly, as such horses sometimes are. He dismounted, took the saddle from the lame horse and strapped it on the borrowed one, and was just about to swing himself on to its back, leaving his own horse for the prince when again the prince rebuffed him with a warm smile. "I am the one who fell," he said. "I shall ride old Shaggy." With that, he threw himself on to the saddle, caught the reins of his limping horse, and rode on at the head of his companions.

As Adelgunda watched him riding so tall and erect on the strong but homely drayhorse, he seemed as handsome as a dream. She knew that from then on she would think about him every hour of every day of her life.

She got up from her hiding-place and walked home in a dream. And she was still dreaming when she went to her room and braided pearls in her hair and put on a white gown with silver embroidery.

Only when a lady-in-waiting knocked on the door with a message from her father to hurry to meet their distinguished guest did she come to her senses. She started in fright, for she had suddenly realized that she could not meet the prince and let him look into her eyes. They would tell him, plainly and clearly, that to her he was the finest man on earth, and that she would think about him every hour of every day of her life. A little noble maiden must never make such a confession to a man, much less to a prince who was so far above her in birth and rank.

Yet Adelgunda said, "Tell my father I am coming," for of course now it was too late to run and hide in the forest.

Instead, she ran to her mother's old room, opened a cupboard, and picked out the thickest white veil she could find. She had never worn a veil over her face before, because she had never needed to hide her face or her thoughts. But now she did. Quickly she threw the veil over her head and walked into the hall where they were waiting for her.

A murmur of surprise rose from everyone in the room as she stepped over the threshold. After she had greeted their honoured guest, her father asked, "Why are you wearing a veil, Adelgunda?"

"Forgive me, Father, but I am not used to the company of princes," she answered.

Sir Hubert smiled and turned to Prince Sigmund. "I am sure she will soon be more confident," he said.

They sat down at the table, with the prince between the knight and his daughter. The prince had eyes for no one but Adelgunda. She seemed to him graceful and gentle; her voice was musical and her words were wise. When she lifted her veil a little to put a wine goblet to her lips, he caught a glimpse of her face, and that made him even more impatient to see it unveiled.

After the meal, they rose from the table, but Adelgunda slipped behind the other guests in the hope of being able to leave the room unnoticed, and then run from the castle. However, the prince still had his eyes on her, and suddenly she found him barring her way.

"I have heard about your eloquent eyes, noble maid," he said. "Won't you let me have the pleasure of seeing them, as others do?"

She bowed her head low. "I cannot," she whispered.

"Then I must believe you have seen something in me

that you do not wish your eyes to speak of."

"Oh, no. No," she exclaimed in a troubled voice.

"Then lift your veil."

But Adelgunda stayed still, wishing she could die.

Her father joined them and looked at Adelgunda with puzzled brows. "What sort of childishness is this?" he asked. "Take off your veil at once."

"I cannot," Adelgunda replied in a voice so low it could hardly be heard.

The prince froze. He stopped Sir Hubert, who was about to tear the veil from his daughter's head, and bade the company a stiff farewell. He did not wish to force Adelgunda to obey him. He and his retinue rode quickly from the castle, and the girl remained standing in the hall, weeping bitterly and without a word of answer to all her father's reproaches.

Word spread quickly throughout the realm that Adelgunda had not let the prince look into her eyes. People asked each other what she could have seen in him that she could not speak of. And so strong was their faith in the girl's gift of reading people's minds that now they whispered that she must have discovered something wicked in the prince, although he had always been thought of as good and righteous.

The whispers spread farther and farther, until at last they reached the court of the powerful king whose daughter Sigmund was wooing. When the princess heard what was being said of Sigmund, she refused even to discuss marriage, and asked him to leave at once. Not until Adelgunda had lifted her veil, she said, and shown that her eyes had nothing evil to say of him, might he return.

The prince went back to his own kingdom angered by this insult, and yet even at home he saw only mistrust and suspicion in people's eyes. So his anger turned to sorrow, and he locked himself in his rooms, cursing the day he had met Adelgunda.

There was one person, however, who was even more grieved than the prince by all that had happened, and that was Adelgunda herself. When she heard how he had suffered for her sake, all she could think about was that she must do everything she could to absolve him from blame.

She went to her father and asked him to go to court and request the king to call together all the knights and ladies of the realm on a certain day—as many people as possible from far and near. Then she would agree to say something about the prince which would dispel all their suspicions.

Sir Hubert set out at once to deliver his daughter's message, which was received with pleasure by both the king and prince. Adelgunda, they believed, would soon appear without her veil, and then everyone would see that her eyes had nothing evil to tell.

From every corner of the kingdom knights and liegemen were summoned, and their wives and daughters came, too. On the appointed day, half the throne room was filled with nobility, and the burghers and peasants so crowded the other half that no one could move an elbow.

When all the guests were assembled, a door was opened, and Adelgunda and her father entered.

But when they saw that Adelgunda was still wearing her veil, the faces of the king and prince darkened, and their guests were offended.

As she reached the throne, she curtsied deeply to the king, and even more deeply to Prince Sigmund. Indeed, she made such a long, low curtsy that the prince sprang up and offered her his hand.

She turned to the king, and then to the whole gathering. "I have heard that some people are suspicious of Prince Sigmund because I did not wish to lift my veil before him. I have come here today to tell you what my eyes have seen. They have seen that there is no more chivalrous, noble, and good man than he on the whole wide earth."

"Then lift your veil, and let us see that your lips do not tell us one thing and your eyes another," said the king.

"That I cannot do," she answered.

"Then no one will believe you," said the old king, his eyes ablaze.

"No one will believe you," everyone called out angrily.

The little maiden stood where she was, with her head still bowed. Then she took one step towards Prince Sigmund, and slowly lifted the veil from her pale, beautiful face.

The eyes that rested on the prince shone like two wonderful stars and told him, plainly and clearly, what a young maiden must never say to any man, much less to a prince. And it was not only the prince who saw what they said; everyone present saw, too. Now they knew why she had not wanted to lift her veil, and suddenly the throne room was so still you could have heard a handkerchief flutter to the floor.

"May I go now?" asked Adelgunda. "Come, Father."

She took Sir Hubert's hand, and they walked slowly through the throng of people, who opened a path for them.

But before they had reached the door, a voice rang out over the heads of the guests. "Close the doors."

It was the prince speaking, and the guards hastened to obey him. Then the prince threw himself on his knees before the king.

"My Father," he pleaded. "Will we let the queen depart?"

"The queen?" asked the king.

"Yes, the queen. For is she not a queen among women? To me at least, there will never be anyone else."

The king looked at the upturned faces before him. "Do all of you, too, say that she is a queen? he asked.

A roar of "Yes" rose from every corner of the room, from nobles and peasants, from young and old. It echoed and rang until the old castle walls reverberated.

"Since you all say so, so be it," said the old king. "We will not let the queen depart."

He rose, stepped from his throne, and walked the length of the room until he stood in front of the noble maiden. Then he took her by the hand and led her slowly back through the joyous crowd. Before the throne, he placed her hand in the young prince's. Then everyone saw that Prince Sigmund's eyes, too, could speak. They told Adelgunda something very similar to what her eyes had told him.

The two stood in silence, hand in hand, while cheers rose around them, so strong and loud, it seemed they would never stop.

A Letter from D.H. Lawrence to Frieda Lawrence

Waldbröl-Mittwoch, 1902

Can't you feel how certainly I love you and how certainly we shall be married? Only let us wait just a short time, to get strong again. Two shaken, rather sick people together would be a bad start. A little waiting, let us have, because I love you. Or does the waiting make you worse?—no, not when it is only a time of preparation. Do you know, like the old knights, I seem to want a certain time to prepare myself—a sort of vigil with myself. Because it is a great thing for me to marry you, not a quick, passionate coming together. I know in my heart "here's my marriage." It feels rather terrible—because it is a great thing in my life—it is *my* life—I am a bit awe-inspired—I want to get used to it. If you think it is fear and indecision, you wrong me. It is *you* who would hurry, who are undecided. It's the very strength and inevitability of the oncoming thing that makes me wait, to get in harmony with it. Dear God, I am marrying you, now, don't you see. It's a far greater thing than ever I knew. Give me till next week-end, at least. If you love me, you will understand.

If I seem merely frightened and reluctant to you —you must forgive me.

I try, I will always try, when I write to you, to write the truth as near the mark as I can get it. It frets me, for fear you are disappointed in me, and for fear you are too much hurt. But you are strong when necessary.

You have got all myself—I don't even flirt—it would bore me very much—unless I got tipsy. It's a funny thing, to feel one's passion—sex desire—no longer a sort of wandering thing, but steady, and calm. I think, when one loves, one's very sex passion becomes calm, a steady sort of force, instead of a storm. Passion, that nearly drives one mad, is far away from real love. I am realizing things that I never thought to realize. Look at that poem I sent you—I would never write that to you. I shall love you all my life. That also is a new idea to me. But I believe it.

Auf Wiedersehen,

D. H. Lawrence

Paul Helleu Sketching with His Wife
by John Singer Sargent
1889

Frieda Lawrence: Memoirs and Correspondence

When I first met him, and with absolute determination he wanted to marry me, it seemed just madness and it was—I was older than he, I had three children and a husband and a place in the world. And he was nobody, and poor. He took me away from it all and I had to be his wife if the skies fell, and they nearly did. The price that I had to pay was almost more than I could afford with all my strength. To lose those children, those children that I had given myself to, it was a wrench that tore me to bits. Lawrence suffered tortures too. I believe he often felt: have I really the right to take this woman from her children? Towards my first husband too, he felt strongly. Do you remember the poem "Meeting on the Mountains," where he meets a peasant with brown eyes?

But then, can I describe what it was like when we were first together? It just had to be. What others find in other ways, the oneness with all that lives and breathes, the peace of all peace, it does pass all understanding, that was between us, never to be lost completely. Love can be such a little thing with little meaning, then it can be a big one.

Everything seemed worth while, even trivial happenings; living with him was important and took on an air of magnificence.

After the first shock and surprise of this being together, as if a big wave had lifted us high on its crest to look at new horizons, it dawned on me: maybe this is a great man I am living with. I wish I knew what greatness consists of; if it were so obvious right away, it would not be great, because it's a man's uniqueness that makes him great.

We weren't soulful, Tristram and Isolde-ish. There wasn't time for tragedy. This new world of freedom and love kept us in its hold. His thoughts and impulses came up from such deep roots always more and more. I was on the alert all the time. The experience put us apart from other people that had not experienced it the same as we had. It made a barrier.

We quarreled so fiercely. But it was never mean or sneaky. We had come so close to each other, so we met each other without holding back, naked and direct.

Resting

by John Singer Sargent

1875

When in Disgrace with Fortune and Men's Eyes
by William Shakespeare

When in disgrace with fortune and men's eyes,
I all alone beweep my outcast state,
And trouble deaf heaven with my bootless cries,
And look upon myself, and curse my fate,
Wishing me like to one more rich in hope,
Featured like him, like him with friends possess'd,
Desiring this man's art and that man's scope,
With what I most enjoy contented least;
Yet in these thoughts myself almost despising,
Haply I think on thee, and then my state,
Like to the lark at break of day arising
From sullen earth, sings hymns at heaven's gate;
 For thy sweet love remember'd such wealth brings
 That then I scorn to change my state with kings.

Hindu Temple Sculpture
Khajurāho, India
Tenth to Eleventh Century

The River-Merchant's Wife
A Letter

by Rihaku

Translated by Ezra Pound

While my hair was still cut straight across my forehead
I played about the front gate, pulling flowers.
You came by on bamboo stilts, playing horse,
You walked about my seat, playing with blue plums.
And we went on living in the village of Chokan:
Two small people, without dislike or suspicion.
At fourteen I married My Lord you.
I never laughed, being bashful.
Lowering my head, I looked at the wall.
Called to, a thousand times, I never looked back.

At fifteen I stopped scowling,
I desired my dust to be mingled with yours
For ever and for ever and for ever.
Why should I climb the look out?

At sixteen you departed,
You went into far Ku-to-yen, by the river of swirling eddies,
And you have been gone five months.
The monkeys make sorrowful noise overhead.

You dragged your feet when you went out.
By the gate now, the moss is grown, the different mosses,
Too deep to clear them away!
The leaves fall early this autumn, in wind.
The paired butterflies are already yellow with August
Over the grass in the West garden;
They hurt me. I grow older.
If you are coming down through the narrows of the river Kiang
Please let me know beforehand,
And I will come out to meet you
        As far as Cho-fu-Sa.

Japanese Screen
Anonymous

The Heart's Friend
A Shoshone Love Song

Fair is the white star of twilight,
And the sky clearer
At the day's end;
But she is fairer, and she is dearer,
She, my heart's friend!

Fair is the white star of twilight,
And the moon roving
To the sky's end;
But she is fairer, better worth loving,
She, my heart's friend.

Indian Elopement
by Alfred Jacob Miller

Illustration
by Sempé
1981

"It looks like they're working things out between them."

ENDURING LOVE

Lovers with Flowers
by Marc Chagall
1927

A Dedication to My Wife
by T. S. Eliot

To whom I owe the leaping delight
That quickens my senses in our wakingtime
And the rhythm that governs the repose of our sleepingtime,
    The breathing in unison

Of lovers whose bodies smell of each other
Who think the same thoughts without need of speech
And babble the same speech without need of meaning.

No peevish winter wind shall chill
No sullen tropic sun shall wither
The roses in the rose-garden which is ours and ours only

But this dedication is for others to read:
These are private words addressed to you in public.

Lady Agnew
by John Singer Sargent
Circa 1892–1893

If in the Years to Come
You Should Recall
by Edna St. Vincent Millay

If in the years to come you should recall,
When faint at heart or fallen on hungry days,
Or full of griefs and little if at all
From them distracted by delights or praise;
When failing powers or good opinion lost
Have bowed your neck, should you recall to mind
How of all men I honoured you the most,
Holding you noblest among mortal-kind:
Might not my love—although the curving blade
From whose wide mowing none may hope to hide,
Me long ago below the frosts had laid—
Restore you somehow to your former pride?
Indeed I think this memory, even then,
Must raise you high among the run of men.

Blue Eyes
by Henri Matisse
1935

"What a strange creature!" he exclaimed. "Heaven made you as you are, but for sheer obstinacy you put all the rest of your sex in the shade. No other wife could have steeled herself to keep so long out of the arms of a husband she had just got back after nineteen years of misadventure...."

"You too are strange," said the cautious Penelope. "I am not being haughty or indifferent.... But I have too clear a picture of you in my mind as you were when you sailed from Ithaca in your long-oared ship. Come, Eurycleia, make him a comfortable bed outside the bedroom that he built so well himself. Place the big bed out there, and make it up with rugs and blankets, and with laundered sheets."

This was her way of putting her husband to the test. But Odysseus flared up at once and rounded on his loyal wife. "Penelope," he cried, "you exasperate me! Who, if you please, has moved my bed elsewhere? Short of a miracle, it would be hard even for a skilled workman to shift it somewhere else, and the strongest young fellow alive would have a job to budge it. For a great secret went into the making of that complicated bed; and it was my work and mine alone. Inside the court there was a long-leaved olive-tree, which had grown to full height with a stem as thick as a pillar. Round this I built my room of close-set stone-work, and when that was finished, I roofed it over thoroughly, and put in a solid, neatly fitted, double door. Next I lopped all the twigs off the olive, trimmed the stem from the root up, rounded it smoothly and carefully with my adze and trued it to the line, to make my bedpost. This I drilled through where necessary, and used as a basis for the bed itself, which I worked away at till that too was done, when I finished it off with an inlay of gold, silver, and ivory, and fixed a set of purple straps across the frame.

"There is our secret, and I have shown you that I know it. What I don't know, madam, is whether my bedstead stands where it did, or whether someone has cut the tree-trunk through and shifted it elsewhere."

Her knees began to tremble as she realized the complete fidelity of his description. All at once her heart melted. Bursting into tears she ran up to Odysseus, threw her arms round his neck and kissed his head. "Odysseus," she cried, "do not be cross with me, you who were always the most reasonable of men. All our unhappiness is due to the gods, who couldn't bear to see us share the joys of youth and reach the threshold of old age together. But don't be angry with me now, or hurt because the moment when I saw you first I did not kiss you as I kiss you now. For I had always had the cold fear in my heart that somebody might come here and bewitch me with his talk.... But now all's well. You have faithfully described our token, the secret of our bed, which no one ever saw but you and I and one maid.... You have convinced your unbelieving wife."

Penelope's surrender melted Odysseus' heart, and he wept as he held his dear wife in his arms, so loyal and so true. Sweet moment too for her, sweet as the sight of land to sailors struggling in the sea, when the Sea-god by dint of wind and wave has wrecked their gallant ship. What happiness for the few swimmers that have fought their way through the white surf to the shore, when, caked with brine but safe and sound, they tread on solid earth! If that is bliss, what bliss it was for her to see her husband once again! She kept her white arms round his neck and never quite let go.

detail from

A Greek Vase
Fourth century

Small Horses Ride in a
Measure of Time
by Colette Inez

Albums of summer when you
were perched on a stubby horse,
how light filled up the emptiness
of the straggling path.
Your eyes, round and dark,
didn't seem to see
more than was needed for the pose.

On another path at the whim
of the clouds, I slipped a foot
into a stirrup and sat on a small,
gray horse. In the picture, light eats
the darkside of the shrubs, shadows
on my face.

Now the horses ride in a measure
of lost time. The camera has stopped
our childhood in its revery. We leave
that frontier for this green film
of leaves in an almost overlavish
summer—snapshots of winter
in a frozen spool—and come to love

despite the dark photographer
trailing our steps out of the frame
and into these red kisses. Geraniums
and the lip of the moon
in the shot on the path
where we blur in the dusk, two
faint lines who don't seem to need
more than is seen in the woods.

Le Repos
by Marc Chagall
1975

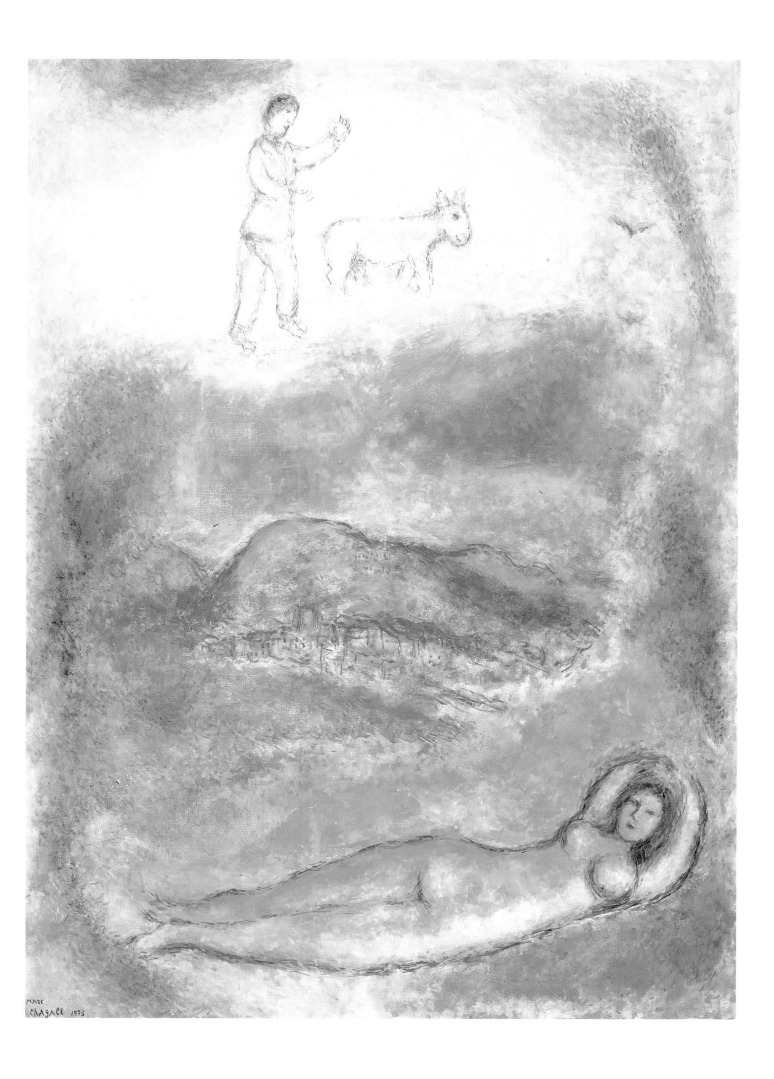

Three Times in Love
by Robert Graves

You have now fallen three times in love
With the same woman, first indeed blindly
And at her blind insistence;

Next with your heart alive to the danger
Of what hers might conceal, although such passion
Strikes nobly and for ever;

Now at last, deep in dream, transported
To her rose garden on the high ridge,
Assured that there she can deny you
No deserved privilege,
However controvertible or new.

The Dressing Gown
by Pierre Bonnard
Circa 1892

Fidelity
by D. H. Lawrence

Fidelity and love are two different things, like a flower and a gem.
And love, like a flower, will fade, will change into something else
or it would not be flowery.

O flowers they fade because they are moving swiftly; a little torrent of life
leaps up to the summit of the stem, gleams, turns over round the bend
of the parabola of curved flight,
sinks, and is gone, like a comet curving into the invisible.

O flowers they are all the time travelling
like comets, and they come into our ken
for a day, for two days, and withdraw, slowly vanish again.

And we, we must take them on the wing, and let them go.
Embalmed flowers are not flowers, immortelles are not flowers;
flowers are just a motion, a swift motion, a coloured gesture;
that is their loveliness. And that is love.

But a gem is different. It lasts so much longer than we do
so much much much longer
that it seems to last forever.
Yet we know it is flowing away
as flowers are, and we are only slower,
the wonderful slow flowing of the sapphire!

All flows, and every flow is related to every other flow.
Flowers and sapphires and us, diversely streaming.

In the old days, when sapphires were breathed upon and brought forth
during the wild orgasms of chaos
time was much slower, when the rocks came forth.
It took eons to make a sapphire, eons for it to pass away

And a flower it takes a summer.

And man and woman are like the earth, that brings forth flowers
in summer, and love, but underneath is rock.
Older than flowers, older than ferns, older than foraminiferae
older than plasm altogether is the soul of a man underneath.

And when, throughout all the wild orgasms of love
slowly a gem forms, in the ancient, once-more-molten rocks
of two human hearts, two ancient rocks, a man's heart and a woman's,
that is the crystal of peace, the slow hard jewel of trust,
the sapphire of fidelity.
The gem of mutual peace emerging from the wild chaos of love.

Sarcophagus from Cerveteri
Seventh to Sixth Century B.C.

A Letter
from Nathaniel Hawthorne
to Sophia Peabody

Boston, 17 April, 1839

My Dearest,—I feel pretty secure against intruders, for the bad weather will defend me from foreign invasion; and as to Cousin Haley, he and I had a bitter political dispute last evening, at the close of which he went to bed in high dudgeon, and probably will not speak to me these three days. Thus you perceive that strife and wrangling, as well as east-winds and rain, are the methods of a kind Providence to promote my comfort, —which would not have been so well secured in any other way. Six or seven hours of cheerful solitude! But I will not be alone. I invite your spirit to be with me,—at any hour and as many hours as you please, —but especially at the twilight hour, before I light my lamp. I bid you at that particular time, because I can see visions more vividly in the dusky glow of firelight than either by daylight or lamplight. Come, and let me renew my spell against headache and other direful effects of the east-wind. How I wish I could give you a portion of my insensibility! and yet I should be almost afraid of some radical transformation, were I to produce a change in that respect. If you cannot grow plump and rosy and tough and vigorous without being changed into another nature, then I do think, for this short life, you had better remain just what you are. Yes; but you will be the same to me, because we have met in Eternity, and there our intimacy was formed. So get well as soon as you possibly can, and I shall never doubt that you are the same Sophie who have so often leaned upon my arm and needed its superfluous strength. I never, till now, had a friend who could give me repose; all have disturbed me, and whether for pleasure or pain, it was still disturbance. But peace overflows from your heart into mine. Then I feel that there is a Now, and that Now must be always calm and happy, and that sorrow and evil are but phantoms that seem to flit across it...

When this week's first letter came, I held it a long time in my hand, marvelling at the superscription. How did you contrive to write it? Several times since I have pored over it, to discover how much of yourself mingled with my share of it; and certainly there is grace flung over the fac-simile, which never was seen in my harsh, uncouth autograph, and yet none of the strength is lost. You are wonderful.

What a beautiful day! and I had a double enjoyment of it—for your sake and my own. I have been to walk, this afternoon, to Bunker's Hill and the Navy Yard, and am tired, because I had not your arm to support me.

God keep you from east-winds and every other evil.

Your own friend,

N. H.

The Kiss
by Edvard Munch
1902

A Letter
from Sophia Peabody
to Nathaniel Hawthorne

31 December, 1839

Best Beloved,—I send you some allumettes wherewith to kindle the taper. There are very few but my second finger could no longer perform extra duty. These will serve till the wounded one be healed, however. How beautiful is it to provide even this slightest convenience for you, dearest! I cannot tell you how much I love you, in this back-handed style. My love is not in this attitude,—it rather bends forward to meet you.

What a year has this been to us! My definition of Beauty is, that it is love, and therefore includes both truth and good. But those only who love as we do can feel the significance and force of this.

My ideas will not flow in these crooked strokes. God be with you. I am very well, and have walked far in Danvers this cold morning. I am full of the glory of the day. God bless you this night of the old year. It has proved the year of our nativity. Has not the old earth passed away from us?—are not all things new?

Your Sophie

Woman with a Rose
by Edmond Aman-Jean
1891

Let Me Not
to the Marriage of
True Minds
by William Shakespeare

Let me not to the marriage of true minds
Admit impediments. Love is not love
Which alters when it alteration finds,
Or bends with the remover to remove.
Oh, no! it is an ever-fixéd mark
That looks on tempests and is never shaken;
It is the star to every wandering bark,
Whose worth's unknown, although his height be taken.
Love's not Time's fool, though rosy lips and cheeks
Within his bending sickle's compass come;
Love alters not with his brief hours and weeks,
But bears it out even to the edge of doom.
  If this be error and upon me proved,
  I never writ, nor no man ever loved.

Man and Woman with
Spinning Wheel
by Pieter Pieterszoon
Circa 1575–1580

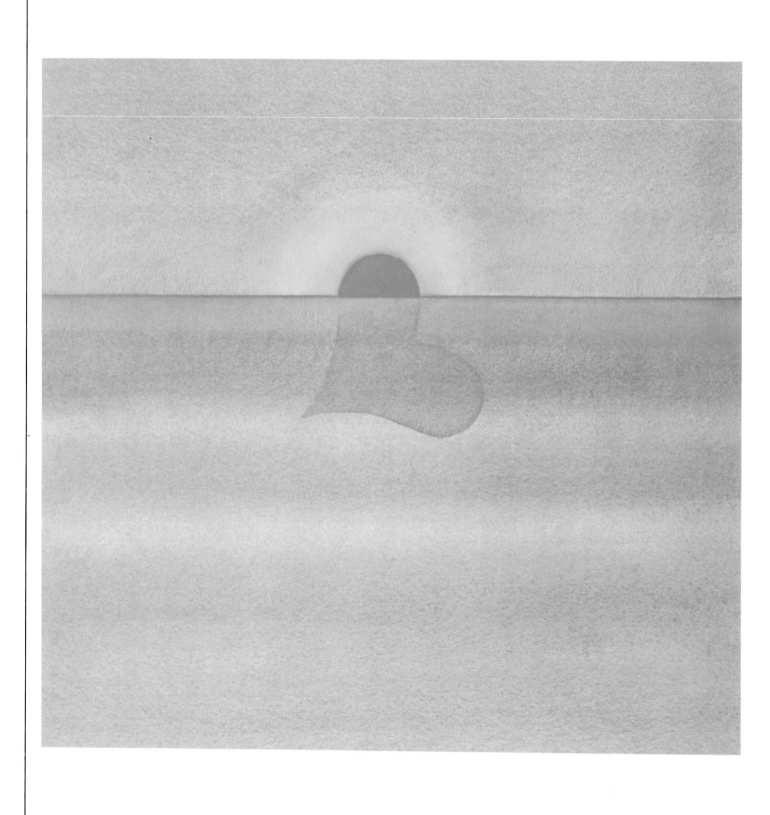

MEDITATIONS

Naked Love

by Folon

1981

"Love is the only thing you get more of by giving it away."

Tom Wilson

The Kiss
by Constantin Brancusi
Circa 1908

Melody
by Alberto De Lacerda

The infinite tenderness of that infinite melody
Carried to the last consequence
Would move mountains the mountains of hatred of ignorance of distance
From man to man from father to son from woman to man
From body to body

The beautiful circle of that melody
Carried to the extreme limit of the earth the bitter earth
Would bring the light that we long for every day
That flowers
The grave sweetness to the heart of all men all women of every race

That melody
Explored to the last cavern of golden stalactites
Would bring
Not any utopia
But the sacred gestures of everyday life
Monday Tuesday Wednesday Thursday Friday Saturday
Sunday
In a dance without questions
In which to be born to die to feed and to love
To sleep embracing another body
Would be part of an endless river
A dance without questions

Around Her
by Marc Chagall
1945

A Tree, A Rock, A Cloud
by Carson McCullers

It was raining that morning, and still very dark. When the boy reached the streetcar café he had almost finished his route and he went in for a cup of coffee. The place was an all-night café owned by a bitter and stingy man called Leo. After the raw, empty street, the café seemed friendly and bright: along the counter there were a couple of soldiers, three spinners from the cotton mill, and in a corner a man who sat hunched over with his nose and half his face down in a beer mug. The boy wore a helmet such as aviators wear. When he went into the café he unbuckled the chin strap and raised the right flap up over his pink little ear; often as he drank his coffee someone would speak to him in a friendly way. But this morning Leo did not look into his face and none of the men were talking. He paid and was leaving the café when a voice called out to him:

"Son! Hey Son!"

He turned back and the man in the corner was crooking his finger and nodding to him. He had brought his face out of the beer mug and he seemed suddenly very happy. The man was long and pale, with a big nose and faded orange hair.

"Hey Son!"

The boy went toward him. He was an undersized boy of about twelve, with one shoulder drawn higher than the other because of the weight of the paper sack. His face was shallow, freckled, and his eyes were round child eyes.

"Yeah Mister?"

The man laid one hand on the paper boy's shoulders, then grasped the boy's chin and turned his face slowly from one side to the other. The boy shrank back uneasily.

"Say! What's the big idea?"

The boy's voice was shrill; inside the café it was suddenly very quiet.

The man said slowly, 'I love you.'

All along the counter the men laughed. The boy, who had scowled and sidled away, did not know what to do. He looked over the counter at Leo, and Leo watched him with a weary, brittle jeer. The boy tried to laugh also. But the man was serious and sad.

"I did not mean to tease you, Son," he said. "Sit down and have a beer with me. There is something I have to explain."

Cautiously, out of the corner of his eye, the paper boy questioned the men along the counter to see what he should do. But they had gone back to their beer or their breakfast and did not notice him. Leo put a cup of coffee on the counter and a little jug of cream.

"He is a minor," Leo said.

The paper boy slid himself up onto the stool. His ear beneath the upturned flap of the helmet was very small and red. The man was nodding at him soberly. "It is important," he said. Then he reached in his hip pocket and brought out something which he held up in the palm of his hand for the boy to see.

"Look very carefully," he said.

The boy stared, but there was nothing to look at very carefully. The man held in his big, grimy palm a photograph. It was the face of a woman, but blurred, so that only the hat and the dress she was wearing stood out clearly.

"See?" the man asked.

The boy nodded and the man placed another picture in his palm. The woman was standing on a beach in a bathing suit. The suit made her stomach very big, and that was the main thing you noticed.

"Got a good look?" He leaned over closer and finally asked: "You ever seen her before?"

The boy sat motionless, staring slantwise at the man. "Not so I know of."

"Very well." The man blew on the photographs and put them back into his pocket. "That was my wife."

"Dead?" the boy asked.

Slowly the man shook his head. He pursed his lips as though about to whistle and answered in a long-drawn way: "Nuuu—" he said. "I will explain."

The beer on the counter before the man was in a large brown mug. He did not pick it up to drink. Instead he bent down and, putting his face over the rim, he rested there for a moment. Then with both hands he tilted the mug and sipped.

"Some night you'll go to sleep with your big nose in a mug and drown," said Leo. "Prominent transient drowns in beer. That would be a cute death."

The paper boy tried to signal to Leo. While the man was not looking he screwed up his face and worked his mouth to question soundlessly: 'Drunk?' But Leo only raised his eyebrows and turned away to put some pink strips of bacon on the grill. The man pushed the mug away from him, straightened himself, and folded his loose crooked hands on the counter. His face was sad as he looked at the paper boy. He did not blink, but from time to time the lids closed down with delicate gravity over his pale green eyes. It was nearing dawn and the boy shifted the weight of the paper sack.

"I am talking about love," the man said. "With me it is a science."

The boy half slid down from the stool. But the man raised his forefinger, and there was something about him that held the boy and would not let him go away.

"Twelve years ago I married the woman in the photograph. She was my wife for one year, nine months,

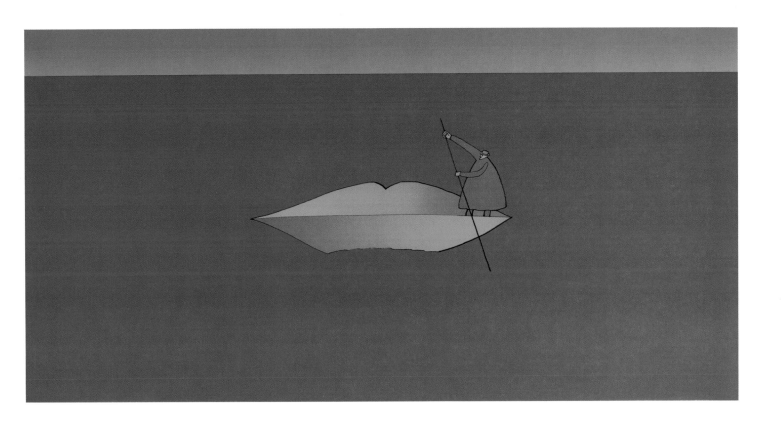

Lily Love Me

by Folon

1975

three days, and two nights. I loved her. Yes...." He tightened his blurred, rambling voice and said again: "I loved her. I thought also that she loved me. I was a railroad engineer. She had all home comforts and luxuries. It never crept into my brain that she was not satisfied. But do you know what happened?"

"Mgneeow!" said Leo.

The man did not take his eyes from the boy's face. "She left me. I came in one night and the house was empty and she was gone. She left me."

"With a fellow?" the boy asked.

Gently the man placed his palm down on the counter. "Why naturally, Son. A woman does not run off like that alone."

The café was quiet, the soft rain black and endless in the street outside. Leo pressed down the frying bacon with the prongs of his long fork. 'So you have been chasing the floozie for eleven years. You frazzled old rascal.'

For the first time the man glanced at Leo. "Please don't be vulgar. Besides, I was not speaking to you." He turned back to the boy and said in a trusting and secretive undertone. "Let's not pay any attention to him. O.K.?"

The paper boy nodded doubtfully.

"It was like this," the man continued. "I am a person who feels many things. All my life one thing after another has impressed me. Moonlight. The leg of a pretty girl. One thing after another. But the point is that when I had enjoyed anything there was a peculiar sensation as though it was laying around loose in me. Nothing seemed to finish itself up or fit in with the other things. Women? I had my portion of them. The same. Afterwards laying around loose in me. I was a man who had never loved."

Very slowly he closed his eyelids, and the gesture was like a curtain drawn at the end of a scene in a play. When he spoke again his voice was excited and the words came fast—the lobes of his large, loose ears seemed to tremble.

"Then I met this woman. I was fifty-one years old and she always said she was thirty. I met her at a filling station and we were married within three days. And do you know what it was like? I just can't tell you. All I had ever felt was gathered together around this woman. Nothing lay around loose in me anymore but was finished up by her."

The man stopped suddenly and stroked his long nose. His voice sank down to a steady and reproachful undertone. "I'm not explaining this right. What happened was this. There were these beautiful feelings and loose little pleasures inside me. And this woman was something like an assembly line for my soul. I run these little pieces of myself through her and I come out complete. Now do you follow me?"

"What was her name?" the boy asked.

"Oh," he said. "I called her Dodo. But that is immaterial."

"Did you try to make her come back?"

The man did not seem to hear. "Under the circumstances you can imagine how I felt when she left me."

Leo took the bacon from the grill and folded two strips of it between a bun. He had a gray face, with slitted eyes, and a pinched nose saddled by faint blue shadows. One of the mill workers signaled for more coffee and Leo poured it. He did not give refills on coffee free. The spinner ate breakfast there every morning, but the better Leo knew his customers the stingier he treated them. He nibbled his own bun as though he grudged it to himself.

"And you never got hold of her again?"

The boy did not know what to think of the man, and his child's face was uncertain with mingled curiosity and doubt. He was new on the paper route; it was still strange to him to be out in the town in the black, queer early morning.

"Yes," the man said. "I took a number of steps to get her back. I went around trying to locate her. I went to Tulsa where she had folks. And to Mobile. I went to every town she had ever mentioned to me, and I hunted down every man she had formerly been connected with. Tulsa, Atlanta, Chicago, Cheehaw, Memphis.... For the better part of two years I chased around the country trying to lay hold of her."

"But the pair of them had vanished from the face of the earth!" said Leo.

"Don't listen to him," the man said confidentially. "And also just forget those two years. They were not important. What matters is that around the third year a curious thing begun to happen to me."

"What?" the boy asked.

The man leaned down and tilted his mug to take a sip of beer. But as he hovered over the mug his nostrils fluttered slightly; he sniffed the staleness of the beer and did not drink. "Love is a curious thing to begin with. It was a kind of mania. But then as time went on I tried to remember her. But do you know what happened?"

"No," the boy said.

"When I laid myself down on a bed and tried to think about her my mind became a blank. I couldn't see her. I would take out her pictures and look. No good. Nothing doing. A blank. Can you imagine it?"

"Say Mac." Leo called down the counter. "Can you imagine this bozo's mind a blank!"

Slowly, as though fanning away flies, the man waved his hand. His green eyes were concentrated and fixed on the shallow little face of the paper boy.

"But a sudden piece of glass on a sidewalk. Or a nickel tune in a music box. A shadow on a wall at night. And I would remember. It might happen in a street and I would cry or bang my head against a lamppost. You follow me?"

"A piece of glass..." the boy said.

"Anything. I would walk around and I had no power of how and when to remember her. You think you can put up a kind of shield. But remembering don't come to a man face forward—it corners around sideways. I was at the mercy of everything I saw and heard. Suddenly instead of me combing the countryside to find her she begun to chase me around in my very soul. *She* chasing *me*, mind you! And in my soul."

The boy asked finally, "What part of the county were you in then?"

"Ooh," the man groaned. "I was a sick mortal. It was like smallpox. I confess, Son, that I boozed. I fornicated. I committed any sin that suddenly appealed to me. I am loath to confess it but I will do so. When I recall that period it is all curdled in my mind, it was so terrible."

The man leaned his head down and tapped his forehead on the counter. For a few seconds he stayed bowed over in this position, the back of his stringy neck covered with orange furze, his hands with their long warped fingers held palm to palm in an attitude of prayer. Then the man straightened himself; he was smiling and suddenly his face was bright and tremulous and old.

"It was in the fifth year that it happened," he said. "And with it I started my science."

Leo's mouth jerked with a pale, quick grin. "Well none of we boys are getting any younger," he said. Then with sudden anger he balled up a dishcloth he was holding and threw it down hard on the floor. "You draggle-tailed old Romeo."

"What happened?" the boy asked.

The old man's voice was high and clear. "Peace," he answered.

"Huh?"

"It is hard to explain scientifically. Son," he said. "I guess the logical explanation is that she and I had fleed around from each other for so long that finally we just got tangled up together and lay down and quit. Peace. A queer and beautiful blankness. It was spring in Portland and the rain came every afternoon. All evening I just stayed there on my bed in the dark. And that is how the science come to me."

The windows in the streetcar were pale blue with light. The two soldiers paid for their beers and opened the door—one of the soldiers combed his hair and wiped off his muddy puttees before they went outside. The three mill workers bent silently over their breakfasts. Leo's clock was ticking on the wall.

"It is this. And listen carefully. I meditated on love and reasoned it out. I realized what is wrong with us. Men fall in love for the first time. And what do they fall in love with?"

The boy's soft mouth was partly open and he did not answer.

"A woman," the old man said. "Without science, with nothing to go by, they undertake the most dangerous and sacred experience in God's earth. They fall in love with a woman. Is that correct, Son?"

"Yeah," the boy said faintly.

"They start at the wrong end of love. They begin at the climax. Can you wonder it is so miserable? Do you know how men should love?"

The old man reached over and grasped the boy by the collar of his leather jacket. He gave him a gentle little shake and his green eyes gazed down unblinking and grave.

"Son, do you know how love should be begun?"

The boy sat small and listening and still. Slowly he shook his head. The old man leaned closer and whispered:

"A tree. A rock. A cloud."

It was still raining outside in the street: a mild, gray, endless rain. The mill whistle blew for the six o'clock shift and the three spinners paid and went away. There was no one in the café but Leo, the old man, and the little paper boy.

"The weather was like this in Portland," he said. "At the time my science was begun. I meditated and I started very cautious. I would pick up something from the street and take it home with me. I bought a goldfish and I concentrated on the goldfish and I loved it. I graduated from one thing to another. Day by day I was getting this technique. On the road from Portland to San Diego—"

"Aw shut up," screamed Leo suddenly. "Shut up! Shut up!"

The old man still held the collar of the boy's jacket; he was trembling and his face was earnest and bright and wild. "For six years now I have gone around by myself and built up my science. And now I am a master, Son. I can love anything. No longer do I have to think about it even. I see a street full of people and a beautiful light comes in me. I watch a bird in the sky. Or I meet a traveler on the road. Everything, Son. And anybody. All stranger and all loved! Do you realize what a science like mine can mean?"

The boy held himself stiffly, his hands curled tight around the counter edge. Finally he asked: "Did you ever really find that lady?"

"What? What say, Son?"

"I mean," the boy asked timidly. "Have you fallen in love with a woman again?"

The old man loosened his grasp on the boy's collar. He turned away and for the first time his green eyes had a vague and scattered look. He lifted the mug from the counter, drank down the yellow beer. His head was shaking slowly from side to side. Then finally he answered: "No, Son. You see that is the last step in my science. I go cautious. And I am not quite ready yet."

"Well!" said Leo. "Well well well."

The old man stood in the open doorway. "Remember," he said. Framed there in the gray damp light of the early morning he looked shrunken and seedy and frail. But his smile was bright. "Remember I love you," he said with a last nod. And the door closed quietly behind him.

The boy did not speak for a long time. He pulled down the bangs on his forehead and slid his grimy little forefinger around the rim of his empty cup. Then without looking at Leo he finally asked:

"Was he drunk?"

"No," said Leo shortly.

The boy raised his clear voice higher. "Then was he a dope fiend?"

"No."

The boy looked up at Leo, and his flat little face was desperate, his voice urgent and shrill. "Was he crazy? Do you think he was a lunatic?" The paper boy's voice dropped suddenly with doubt. "Leo? Or not?"

But Leo would not answer him. Leo had run a night café for fourteen years, and he held himself to be a critic of craziness. There were the town characters and also the transients who roamed in from the night. He knew the manias of all of them. But he did not want to satisfy the questions of the waiting child. He tightened his pale face and was silent.

So the boy pulled down the right flap of his helmet and as he turned to leave he made the only comment that seemed safe to him, the only remark that could not be laughed down and despised:

"He sure has done a lot of traveling."

Woman with Flower
by Naomi Long Madgett

I wouldn't coax the plant if I were you.
Such watchful nurturing may do it harm.
Let the soil rest from so much digging
And wait until it's dry before you water it.
The leaf's inclined to find its own direction;
Give it a chance to seek the sunlight for itself.

Much growth is stunted by too careful prodding,
Too eager tenderness.
The things we love we have to learn to leave alone.

Illustration
by W. Steig
1978

W. Steig

from

Letters to a Young Poet
by Rainer Maria Rilke

May 14, 1904, Rome

To love is good, too: love being difficult. For one human being to love another: that is perhaps the most difficult of all our tasks, the ultimate, the last test and proof, the work for which all other work is but preparation. For this reason young people, who are beginners in everything, cannot yet know love: they have to learn it. With their whole being, with all their forces, gathered close about their lonely, timid, upward-beating heart, they must learn to love. But learning-time is always a long, secluded time, and so loving, for a long while ahead and far on into life, is—solitude, intensified and deepened loneness for him who loves. Love is at first not anything that means merging, giving over, and uniting with another (for what would a union be of something unclarified and unfinished, still subordinate—?), it is a high inducement to the individual to ripen, to become something in himself, to become world, to become world for himself for another's sake, it is a great exacting claim upon him, something that chooses him out and calls him to vast things.

from Les Metamorphoses d'Ovid

The Love of Jupiter and Semele
by Pablo Picasso
1930–1931

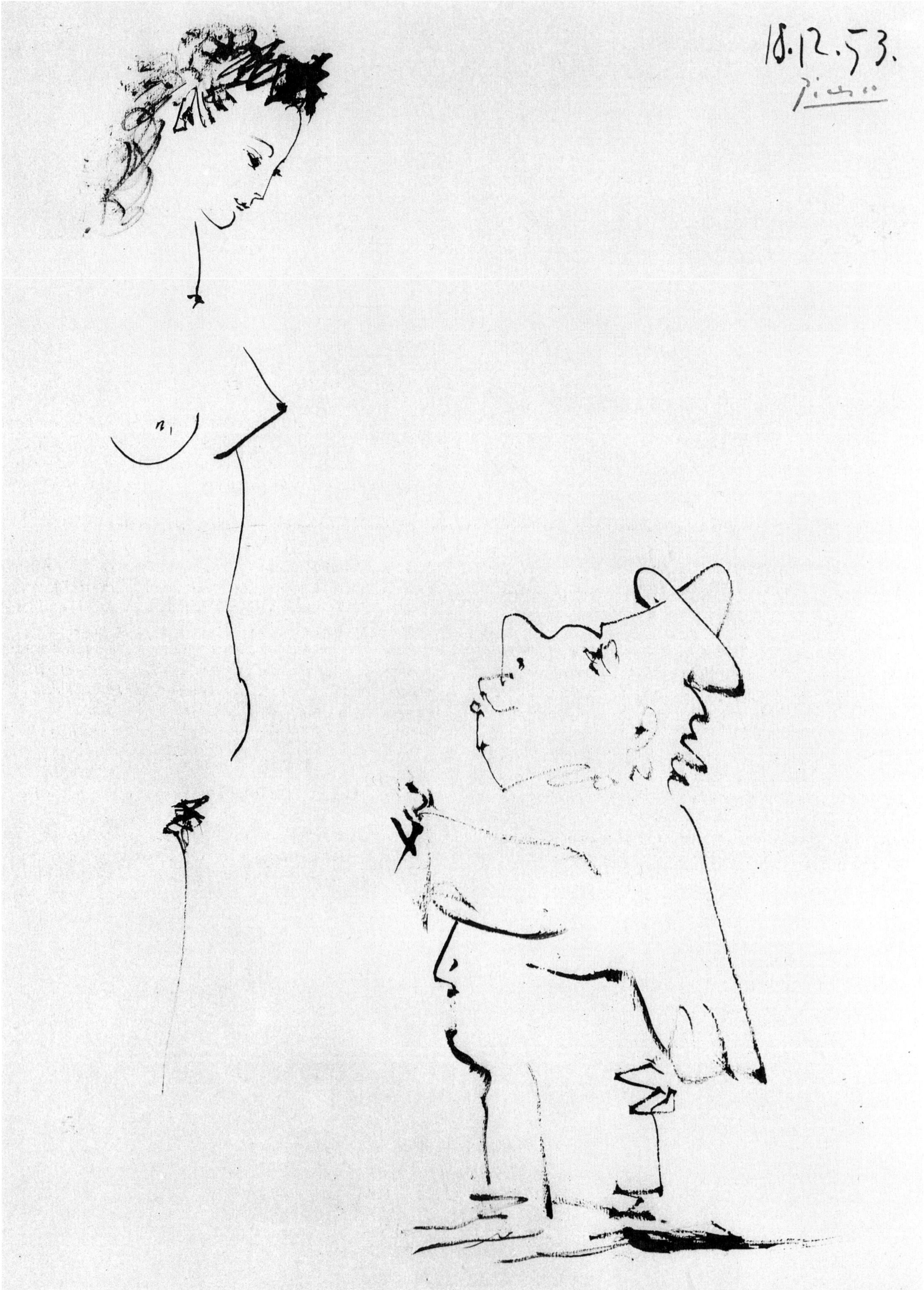
18.12.53.

The Apollo of Bellac
by Jean Giraudoux

CAST

AGNES	MR. LEPEDURA
THERESE	MR. RASEMUTTE
THE CLERK	MR. SCHULTZ
THE MAN	THE PRESIDENT
THE VICE-PRESIDENT	CHEVREDENT
MR. CRACHETON	THE CHAIRMAN OF THE BOARD

The Man from Bellac is not Apollo. The Man from Bellac is a little shabby fellow who doesn't know where his next meal is coming from. He is a vagabond and a poet, therefore an inventor. He dreams things up, but he does nothing and he has nothing. He was cast very sensibly on the Ford Omnibus television program, when Claude Dauphin played the role—a fine character-actor, not a matinee idol. The Man from Bellac must evoke Apollo, but visually he must remain the shabby little figure throughout the play. The moment he is cast as a big beautiful man with curly ringlets, the play is spoiled.

Translated by Maurice Valency

SCENE: *The reception room of The International Bureau of Inventions, S.A.*

This is a large, well-appointed room on the second floor of a magnificent office building in Paris. The French windows are open and afford us a view of tree-tops. There is an elaborate crystal chandelier hanging from the ceiling. The morning sun plays upon it. On a pedestal large enough to conceal a man a bust of Archimedes is set. Four doors open off the room. Three of them are marked Private. These lead into the office of the President, Right, and the First Vice-President rear Right, and the Directors' Conference Room rear Left. The effect is French and very elegant, perhaps a trifle oppressive in its opulence.

Behind a period desk sits the RECEPTION CLERK. *The desk has an ivory telephone and a row of signal lights. It has also a period blotter on which the clerk is writing something in an appointment book. The Clerk is well on in years and his face makes one think of a caricature by Daumier.*

TIME: *Autumn in Paris. The present or shortly before.*

AT RISE: THE CLERK *is writing with a meticulous air. The outer door opens.* AGNES *comes in timidly from outer door, and stands in front of the desk.* THE CLERK *does not look up.*

continued

Woman and Dwarf
by Pablo Picasso
1953

AGNES   Er—

CLERK   Yes?

AGNES   Is this the International Bureau of Inventions, Incorporated?

CLERK   Yes.

AGNES   Could I please see the Chairman of the Board?

CLERK   *(Looks up)*   The Chairman of the Board? No one sees the Chairman of the Board.

AGNES   Oh.

(The outer door opens again. THERESE sweeps into the room. She is blonde, shapely, thirty-five, dressed in expensive mink. CLERK rises respectfully.)

CLERK   Good morning, Madame.

THERESE   Is the President in?

CLERK   Yes, Madame. Of course.

(THERESE walks haughtily to President's door. CLERK opens it for her and closes it behind her. He goes back to his desk where AGNES is waiting.)

AGNES   Could I see the President?

CLERK   No one sees the President.

AGNES   But I have—

CLERK   What type of invention? Major? Intermediate? Minor?

AGNES   I beg pardon?

CLERK   Assistant Secretary to the Third Vice-President. Come back Tuesday. Name?

AGNES   My name?

CLERK   You have a name, I presume?

(THE MAN FROM BELLAC appears suddenly from outer door. He is nondescript, mercurial, shabby.)

MAN   Yes. The young lady has a name. But what permits you to conclude that the young lady's invention is as minor as all that?

CLERK   Who are you?

MAN   What chiefly distinguishes the inventor is modesty. You should know that by now. Pride is the invention of non-inventors.

(A STREET SINGER, accompanied by violin and accordian, begins "La Seine" outside the windows. CLERK crosses to close them.)

AGNES   *(To the MAN)*   Thanks very much, but—

MAN   To the characteristic modesty of the inventor, the young lady adds the charming modesty of her sex— *(He smiles at AGNES)* But—
    (CLERK closes one of the windows.)
    how can you be sure, you, that she has not brought us at last the invention which is destined to transform the modern world?

CLERK   *(Closes the other window)*   For world-transformations it's the Second Vice President. Mondays ten to twelve.

MAN   Today is Tuesday.

CLERK   Now how can I help that?

MAN   So! While all humanity awaits with anguish the discovery which will at last utilize the moon's gravitation for the removal of corns, and when we have every reason to believe that in all likelihood Mademoiselle—Mademoiselle?

AGNES   Agnes.

MAN   Mademoiselle Agnes has this discovery in her handbag—You tell her to come back Monday.

CLERK   *(Nervously)*   There is going to be a Directors' meeting in just a few minutes. The Chairman of the Board is coming. I must beg you to be quiet.

MAN   I will not be quiet. I am quiet Mondays.

CLERK   Now, please. I don't want any trouble.

MAN   And the Universal Vegetable? Five continents are languishing in the hope of the Universal Vegetable which will once and for all put an end to the ridiculous specialization of the turnip, the leek and the stringbean, which will be at one and the same time bread, meat, wine and coffee, and yield with equal facility cotton, potassium, ivory and wool. The Universal Vegetable which Paracelsus could not, and Burbank dared not, imagine! Yes, my friend. And while in this handbag, which with understandable concern she clutches to her charming bosom, the seeds of the Universal Vegetable await only the signal of your President to burst upon an expectant world, you say—come back Monday.

AGNES   Really, sir—

CLERK   If you wish an appointment for Monday, Mademoiselle—

MAN   She does not wish an appointment for Monday.

CLERK   *(Shrugs)*   Then she can go jump in the lake.

MAN   What did you say?

CLERK   I said: She can go jump in the lake. Is that clear?

MAN   That's clear. Perfectly clear. As clear as it was to Columbus when—
    (The buzzer sounds on the CLERK's desk. A light flashes on.)

CLERK   Excuse me. (He crosses to the VICE PRESIDENT'S door, knocks and enters.)
    (MAN smiles. AGNES smiles back wanly.)

AGNES   But I'm not the inventor of the Universal Vegetable.

MAN   I know. I am.

AGNES   I'm just looking for a job.

MAN   Typist?

ANGES   Not really.

MAN   Stenographer?

AGNES   Not at all.

MAN   Copy-reader, translator, book-keeper, editor, file-clerk—stop me when I come to it.

AGNES   You could go on like that for years before I could stop you.

MAN   Well then—your specialty? Charm? Coquetry, devotion, seduction, flirtation, passion, romance?

AGNES   That's getting warmer.

MAN   Splendid. The best career for a female is to be a woman.

AGNES   Yes, but—men frighten me.

MAN   Men frighten you?

AGNES   They make me feel weak all over.

MAN   That clerk frightens you?

AGNES   Clerks, presidents, janitors, soldiers. All a man has to do is to look at me, and I feel like a shoplifter caught in the act.

MAN   Caught in what act?

AGNES   I don't know.

MAN   Perhaps it's their clothes that frighten you. Their vests? Their trousers?

AGNES   *(Shakes her head)*   I feel the same panic on the beach when they don't wear their trousers.

MAN   Perhaps you don't like men.

AGNES   Oh, no, I like them. I like their dog-like eyes, their hairiness, their big feet. And they have special organs which inspire tenderness in a woman—. Their Adam's apple, for instance, when they eat dinner or make speeches. But the moment they speak to me, I begin to tremble—

MAN *(He looks appraisingly at her a moment)* You would like to stop trembling?

AGNES Oh yes. But—*(She shrugs hopelessly.)*

MAN Would you like me to teach you the secret?

AGNES Secret?

MAN Of not trembling before men. Of getting whatever you want out of them. Of making the directors jump, the presidents kneel and offer you diamonds?

AGNES Are there such secrets?

MAN One only. It is infallible.

AGNES Will you really tell it to me?

MAN Without this secret a girl has a bad time of it on this earth. With it, she becomes Empress of the World.

AGNES Oh tell it to me quickly.

MAN *(Peering about the room)* No one is listening?

AGNES *(Whispers)* No one.

MAN Tell them they're handsome.

AGNES You mean, flatter them? Tell them they're handsome, intelligent, kind?

MAN No. As for the intelligence and the kindness, they can shift for themselves. Tell them they're handsome.

AGNES All?

MAN All. The foolish, the wise, the modest, the vain, the young, the old. Say it to the professor of philosophy and he will give you a diploma. Say it to the president here, and he will give you a job.

AGNES But to say a thing like that, one has to know a person well—

MAN Not at all. Say it right off. Say it before he has a chance even to open his mouth.

AGNES But one doesn't say a thing like that before people.

MAN Before people. Before all the world. The more witnesses, the better.

AGNES But if they're not handsome—and for the most part they're not, you know—how can I tell them that they are?

MAN Surely you're not narrow-minded, Agnes?
(She shrugs, not quite sure.)
The ugly, the pimply, the crippled, the fat. Do you wish to get on in this world? Tell them they're handsome.

AGNES Will they believe it?

MAN They will believe it because they've always known it. Every man, even the ugliest, feels in his heart a secret alliance with beauty. When you tell him he's handsome, he will simply hear outwardly the voice he has been listening to inwardly all his life. And those who believe it the least will be the most grateful. No matter how ugly they may have thought themselves, the moment they find a woman who thinks them handsome, they grapple her to their hearts with hooks of steel. For them, she is the magic glass of truth, the princess of an enchanted world. When you see a woman who can go nowhere without a staff of admirers, it is not so much because they think she is beautiful, it is because she has told them they are handsome.

AGNES There are women then who already know this secret?

MAN Yes. But they know it without really knowing it. And usually they evade the issue, they go beside the point. They tell the hunchback he is generous, the wall-eyed that he's strong. There's no profit in that. I've seen a woman throw away a cool million in diamonds and emeralds because she told a club footed lover that he walked swiftly, when all he wanted to hear was—you know what. And now—to work. The President is in every day to those who come to tell him he's handsome.

AGNES I'd better come back another day. I have to have training. I have a cousin who's not at all bad-looking—I'll practice on him tomorrow, and then the next day I'll—

MAN You can practice right now. On the receptionist.

AGNES That monster?

MAN The monster is perfect for your purpose. After that, the Vice President. I know him. He's even better. Then the President.
The VICE PRESIDENT's *door opens. The* CLERK *comes in.)*

CLERK *(Into the doorway)* Very good, sir.

VOICE And another thing—

CLERK *(Turns)* Yes sir?

VOICE When the Chairman of the Board—
(CLERK goes back in and closes the door.)

AGNES No, I can't!

MAN *(Indicating the bust of Archimedes at rear)* Begin with this bust then.

AGNES Whose is it?

MAN What does it matter? It's the bust of a man. It's all ears. Speak!

AGNES *(Shuddering)* It has a beard.

MAN Begin with what you like. With this chair. With this clock.

AGNES They're not listening.

MAN This fly, then. See? He's on your glove. He's listening.

AGNES Is he a male?

MAN Yes. Speak. Tell him.

AGNES *(With an effort)* How handsome he is!

MAN No, no, no. Say it to him.

AGNES How handsome you are!

MAN You see? He's twirling his moustache. Go on. More. More. What is a fly especially vain of?

AGNES His wings? His eyes?

MAN That's it. Tell him.

AGNES How beautiful your wings are, beautiful fly! They sparkle in the sun like jewels. And your eyes—so large, so sad, so sensitive!

MAN Splendid. Shoo him away now. Here comes the clerk.

AGNES He won't go. He's clinging to me.

MAN Naturally.

AGNES *(To the fly)* You're bowlegged. *(She smiles)* He's gone.

MAN You see? And now—
(The VICE PRESIDENT's *door open slowly.)*
Here he comes.

AGNES *(In panic)* What must I say?

MAN "How handsome you are."
(CLERK comes in and walks to his desk.)

MAN *(disappears behind the bust of Archimedes.)*

AGNES *(After an agony of indecision)* How handsome you are!

CLERK *(Stops dead)* What?

AGNES I said, how handsome you are!

CLERK Do you get this way often?

AGNES It's the first time in my life that I've ever—

CLERK *(Finishing the sentence for her)* Called a chimpanzee handsome? Thanks for the compliment. But—why?

AGNES You're right. Handsome is not the word. I should have said beautiful. Because, mind you, I never judge a face by the shape of the nose or the arch of the brow. To me, what counts is the ensemble.

CLERK So what you're telling me is: your features are ugly, but they go beautifully together. Is that it?

AGNES It serves me right. Very well—It's the first time I've ever told a man he was handsome. And it's going to be the last.

CLERK Now don't get excited, please. I know girls. At your age a girl doesn't calculate; she says whatever comes into her head. I know you meant it. Only —why did you say it so badly?
(MAN sticks his head out and makes a face at AGNES behind the CLERK's back.)

AGNES *(To the MAN)* Did I say it badly? *(To the CLERK, who thinks it is said to him)* I thought you were handsome. I may have been wrong.

CLERK Women are blind as bats. Even if there were something good about me, they'd never see it. What's so good about me? My face? God, no. My figure? Not at all. Only my shadow. But of course you didn't notice that.

AGNES Is that what you think? And when you leaned over to close the window, I suppose your shadow didn't lean over with you? And when you walked into the Vice President's office, did you put your shadow away in a drawer? *(She strokes his shadow with her hand)* How could I help noticing a shadow like that?

CLERK You notice it now because I direct your attention to it.

AGNES Have it your way. I thought I was looking at you, but what I saw was your shadow.

CLERK Then you shouldn't say, what a handsome man. You should say, what a handsome shadow.
(He opens the window, the room is filled with music It is still "La Seine.")

AGNES From now on, I shall say no more about it.

CLERK *(Returning to desk)* Don't be angry, my dear. It's only because I'm a man of years and I have a right to warn you. I have a daughter of your age. I know what girls are. One day they see a fine shadow, and at once their heads are turned, the silly geese, and they think the man himself is handsome. Oh, I don't deny it, it's a rare thing, a fine shadow. And believe me it lasts—you don't keep your hair, you don't keep your skin, but your shadow lasts all your life. Even longer, they say. But that's not the point. These little fools invariably insist on confusing the shadow with the man, and if the idiot lets himself be talked into it, in a moment it's all over and they've ruined their lives for nothing, the

---

Illustration
by W. Steig
1977

---

nitwits. No, my dear. Heed an old man's warning. You can't live your life among shadows.

(MAN *sticks out his head and lifts an admonishing finger.*)

AGNES   How handsome you are!

CLERK   You know why? It's because when I'm angry I show my teeth. And the fact is, they are rather good. My dentist says they're perfect. It's no credit to me—It's because I eat hard foods. And when you—

(The buzzer sounds again.)

Ah—the Vice President needs me again. Wait just a minute, my dear. I'll make sure that he sees you at once. I'll say it's my niece.

AGNES *(As he bends over to close a drawer)*   How beautiful it is, your shadow, when it leans over. One would say it belonged to Rodin's Thinker!

CLERK *(Delighted)*   Come, now, that will do. If you were my daughter, I'd give you a good slap on the—. Sit down a minute. I'll get him for you. *(Crosses to the* VICE PRESIDENT'S *door and goes out.)*

(MAN *comes out from behind the bust. The music stops.)*

MAN   Well, its a start.

AGNES   I think I'm better with flies.

MAN   Because in your mind the idea of beauty is inseparable from the idea of the caress. Women have no sense of the abstract—a woman admiring the sky is a woman caressing the sky. In a woman's mind beauty is something she needs to touch. And you didn't want to touch the clerk, not even his shadow.

AGNES   No.

MAN   With my method, it's not your hands that must speak, not your cheek, nor your lips—. It's your brain.

AGNES   I had a narrow squeak. I almost lost him.

MAN.   Yes, he had you there with his shadow. You're not ready to tackle a Vice President. No. Not yet.

AGNES   But there's no time. What shall I do?

MAN   Practice. Practice on me.

AGNES   You expect me to tell you you're handsome?

MAN   Is it so difficult?

AGNES   Not at all. Only—

MAN   Think. Think before you speak.

AGNES   Oh, you're not bad at all, you know, when you tease one like this.

MAN   Very feeble. Why when I tease one like this? The rest of the time, I'm not handsome?

AGNES   Oh yes. Always. Always.

MAN   Better. Now, it's no longer your hands that are speaking.

AGNES   With you, all the same, they murmur a little something.

MAN   Good.

AGNES   The mass of your body is beautiful. The outline is beautiful. The face matters little.

MAN   What nonsense is this? My face matters little?

AGNES *(Recovering quickly)*   No more than the face of Rodin's Thinker.

MAN   In his case, doubtless the feet have more importance. Look here, Agnes, these little allusions to famous statues are ingenious. But is Rodin's Thinker the only one you know?

AGNES   Except for the Venus of Milo. But she wouldn't be much use to me with men.

MAN   That remains to be seen. In any case, we'd better extend your repertory. Forget The Thinker. Michelangelo's David is very good. Or his Moses. But best of all—the Appolo of Bellac—

AGNES   The Apollo of Bellac?

MAN   It doesn't exist. It will do perfectly.

AGNES   What does it look like?

MAN   A little like me, I think. I too come from Bellac. It's a little town in Limousin. I was born there.

AGNES   But they say the men of Limousin are so ugly. How does it happen that you are so handsome?

MAN   My father was a very handsome man, and he— Oh-oh. Good for you. *(He applauds.)*

AGNES *(Pursuing her advantage)*   Oh never! Not with you! You taught me the secret. With you I could be no other than honest.

MAN   At last. You understand.

(The VICE PRESIDENT'S *door opens.)*

Here we are. *Goes behind the bust.)*

CLERK *(Comes in, smiling tenderly)*   The Vice President will be out in a moment, my dear. No need to put yourself out. A shadow like his, you may see every day—in the zoo. *(He takes some papers from his desk and goes into where the Directors will meet.)*

AGNES *(Whispers)*   Help! Help!

(MAN *thrusts his head out.)*

I feel faint!

MAN   Practice. Practice.

AGNES *(Desperately)*   On whom? On what?

MAN   On anything. The telephone.

AGNES *(She speaks to the telephone)*   How handsome you are, my little telephone! *(She strokes it gently.)*

MAN   No! Not with the hands.

AGNES   But it's so much easier that way.

CLERK   I know. Try the chandelier. That's the one thing you can't touch.

AGNES   How handsome you are, my little, my great chandelier!

(The music begins again. Another tune.)

Only when you're all lit up? Oh, don't say that. Other chandeliers, yes. Street lamps, store-fixtures, yes. Not you. See—you are full of sunshine. You are the chandelier of the sun. A desk lamp needs to be lit. A planet needs to be lit. But you have radiance of your own. You are as beautiful as a galaxy of stars, even more beautiful, for a galaxy is only an imitation chandelier, a cluster of uncertain lights swinging precariously in the eternal darkness. But you are a creature of crystal with lamps of ivory and gold, a living miracle!

(The chandelier lights up by itself.)

MAN   Bravo!

VICE PRESIDENT *(The door opens. The* VICE PRESIDENT *comes in. His manner is important. His face is that of a gargoyle)*   My dear young lady, I have exactly two minutes to give you. *(He crosses to close the window.)*

AGNES *(Whispering in awe)*   Oh!

VICE PRESIDENT *(Stops and turns)*   Why do you stare at me like that? You've seen me before?

AGNES *(In a tone of wonder)*   No! On the contrary.

VICE PRESIDENT   And what does that mean, no, on the contrary?

AGNES   I was expecting to see the usual Vice President, stoop-shouldered, paunchy, bald— And all at once, I see you!

(VICE PRESIDENT *freezes in his tracks.* MAN *thrusts out his head. He raises a warning finger.*)

(*Hastily*) How handsome you are!

VICE PRESIDENT   What? (*He turns.*)

AGNES   Nothing. I beg your pardon.

VICE PRESIDENT   I heard you distinctly. You said I was handsome. Don't deny it. (*He steps closer to her*) (*music swells up.*) You know, it gave me rather a shock to hear you say it. However, it can't be true. If I were really— what you said—wouldn't some woman have told me before this?

AGNES   Oh, the fools! The fools!

VICE PRESIDENT   Whom are you calling fools, Mademoiselle? My sister, my mother, my niece?

AGNES (*Giving up all at once. In a formal tone*)   Mr. Vice President, the truth is I am looking for a position. And I happened to hear through a friend of one of your directs, Mr. Lepédura—

(MAN *thrusts out his head.*)

VICE PRESIDENT   Never mind Monsieur Lepédura. We are discussing me. As you probably know, I am one of the world's authorities in the fields of dreams. It is I who work with those who are able to invent only while they sleep, and I have been able to extract from their dreams such extraordinary devices as the book that reads itself and the adjustable Martini, wonders of modern science which without my help would have remained mere figments of the imagination. If you appeared to me in a dream and told me I was handsome, I should have understood at once. But we are in a waking state, or are we? One moment. (*He pinches himself*) Ow! I am awake. Permit me.

(*Pinches her.*)

AGNES   Ow!

VICE PRESIDENT   We're not dreaming, Mademoiselle. And now, my dear—(*He takes her hand*) Why did you say I was handsome? To flatter me?—I can see you are incapable of such baseness. To make fun of me? No—your eye is gentle, your lips attract— Why did you say it, Mademoiselle?

AGNES   I say you are handsome because you are handsome. If your mother finds you ugly that's not my concern.

VICE PRESIDENT   I cannot permit you to form so low an opinion of my mother's taste. Even when I was a boy, my mother used to say I had the hands of an artist.

AGNES   If your niece prefers Charles Boyer—

VICE PRESIDENT   My niece? Only yesterday at dinner she was saying that my eyebrows could have been drawn by El Greco.

AGNES   If your sister—

VICE PRESIDENT   My sister has never quite admitted that I am handsome, no, but she always said that there was something distinctive about my face. A friend of hers, a history teacher, told her it's because in certain lights, I resemble Lodovico Sforza. (*He makes a deprecating gesture.*)

AGNES   Lodovico Sforza? Never. The Apollo of Bellac, yes.

VICE PRESIDENT   The Apollo of Bellac?

AGNES   Wouldn't you say? Quite objectively?

VICE PRESIDENT   Well—if you really think so—perhaps just a little. Although Lodovico Sforza, you know— I've seen engravings—

AGNES   When I say the Apollo of Bellac, I mean, naturally, the Apollo of Bellac in a beautifully tailored suit. You see, I am frank. I say what I think. Yes, Mr. Vice President. You have the fault of all really handsome men—you dress carelessly.

VICE PRESIDENT (*Smiling*)   What insolence! And this from a girl who tells every man she meets that he's handsome!

AGNES   I have said that to two men only in all my life. You are the second.

(CLERK *comes in.*)

VICE PRESIDENT   What is it? Don't you see I'm busy?

CLERK   The Directors are on the way up, sir. It's time for the meeting.

VICE PRESIDENT   I'll be right in.

(CLERK *goes into the Directors' room.*) I'm sorry, Mademoiselle. I must go to this meeting. But we must certainly continue this wonderful conversation. Won't you come back and lunch with me? You know, my secretary is impossible. I'm having her transfered to the sales department. Now you're a first-rate typist, I'm told—

AGNES   I don't type. I play the piano.

VICE PRESIDENT   Ah, that's wonderful. And you take dictation?

AGNES   In longhand, yes.

VICE PRESIDENT   That's much the best way. That gives one time to think. Would you like to be my secretary?

AGNES   On one condition.

VICE PRESIDENT   A condition?

AGNES   On condition that you never wear this awful jacket again. When I think of these wonderful shoulders in that ill-fitting suit—!

VICE PRESIDENT   I have a beautiful blue silk suit. But it's for summer—It's a little light for the season.

AGNES   As you please.

VICE PRESIDENT   I'll wear it tomorrow.

AGNES   Good-bye.

VICE PRESIDENT   Don't forget. Lunch. (*He goes out, smiling, by way of the door to the Directors' room. The street music stops.*)

(MAN *peers out from behind the bust.*)

AGNES   I kept my hands behind my back the whole time. I pretended I had no hands. Now I can hardly move my fingers.

MAN   Here come the rest of the apes. Go to work.

AGNES   On the first?

MAN   On all. One after the other.

AGNES   But—

(CLERK *throws open the doors of the Directors' room. The street music starts again. We have a glimpse of the Directors' table with chairs pulled back ready to receive the Directors. The* VICE PRESIDENT *is seen inside. He is posturing in front of a bookcase in the glass door of which he sees himself reflected, and he is trying vainly to give a smartly tailored appearance to his coat.* CLERK *glances at him in astonishment, then he stands by the outer door to announce the Directors as they appear. They come in through the outer door*

*and cross the length of the reception room, one by
one in time to the music, which is a waltz.)*

CLERK   Mr. Cracheton.

> (MR. CRACHETON *comes in, a lugubrious type, stiff and
> melancholy.)*

AGNES   How handsome he is!

CRACHETON *(He snaps his head about as if shot. His
expression changes. He smiles. In a low voice)*
Charming girl! *(He goes into the Directors' room,
looking all the while over his shoulder.)*

CLERK   Mr. Lepédura.

LEPÉDURA *(Appears. He has a face full of suspicion
and worry. As he passes* AGNES, *he tips his derby
perfunctorily, recognizing her)*   Good morning.

AGNES   How handsome you are!

LEPÉDURA *(Stops dead)*   Who says so?

AGNES   Your wife's friend, the Baroness Chagrobis.
She thinks you're wonderful.

LEPÉDURA *(A changed man, gallant and charming)*   She
thinks I'm wonderful? Well, well, give her my love
when you see her. And tell her I mean to call
her up shortly myself. She has a pretty thin time
of it with the Baron, you know. We have to be
nice to her. Is she still at the same address?

AGNES   Oh yes. I'll tell her you're as handsome as ever.

LEPÉDURA   Now don't exaggerate, my dear. We don't
want to disappoint her. *(He gives her a radiant
smile, and goes in, full six inches taller and many
pounds lighter. To the* CLERK) *Delightful girl!*

CLERK   Mr. Rasemutte and Mr. Schultz.

> *(They enter together, Mutt and Jeff.)*

AGNES   How handsome he is!

> (BOTH *stop as if at a signal.)*

RASEMUTTE   To which of us, Mademoiselle—

SCHULTZ   —Do you refer?

AGNES   Look at each other. You will see.

> *(They look at each other anxiously, and* BOTH *smile
> radiantly.)*

RASEMUTTE   Charming creature!

SCHULTZ   Lovely girl!

> *(*SCHULTZ *offers* RASEMUTTE *his arm. They walk into
> the Directors' room arm in arm like characters in
> "Alt Wien."* CLERK *blows* AGNES *a kiss, follows them in
> and closes the doors behind them.* MAN *pokes his head
> out from behind Archimedes. He shakes his head
> ruefully.)*

AGNES   I'm not doing it well? You're sad?

MAN   You're doing it much too well. I'm frightened.

AGNES   You?

MAN   Like Frankenstein.

> *(The door of the Directors' room is flung open.)*

CLERK   The President!

> *(As the* PRESIDENT *enters the room, we catch a glimpse
> of the* DIRECTORS. *Each has a mirror in his hand.
> While one combs his hair into waves, another settles
> his tie. Another preens his whiskers. The* VICE PRESI-
> DENT *has taken off his jacket.)*

PRESIDENT   So you're the cause of it all, Miss—Miss—?

AGNES   Agnes.

PRESIDENT   Miss Agnes, for fifteen years this organiza-
tion has been steeped in melancholy, jealousy and
suspicion. And now suddenly this morning, everything is changed. My reception clerk, ordinarily a
species of hyena—

> *(The* CLERK *smiles affably.)*

has become so affable he even bows to his own
shadow on the wall—

> (CLERK *contemplates his silhouette in the sunshine
> with a nod of approval. It nods back.)*

The First Vice President, whose reputation for
stuffiness and formality has never been seriously
challenged, insists on sitting at the Directors'
Meeting in his shirtsleeves, God knows why. In the
Directors' Room, around the table, mirrors flash
like sunbeams in a forest, and my Directors gaze
into them with rapture. Mr. Lepédura contemplates
with joy the Adam's apple of Mr. Lepédura.
Mr. Rasemutte stares with pride at the nose of Mr.
Rasemutte. They are all in love with themselves
and with each other. How in the world did you
bring about this miracle, Miss Agnes? What was
it you said to them?

AGNES   How handsome you are!

PRESIDENT   I beg your pardon?

AGNES   I said to them, to each of them, "How handsome
you are!"

PRESIDENT   Ah! You conveyed it to them subtly by
means of a smile, a wink, a promise—

AGNES   I said it in a loud clear voice. Like this: How
handsome you are!

> *(In the Directors' room , all heads turn suddenly.*
> CLERK *closes the doors.)*

PRESIDENT   I see. Like a child winding up a mechanical
doll. Well, well! No wonder my mannikins are
quivering with the joy of life.

> *(There is a round of applause from the Directors'
> Room.)*

Listen to that. It's Mr. Cracheton proposing the
purchase of a new three-way mirror for the men's
room. Miss Agnes, I thank you. You have made a
wonderful discovery.

AGNES   *(Modestly)* Oh, it was nothing.

PRESIDENT   And the President? How does it happen
that you don't tell the President?

AGNES   How handsome he is?

PRESIDENT   He's not worth the trouble, is that it?
(She looks at him with a smile full of meaning.)
You've had enough of masculine vanity for one
morning?

AGNES   Oh, Mr. President—you know the reason as
well as I.

PRESIDENT   No. I assure you.

AGNES   But—I don't need to tell *you*. You *are* handsome.

PRESIDENT *(Seriously)*   Would you mind repeating that?

AGNES   You are handsome.

PRESIDENT   Think carefully, Miss Agnes. This is a
serious matter. Are you quite sure that to you I
seem handsome?

AGNES   You don't seem handsome. You are handsome.

PRESIDENT   You would be ready to repeat that before
witnesses? Think. Much depends upon your answer.
I have grave decisions to make today, and the
outcome depends entirely upon you. Have you
thought? Are you still of the same opinion?

AGNES   Completely.

PRESIDENT   Thank heaven. *(He goes to his private door,
opens it and calls)* Chevredent!

> (CHEVREDENT *comes in. She is a thin, sour woman*

with an insolent air. Her nose is pinched. Her chin is high. Her hair is drawn up tightly. When she opens her mouth she appears to be about to bite.)

CHEVREDENT   Yes? *(She looks at* AGNES *and sniffs audibly.)*

PRESIDENT   Chevredent, how long have you been my private secretary?

CHEVREDENT   Three years and two months. Why?

PRESIDENT   In all that time there has never been a morning when the prospect of finding you in my office has not made me shudder.

CHEVREDENT   Thanks very much. Same to you.

PRESIDENT   I wouldn't have put up with you for ten minutes if it had ever occurred to me that I was handsome.

CHEVREDENT   Ha-ha.

PRESIDENT   But because I thought I was ugly, I took your meanness for generosity. Because I thought I was ugly, I assumed that your evil temper concealed a good heart. I thought it was kind of you even to look at me. For I am ugly, am I not?
*(*CHEVREDENT *sneers maliciously.)*
Thank you. And now listen to me. This young lady seems to be far better equipped to see than you. Her eyelids are not red like yours, her pupils are clear, her glance is limpid. Miss Agnes, look at me. Am I ugly?

AGNES   You are beautiful.
*(*CHEVREDENT *shrugs.)*

PRESIDENT   This young lady's disinterested appraisal of my manly charms has no effect on your opinion?

CHEVREDENT   I never heard such rubbish in my life!

PRESIDENT   Quite so. Well, here is the problem that confronts us. I have the choice of spending my working time with an ugly old shrew who thinks I'm hideous or a delightful young girl who thinks I'm handsome. What do you advise?

CHEVREDENT   You intend to replace me with this little fool?

PRESIDENT   At once.

CHEVREDENT   We'll soon see about that, Mr. President. You may have forgotten, but your wife is inside in your office reading your mail. She should know about this.

PRESIDENT   She should. Tell her.

CHEVREDENT   With pleasure. *(She rushes into the President's office, slamming the door after her.)*

AGNES   I'm terribly sorry, Mr. President.

PRESIDENT   My dear, you come like an angel from heaven at the critical moment of my life. Today is my fifteenth wedding anniversary. My wife, with whose fury Chevredent threatens us, is going to celebrate the occasion by lunching with my Directors. I am going to present her with a gift. A diamond.
(He takes out a case and opens it) Like it?

AGNES   How handsome it is!

PRESIDENT   Extraordinary! You praised the diamond in exactly the same tone you used for me. Is it yellow, by any chance? Is it flawed?

AGNES   It is beautiful. Like you.

PRESIDENT   *(His door opens)* We are about to become less so, both of us. *(He puts the case in his pocket)* Here is my wife.

THERESE (THERESE, *the blonde lady, comes in with icy majesty. She looks* AGNES *up and down)* So.

PRESIDENT   Therese, my dear, permit me to present—

THERESE   Quite unnecessary. That will be all, Mademoiselle. You may go.

PRESIDENT   Agnes is staying, my dear. She is replacing Chevredent.

THERESE   Agnes! So she is already Agnes!

PRESIDENT   Why not?

THERESE   And why is Agnes replacing Chevredent?

PRESIDENT   Because she thinks I'm handsome.

THERESE   Are you mad?

PRESIDENT   No. Handsome.

THERESE *(To* AGNES*)*   You think he's handsome?

AGNES   Oh yes.

THERESE   He makes you think of Galahad? Of Lancelot?

AGNES   Oh no. His type is classic. The Apollo of Bellac.

THERESE   The Apollo of Bellac?

PRESIDENT   Have you ever stopped to wonder, Therese, why the good Lord made women? Obviously they were not torn from our ribs in order to make life a torment for us. Women exist in order to tell men they are handsome. And those who say it the most are those who are most beautiful. Agnes tells me I'm handsome. It's because she's beautiful. You tell me I'm ugly. Why?

MAN *(Appears. He applauds)*   Bravo! Bravo!

THERESE   Who is this maniac?

MAN   When one hears a voice which goes to the very heart of humanity, it is impossible to keep silent.

PRESIDENT   My friend—

MAN   From the time of Adam and Eve, of Samson and Delilah, of Antony and Cleopatra, the problem of man and woman has made an impenetrable barrier between man and woman. If, as it seems, we are able to solve this problem once and for all, it will be a work of immeasurable benefit to the human race.

THERESE   And you think we're getting somewhere with it today, is that it?

MAN   Oh, yes.

THERESE   You don't think the final solution could be deferred until tomorrow?

MAN   Till tomorrow? When the President has just posed the problem so beautifully?

AGNES   So beautifully!

THERESE   The beautiful man poses a beautiful problem, eh, Mademoiselle?

AGNES   I didn't say it. But I can say it. I say what I think.

THERESE   Little cheat!

PRESIDENT   I forbid you to insult Agnes!

THERESE   It's she who insults me!

PRESIDENT   When I'm called handsome, it's an insult to you—is that it?

THERESE   I'm no liar.

PRESIDENT   No. You show us the bottom of your heart.

MAN   Agnes is telling the President the truth, Madame. Just as Cleopatra told the truth, just as Isolt told the truth. The truth about men is, they are beautiful, every last one of them; and your husband is right, Madame, the woman who tells it to them never lies.

THERESE   So I am the liar!

MAN *(Gently)*   It's only because you don't see clearly.

All you have to do to see the beauty of men is
to watch as they breathe and move their limbs.
Each has his special grace. His beauty of body. The
heavy ones—how powerfully they hold the ground!
The light ones—how well they hang from the sky!
His beauty of position. A hunchback on the ridge
of Notre Dame makes a masterpiece of Gothic
sculpture. All you have to do is to get him up
there. And, finally, his beauty of function. The
steamfitter has the beauty of a steamfitter. The
president has the beauty of a president. There is
ugliness only when these beauties become confused
—when the steamfitter has the beauty of a president, the president the beauty of a steamfitter.

AGNES   But there is no such confusion here.

THERESE   No. He has the beauty of a garbageman.

PRESIDENT   Thanks very much.

THERESE   My dear, I have known you too long to
deceive you. You have many good qualities. But
you're ugly.

PRESIDENT   Quiet!

THERESE   Yes. Yes. Ugly! This girl, whatever her mo-
tives, is just able to force her lips to whisper her
lies. But with every part of me—my heart, my
lungs, my arms, my eyes—I scream the truth at
you. My legs! You're ugly! Do you hear?

PRESIDENT   I've heard nothing else for years.

THERESE   Because it's true.

MAN   There. And at last she's confessed.

THERESE   Confessed what? What have I confessed?

MAN   Your crime, Madame. You have injured this man.
How could you expect him to be handsome in an
environment that screamed at him constantly that
he was ugly?

PRESIDENT   Ah! Now I understand!

THERESE   What do you understand? What's the matter
with you all? What have I done?

PRESIDENT   Now I understand why I am always embar-
rassed not only in your presence, but in the
presence of everything that belongs to you.

THERESE   Do you know what is he talking about?

PRESIDENT   The sight of your skirt on the back of a
chair shortens my spine by three inches. Can you
expect me to stand up like a man when you come
in? Your stockings on the bureau tell me that I'm
knock-kneed and thick-ankled. Is it any wonder if I
stumble? Your nail file on my desk hisses at me
that my fingers are thick and my gestures clumsy.
What do you expect of me after that? And your
onyx clock with the Dying Gaul on the mantelpiece
—no wonder I always shiver when I go near the
fire. Imagine—for fifteen years that Dying Gaul has
been sneering at me in my own house, and I never
realized why I was uncomfortable. Well, at last I
understand. And this very evening—

THERESE   Don't you dare!

PRESIDENT   This very evening your Dying Gaul shall
die. You will find him in the garbage with the rest
of the conspiracy. Your Dresden china shepherd,
your Arab sheik, your directoire chairs with their
scratchy bottoms—

THERESE   Those chairs belonged to my grandmother!

PRESIDENT   From now on they belong to the garbage.
What are your chairs covered with, Agnes?

AGNES   Yellow satin.

Birth of Venus
Odilon Redon
1912

216

PRESIDENT   I knew it. And the statues on your table?

AGNES   There is only a bowl of fresh flowers on my table. Today it is white carnations.

PRESIDENT   Of course. And over your fireplace?

AGNES   A mirror.

PRESIDENT   Naturally.

THERESE   I warn you, if you so much as touch my chairs, I'll leave you forever.

PRESIDENT   As you please, my dear.

THERESE   I see. So this is my anniversary gift after fifteen years of devotion. Very well. Only tell me, what have you to complain of? In all these years has it ever happened that your roast was too rare? Did I ever give you your coffee too cold, too hot, too light, too sweet? Thanks to me, you are known as a man whose handkerchief is always fresh, whose socks are always new. Have you ever known what it was to have a hole in your toe? Has anyone ever seen a spot on your vest? And yet how you splash in your gravy, my friend! How you go through your socks.

PRESIDENT   Tell me one thing. Do you say I am ugly because you think I am ugly or merely to spite me?

THERESE   Because you are ugly.

PRESIDENT   Thank you, Therese. Go on.

THERESE   Then this woman appears. And at the first glance we can guess the fate of the unhappy creature who marries her. We see it all—the slippers with the inner sole curled up in a scroll. The nightly battle over the newspaper. The pajamas without buttons and always too small. The headaches without aspirin, the soup without salt, the shower without towels—

PRESIDENT   Agnes, one question. Do you tell me I'm handsome because you think I'm handsome or only to make fun of me?

AGNES   Because you're handsome.

PRESIDENT   Thank you, Agnes.

THERESE   You mean because he's rich.

AGNES   If he were the richest man in the world, I'd still say he was handsome.

THERESE   Very well. Marry her if she thinks you're so handsome. Well? What are you waiting for?

PRESIDENT   Nothing.

THERESE   Take him, you, with my compliments. After fifteen years I've had enough. If you like to hear snoring at night—

AGNES   You snore? How wonderful!

THERESE   If you like bony knees—

AGNES   I like legs that have character.

THERESE   Look at that face! Now tell me he has the brow of a Roman Senator.

AGNES   No, Madame.

THERESE   No?

AGNES   The brow of a king.

THERESE   I give up. Goodbye.

PRESIDENT   Goodbye, my love.

(THERESE *rushes out through outer door.*)
And now, Agnes, in token of a happy future, accept this diamond. For me, one life has ended, and another begins.

(CLERK *comes in and signs to him.*)
Forgive me just one moment, Agnes. I must address the Directors. The Chairman of the Board is evidently not coming. I'll be right back. (*He crosses to the door. To the* CLERK) Send down to the florist. I want all the white carnations he has. Agnes, you have made me the happiest of men.

AGNES   The handsomest.

(*The* PRESIDENT *goes out by his door, the* CLERK *by the outer door.*)

MAN   Well, there you are, my dear. You have everything—a job, a husband and a diamond. I can leave?

AGNES   Oh no!

(*The street music starts afresh.*)

MAN   But what more do you want?

AGNES   Look at me. I have changed—haven't I?

MAN   Perhaps just a little. That can't be helped.

AGNES   It's your fault. I have told so many lies! I must tell the truth at last or I shall burst!

MAN   What truth do you want to tell?

AGNES   I want to tell someone who is really beautiful that he is beautiful. I want to tell the most beautiful man in the world that he is the most beautiful man in the world.

MAN   And to caress him, perhaps, just a little?

AGNES   Just a little.

MAN   There is the Apollo of Bellac.

AGNES   He doesn't exist.

MAN   What does it matter whether or not he exists? His beauty is the supreme beauty. Tell him.

AGNES   I can't. Unless I touch a thing I don't see it. You know that. I have no imagination.

MAN   Close your eyes.

AGNES   (*Closes them*)   Yes?

MAN   Suppose, Agnes, it were the God of Beauty himself who visited you this morning? Don't be astonished. Perhaps it's true. Where else could this terrible power have come from? Or this extraordinary emotion you feel? Or this sense of oppression? And suppose that now the god reveals himself?

AGNES   It is you?

MAN   Don't open your eyes. Suppose I stand before you now in all my truth and all my splendor.

AGNES   I see you.

MAN   Call me thou.

AGNES   I see thee.

MAN   How do I seem?

AGNES   You seem—

MAN   I am taller than mortal men. My head is small and fringed with golden ringlets. From the line of my shoulders, the geometricians derived the idea of the square. From my eyebrows the bowmen drew the concept of the arc. I am nude and this nudity inspired in the musicians the idea of harmony.

AGNES   Your heels are winged, are they not?

MAN   They are not. You are thinking of the Hermes of St. Yrieix.

AGNES   I don't see·your eyes.

MAN   As for the eyes, it's as well you don't see them. The eyes of beauty are implacable. My eyeballs are silver. My pupils are graphite. From the eyes of beauty poets derived the idea of death. But the feet of beauty are enchanting. They are not feet that touch the ground. They are never soiled and never captive. The toes are slender, and from them artists derived the idea of symmetry. Do you see me now?

AGNES   You dazzle my eyes.

MAN   But your heart sees me.

AGNES   I'm not so sure. Do not count on me too much, God of Beauty. My life is small. My days are long, and when I come back to my room each evening there are five flights to climb in the greasy twilight amid smells of cooking. These five flights mark the beginning and the end of every event of my life, and oh, if you knew, Apollo, how lonely I am! Sometimes I find a cat waiting in a doorway. I kneel and stroke it for a moment, we purr together and it fills the rest of my day with joy. Sometimes I see a milk bottle that has fallen on its side. I set it right and the gesture comforts me. If I smell gas in the hallway I run and speak to the janitor. It is so good to speak to someone about something. Between the second story and the third, the steps sag. At this turning one abandons hope. At this turning one loses one's balance, and catches at the bannister, gasping with the anguish of those more fortunate ones who clutch at the rail on the heaving deck of a ship. That is my life, Apollo, a thing of shadows and tortured flesh. That is my conscience, Apollo, a staircase full of stale odors. If I hesitate to see you as you are, O beautiful god, it is because I need so much and I have so little and I must defend myself.

MAN   But I have rescued you, Agnes. You possess the secret.

AGNES   I know. From now on, my staircase will be new and full of light, the treads carpeted in velvet and adorned with initials. But to climb it with you would be unthinkable. Go away, God of Beauty. Leave me for always.

MAN   You wish that?

AGNES   If you were merely a handsome man, Apollo, thick and human in your flesh, with what joy I would take you in my arms! How I would love you! But you are too brilliant and too great for my staircase. I would do better to look at my diamond. Go, Apollo. Go away. Before I open my eyes, I implore you, vanish.

MAN   When I vanish, you will see before you an ordinary creature like yourself, covered with skin, covered with clothes.

AGNES   That is my destiny, and I prefer it. Let me kiss your lips, Apollo. And then—

MAN   (He kisses her)   Open your eyes, my dear. Apollo is gone. And I am going.

AGNES   How handsome you are!

MAN   Dear Agnes!

AGNES   Don't go. I will make you rich. I will order the President to buy your invention.

MAN   Which one?

AGNES   The Universal Vegetable. There must be a fortune in it.

MAN   I haven't quite got the hang of it yet. The roots don't hold the earth. I'll be back the moment I've perfected it.

AGNES   You promise?

MAN   We shall plant it together. And now—

AGNES   You are really leaving me? You think I shall marry the President?

MAN   No.

AGNES   Why not?

MAN   He's already married. And his wife has learned a lesson. You will see.

AGNES   Then whom shall I marry, if not the President?

CLERK   (Enters. He crosses to the Directors' room and throws open the door. Announces)   The Chairman of the Board!
      (The CHAIRMAN enters from the outer door.)

MAN   (Whispers)   He is a bachelor.

AGNES   How handsome he is!

MAN   Yes. (He vanishes.)

CHAIRMAN   Mademoiselle—

PRESIDENT   (The PRESIDENT comes in quickly in great excitement)   Agnes! Agnes! A miracle! My wife has just telephoned. I don't know what has come over her. She has thrown out the Dying Gaul and the china shepherd.

AGNES   Give her this diamond.

PRESIDENT   Thank you, Agnes. Thank you.

CHAIRMAN   (Taking her hand)   And who is this charming girl who gives away diamonds?

AGNES   Her name is Agnes.

CHAIRMAN   Dear Agnes!

PRESIDENT   But what's happened to our friend? He isn't here?

AGNES   He is gone.

PRESIDENT   Call him back. He must have lunch with us. Do you know his name?

AGNES   His first name only. Apollo.

PRESIDENT   (Runs to the outer door)   Apollo! Apollo!
      (The DIRECTORS come in, all adorned with white carnations)
      Gentlemen, gentlemen, let's call him! We can't let him go like that. Apollo!
      (They each go to a door or a window save AGNES and the CHAIRMAN who remain standing hand in hand.)

PRESIDENT and DIRECTORS   Apollo! Apollo!

CHAIRMAN   But whom are they shouting at? Is Apollo here?

AGNES   No. He just passed by.

from

Still Life with Woodpecker
by Tom Robbins

When the mystery of the connection goes, love goes. It's that simple. This suggests that it isn't love that is so important to us but the mystery itself. The love connection may be merely a device to put us in contact with the mystery, and we long for love to last so that the ecstasy of being near the mystery will last. It is contrary to the nature of the mystery to stand still. Yet it's always there, somewhere, a world on the other side of the mirror (or the Camel pack), a promise in the next pair of eyes that smile at us. We glimpse it when we stand still.

The romance of new love, the romance of solitude, the romance of objecthood, the romance of ancient pyramids and distant stars are means of making contact with the mystery. When it comes to perpetuating it, however, I got no advice. But I can and will remind you of two of the most important facts I know:

(1) *Everything* is part of it.
(2) It's never too late to have a happy childhood.

Double Portrait with Wine Glass
by Marc Chagall
1917–1918

The Good Angel
by Rafael Alberti

The one I wanted came,
the one I called.

Not the one who sweeps away defenseless skies,
stars without homes,
moons without a country,
snows.
The kind of snows that fall from a hand,
a name,
a dream,
a face.

Not the one who tied death
to his hair.

The one I wanted.

Without scraping air,
without wounding leaves or shaking windowpanes.

The one who tied silence
to his hair.

To scoop out, without hurting me,
a shoreline of sweet light inside my chest
so that my soul could sail.

The Bridal Couple
by Marc Chagall
Circa 1935

from

I and Thou
by Martin Buber

Feelings are "entertained": love comes to pass. Feelings dwell in man; but man dwells in his love. That is no metaphor, but the actual truth. Love does not cling to the *I* in such a way as to have the *Thou* only for its "content," its object; but love is *between I* and *Thou*.... Love is responsibility of an *I* for a *Thou*.

The Bridal Couple
by Rembrandt van Rijn
Circa 1665

"We two form a multitude."

Ovid

above

Seated Man and Woman
Dogon Sculpture

Mali

opposite

King Mycerinus and
Queen Kha Merer Nebty II

Circa 2570 B.C.

below

Loving Couple
Pre-Columbian Terra-cotta Sculpture
Mexico

opposite

Sarcophagus from Cerveteri
Seventh to Sixth Century B.C.

Vajrasattva in Union with
the Supreme Wisdom Visvatara
Tibet, Lamaistic-Tantric

Eighteenth Century

Hoysaleswara Temple Sculpture

Mysore, India

Thirteenth Century

INDEX

ACKNOWLEDGMENTS

ART

Page 1, Hoysaleswara temple sculpture, Mysore, India, 13th century. Photograph: Matthias Oppersdorff/Photo Researchers, Inc.

Page 2, *White Samvara*, a Tanka by an anonymous artist, 19th century. Asian Art Museum of San Francisco; the Avery Brundage Collection.

Pages 4–5, *Equestrian* by Marc Chagall, 1931. Stedelijk Museum, Amsterdam. S.P.A.D.E.M.

Page 7, detail from *Self-Portrait with Isabella Brandt in the Honeysuckle Bower* by Peter Paul Rubens, 1609. Alte Pinakothek, Munich.

Page 8, detail from *Scene at Houghton Farm* by Winslow Homer, c. 1878. Scala/Editorial Photocolor Archives, New York.

Page 12, detail from *Spring in Central Park* by William Zorach, 1914. The Metropolitan Museum of Art, New York; anonymous gift, 1979.

Page 15, detail from King Mycerinus and Queen Kha Merer Nebty II, sculpture from the Valley Temple of Mycerinus, c. 2570 B.C. Courtesy Museum of Fine Arts, Boston; Harvard-Boston Expedition, 11.1738.

Page 16, *Adam and Eve* by an anonymous American artist, c. 1830. Collection of the Whitney Museum of American Art, New York; gift of Edgar William and Bernice Chrysler Garbisch. Photograph: Geoffrey Clements, New York.

Page 20, *Peaceable Kingdom of the Branch* by Edward Hicks, 1830–1840. Abby Aldrich Rockefeller Folk Art Center, Williamsburg, Virginia.

Page 28, *Paolo and Francesca* by William Dyce, 1837. Collection: National Galleries of Scotland, Edinburgh. Photograph: Tom Scott, Edinburgh.

Page 30, Persian fresco at Isfahan, Safavid Period, 16th century. Telarci/Giraudon.

Page 31, *A Bridal Pair* by an anonymous South German master, Upper Rhine Region, c. 1470. The Cleveland Museum of Art, Purchase; Delia E. Holden Fund and L.E. Holden Fund.

Page 32, detail from the back of the throne of Tutankhamen, Egypt, late XVIII Dynasty. Collection: Cairo Museum. Photograph: Werner Forman Archive.

Page 33, Hindu temple sculpture, Khajurāho, India, 10th to 11th century. Photograph: Copyright © Jehangir Gazdar 1979/Woodfin Camp.

Page 34, *Love Scene by Candlelight* by Godfried Schalcken. Courtesy of the Trustees of the National Gallery, London.

Page 35, *A Lady Playing the Theorbo* by Gerard Terborch, mid-17th century. The Metropolitan Museum of Art, New York; bequest of Benjamin Altman, 1913.

Page 36, detail from *Jealousy and Flirtation* by Haynes King, 1874. Victoria and Albert Museum, London, Crown Copyright.

Page 37, *The Glass of Lemonade* by Gerard Terborch, 1663–1664. The Hermitage, Leningrad.

Page 39, *Scene at Houghton Farm* by Winslow Homer, c. 1878. Scala/Editorial Photocolor Archives, New York.

Page 40, *To Jacques Prévert* by Jean-Michel Folon, 1979. By permission of the artist.

Page 41, *He Loves Me* by Maurice Sendak, 1963. Rosenbach Museum & Library, Philadelphia. An illustration by Maurice Sendak from *She Loves Me...She Loves Me Not* by Robert Keeshan. Illustration copyright © 1963 by Maurice Sendak. By permission of Harper & Row, Publishers, Inc.

Page 42, *Daphnis and Chloé* by Pierre Bonnard, 1902. Photo Flammarion. S.P.A.D.E.M.

Page 45, *Reclining Girl* by Richard Williams, 1964. By permission of the artist.

Page 51, detail from *La Revue Blanche* by Pierre Bonnard, 1894. Photo Flammarion. S.P.A.D.E.M.

Page 57, *Woman with Gloves* by Toulouse-Lautrec. Collection: Jeu de Paume, Paris. Photograph: Scala/Editorial Photocolor Archives, New York.

Page 61, *Young Woman in a Ball Gown* by Berthe Morisot, 1879. Collection: Jeu de Paume, Paris. Photograph: Scala/Editorial Photocolor Archives, New York.

Page 64, illustration by William Steig, 1980. Reprinted by permission. Copyright © 1980 The New Yorker Magazine, Inc.

Page 66, *The Proposal* by Adolphe William Bouguereau, 1872. The Metropolitan Museum of Art, New York; gift of Mrs. Elliot L. Kamen, in memory of her father, Bernard R. Armour, 1960.

Page 69, illustration by Elwood H. Smith, 1982. By permission of the artist.

Page 70, *Spring in Central Park* by William Zorach, 1914. The Metropolitan Museum of Art, New York; anonymous gift, 1979.

Pages 74 and 75, illustrations by Walt Lee, 1982. By permission of the artist.

Page 76, *The White Window* by Marc Chagall, 1955. Collection: Kunstmuseum, Basel. Colorphoto Hans Hinz, Allschwil-Basel. S.P.A.D.E.M.

Page 78, *Meditation (Contemplation)* by Pablo Picasso, 1904. Collection: Mrs. Bertram Smith, New York. Photograph: The Museum of Modern Art, New York. S.P.A.D.E.M.

Page 85, *The East Window* by Childe Hassam, 1913. Hirshhorn Museum and Sculpture Garden, Smithsonian Institution, Washington, D.C.

Page 91, *Street Scene* by John Sloan, 1859. The Delaware Art Museum, Wilmington; John Sloan Collection.

Page 97, detail from *The Garden of Love* by Peter Paul Rubens, 1638. Copyright © The Prado, Madrid.

Page 98, illustration by Robert Weber, 1978. Reprinted by permission. Copyright © 1978 The New Yorker Magazine, Inc.

Page 100, *Birthday* by Marc Chagall, 1915. The Museum of Modern Art, New York; acquired through the Lillie P. Bliss bequest. S.P.A.D.E.M.

Page 102, "Qui trop embrasse" from a de luxe album called Quatre Proverbs by Tito, c. 1920.

Page 104, *Sethos I with Queen Hathor*, Egypt, XIX Dynasty. Collection: Archeological Museum, Florence. Photograph: Scala/Editorial Photocolor Archives, New York.

Page 105, detail from the Tomb of Ramses I, Valley of Kings, Thebes. Photograph: John G. Ross.

Page 106, *Man and Woman* by Pierre Bonnard, c. 1906. Collection: Musée National d'Art Moderne, Paris. Photograph: Cliché Musées Nationaux, Paris. S.P.A.D.E.M.

Page 108, *Le Bal à Bougival* by Pierre Auguste Renoir, 1883. Courtesy Museum of Fine Arts, Boston; Anna Mitchell Richards Fund. S.P.A.D.E.M.

Pages 110-111, detail from *Night* by Ferdinand Hodler, 1890. Kunstmuseum, Bern.

Pages 112-113, *Krishna and Radha in the Groves of Brindaban*, Indian painting, 19th to 20th century. The Metropolitan Museum of Art, New York; bequest of Cora Timken Burnett, 1957.

Page 115, *Romance* by Thomas Hart Benton, 1931–1932. The James and Mari Michener Collection, the Archer M. Huntington Art Gallery, the University of Texas at Austin.

Page 116, *Self-Portrait with Isabella Brandt in the Honeysuckle Bower* by Peter Paul Rubens, 1609. Alte Pinakothek, Munich.

Page 119, *Azuma and Yogoro* by Hokusai, c. 1798. Private Collection. Photograph: Courtesy of The Bridgeman Art Library, London.

Page 121, *Symphony in White, No. 2* by James Abbott McNeill Whistler, 1864. The Tate Gallery, London.

Page 122, *The Kiss* by Gustav Klimt, 1907–1908. Öesterreichische Galerie, Vienna.

Page 124, *The Stolen Kiss* by Jean Honoré Fragonard, c. 1761–1765. The Hermitage, Leningrad.

Page 125, *Francesca da Rimini and Paolo Malatesta* by J.A.D. Ingres, 1819. Collection: Musée des Beaux-Arts, Angers. Photograph: Lauros-Giraudon.

Page 126, *The Kiss* by Constantin Brancusi, 1922–1940. Musée National d'Art Moderne, Centre National d'Art et de Culture Georges Pompidou, Paris.

Page 127, *Lovers* by Pablo Picasso. Collection: Barcelona Arte Moderna. Photograph: Scala/Editorial Photocolor Archives, New York.

Page 128, Hindu temple sculpture, Khajurāho, India, 10th to 11th century. Photograph: Copyright © Jehangir Gazdar 1979/Woodfin Camp.

Page 129, *The Kiss* by Francesco Hayez, c. 1859. Collection: Brera Gallery, Milan. Photograph: Scala/Editorial Photocolor Archives, New York.

Page 130, Hindu temple sculpture, Khajurāho, India, 10th to 11th century. Photograph: Copyright © Jehangir Gazdar 1979/Woodfin Camp.

Page 132, *Equestrian* by Marc Chagall, 1931. Stedelijk Museum, Amsterdam. S.P.A.D.E.M.

Page 133, study for *Country Dance* by Pierre Auguste Renoir. Szépmüvészeti Museum, Budapest. S.P.A.D.E.M.

Page 134–135, detail from a Greek red-figure vase by the Brygos painter, 500–480 B.C. Collection: The Louvre, Paris. Photograph: Bulloz.

Page 136, *Two Lovers* by Reza-ye Abbasi (in the royal studio of Shah Abbas). The Metropolitan Museum of Art, New York; Francis M. Weld Fund.

Pages 138–139, *Lovers* by Kitagawa Utamaro, 1788. A woodblock color print from the album Uta-makura. Ukiyo-e school. Photograph: Weidenfeld & Nicolson Publishers, Ltd.

Page 140, *Man and Woman* by Pablo Picasso, 1927. Copyright © Sotheby Parke-Bernet. Agent: Editorial Photocolor Archives, New York.

Page 143, *Danaë* by Gustav Klimt, 1907–1908. Joseph Martin/Scala/Editorial Photocolor Archives, New York.

Page 145, *The Embrace* by Egon Schiele, 1917. The Österreichische Galerie, Vienna. Courtesy Ing Norbert Gradisch.

Page 148, *Village with Dark Sun* by Marc Chagall, 1950. Photograph: Francis G. Mayer/Photo Researchers, Inc.

Page 150, illustration by Edward Koren, 1977. Reprinted by permission. Copyright © 1977 The New Yorker Magazine, Inc.

Page 154, detail from *By the Seashore* by Pierre Auguste Renoir, 1883. The Metropolitan Museum of Art, New York; bequest of Mrs. H.O. Havemeyer, 1929. The H.O. Havemeyer Collection. S.P.A.D.E.M.

Pages 156–157, illustration by John Bauer from "The Ring" by John Bauer from *Great Swedish Fairy Tales*, 1914. Photograph: Bonnier Juveniles International, Stockholm.

Page 160, *Paul Helleu Sketching with His Wife* by John Singer Sargent, 1889. The Brooklyn Museum; Museum Collection Fund.

Page 163, *Resting* by John Singer Sargent, 1875. Sterling and Francine Clark Art Institute, Williamstown, Massachusetts.

Page 164, Hindu temple sculpture, Khajurāho, India, 10th to 11th century. Photograph: Copyright © Jehangir Gazdar 1979/Woodfin Camp.

Page 166, Japanese screen by an anonymous artist. Werner Forman Archive.

Page 168–169, *Indian Elopement* by Alfred Jacob Miller. Courtesy of the Buffalo Bill Historical Center, Cody, Wyoming.

Page 170–171, illustration by Jean-Jacques Sempé, 1981. From *Displays of Affection* by Sempé. Copyright © 1981 by Jean-Jacques Sempé. Published by Workman Publishing Company, Inc., New York.

Page 172, *Lovers with Flowers* by Marc Chagall, 1927. The Israel Museum, Jerusalem. S.P.A.D.E.M.

Page 174, *Lady Agnew* by John Singer Sargent, c. 1892–1893. National Gallery, Edinburgh.

Page 177, *Blue Eyes* by Henri Matisse, 1935. The Baltimore Museum of Art; the Cone Collection, formed by Dr. Claribel Cone and Miss Etta Cone of Baltimore, Maryland. S.P.A.D.E.M.

Page 179, detail from a Greek vase (campanian bell krater, cunai), 4th century. Collection: Museo Nazionale, Naples. Photograph: Scala/Editorial Photocolor Archives, New York.

Page 187, *Le Repos* by Marc Chagall, 1975. St. Paul de Vence. Photograph: Scala/Editorial Photocolor Archives, New York.

Page 182, *The Dressing Gown* by Pierre Bonnard, c. 1892. Scala/Editorial Photocolor Archives, New York.

Page 185, sarcophagus from Cerveteri, 7th to 6th century B.C. The Louvre, Paris.

Page 187, *The Kiss* by Edvard Munch, 1902. Museum of Modern Art, New York; gift of Abby Aldrich Rockefeller.

Page 188, *Woman with a Rose* by Edmond Aman-Jean, 1891. Copyright © Sotheby Parke-Bernet. Agent: Editorial Photocolor Archives, New York.

Page 191, *Man and Woman with Spinning Wheel* by Pieter Pieterszoon, c. 1575–1580. Rijksmuseum, Amsterdam.

Page 192, *Naked Love* by Jean-Michel Folon, 1981. By permission of the artist.

Page 195, *The Kiss* by Constantin Brancusi, c. 1908. Collection: Musée d'Art Moderne, Paris. Photograph: Lauros/Giraudon.

Page 196, *Around Her* by Marc Chagall, 1945. Collection: Musée National d'Art Moderne, Paris. Photograph: Scala/Editorial Photocolor Archives, New York.

LITERATURE

Composition in Aster
by U.S. Lithograph Inc., New York, New York.
Printing in four-color offset on 157 gsm matte-coated paper
by Toppan Printing Co., Ltd., Tokyo, Japan. Bound in Japan
by Toppan Printing Co., Ltd.